Praise for Betty's Work

"Betty Dietz is a visionary whose ability to dialogue with the psychic images from Wanless' Voyager Tarot Deck stems from her familiarity with divination techniques and with dream images from the unconscious. Betty's coaching ability offers persons seeking wisdom and clarity the opportunity to learn from one who picks up the back story most of us miss. I am one of those who has long benefited from Betty's visions and guidance."

~ Rachel Fitzgerald, PhD, psychotherapist and author of
Toni Wolff's Forms: She Moves in Circles: Vital Links to the Archaic Mind
Website: http://www.evolvingdeepforms.com

"When life seems gloomy and hopeless with deaths and conflicts, the cards YOU chose reveal answers and pathways for a brighter outcome. Over a decade of Betty's readings have given me insights and guided me to have peace and enriched my life.
With gratitude, a believer from S. Cal." ~ Eiko Amano, artist and teacher

"Betty has been a mentor, sage, teacher, and spiritual guide to me for nearly fifteen years. Through our work together, I have learned to embrace my shadow self, accept what is beyond my control, explore my emotions, and discover new sources of strength and vitality. My life is enriched by her kindness, generosity, and wisdom." ~ Ron Blandford

"Betty has taught me to use the Voyager Tarot like a flashlight to illuminate areas of darkness, confusion, and doubt. She's like a translator who helps me understand what the universe wants to tell me. When my journey of self discovery begins to stall, I look to Betty to get ideas on how to get around the obstacles in my path. She has an amazing ability to help me turn inspiration into action." ~ Tori van Zanten, Interior Architect and Designer

"When Betty first started doing tarot cards, I didn't believe everything. I'm a skeptic. But then something magical happened. The cards seemed to always know just what to say and when. Except, I realized it wasn't the cards. It was Betty. It didn't matter if I 'believed.' Betty's readings aren't about belief at all. They're about guidance. I know this because I get just as much from reading her blog posts and other writing as I do from personal readings. She shares her insights about life. Betty accepts everyone where they are and speaks deeply from the heart, using her brilliant mind. Really, what I get from her readings is love, guidance and kindness. I don't worry any more about believing or not believing. So whether you believe in cards, in magic, in karma, God, or nothing at all, it doesn't matter. Because Betty will help you believe in the most important thing in your life: yourself." ~ Janet Kornblum, writer and media trainer
http://janetkornblum.com/

"Betty's tarot readings are an experience not to be missed. She brings to the table a very deep knowledge of the cards and how those energies play out in our daily lives. She also combines that knowledge with her insights from much experience, her intuitive abilities, and her skills as a life coach. Her readings have helped me, as well as many others, to move forward in life."

~ James O'Hara, author of *In the Land of Shiva: A Memoir*
Website: jamesohara.com

"Over the years, I have always enjoyed and appreciated Betty Dietz's insightful comments and her usage of the Tarot cards as a vehicle to open discussions, encourage self-reflection, and generally to increase awareness of our own lives and the people we touch. When I first participated in a dinner with Tarot cards at the Dietz home, I was, to be honest, a bit apprehensive and skeptical. However, it soon became clear that the cards were a great tool for opening interesting conversations, especially when bringing together thoughtful people who just may not know each other so well. Betty never fails to create a safe and supportive atmosphere for individuals to open up, perhaps share a glimpse of an issue they are wrestling with, and to take a bit of time to strengthen and train their skills of self-awareness and self-help. Since then, my family and I have been the benefactors of many tasty meals in Betty Dietz's home, where the Tarot cards are often part of the dessert activities, equally anticipated and relished."

~ JM Chan, UCSF Professor

"As social, mindful creatures we desire deeper connections to our community, our family, our friends and ourselves. Using the symbols and structure of tarot, let Betty Dietz be your spiritual guide to build and strengthen the connections you desire. Whether you are confronting a relationship or career challenge or simply desire more clarity in your life, Betty's approach is one you must try and one you're not likely to find elsewhere. I and many of my friends are benefactors of her innovative approach, leading more positive fulfilling lives as a result! Grab a copy of this book and you can too!"

~ Brian Allen

"With this book, Betty Dietz has perfectly melded her specialties as a counselor, a life coach and an interpreter of James Wanless' Voyager Tarot Deck into a guide for those seeking great fulfillment. With each chapter she leads her readers down a path of nurturing their own lives into the kind of lives they most desire. Knowledge of the Voyager Tarot Deck is not necessary for using this wonderful book, but that knowledge could add another layer to the experience."

~ Denise E. Minor, Ph.D

"Drawing on a lifetime of teaching, healing, and observing, Betty Dietz illuminates the Tarot with her insightful, eloquent commentary. Her passion and wisdom, applied to the reality of everyday life, provide a truly powerful perspective on how the cards are speaking to each of us, if we're ready to listen."

~ Sally Araki Aalfs, Ph.D

The Soul of Success

A Guide to Living a Life of Meaning, Purpose, and Abundance

The Soul of Success

A Guide to Living a Life of Meaning, Purpose, and Abundance

Betty Dietz

Dear Mahvash and Ahmad —
Joy to The journey and our
friendship! Love,
Betty

Lark Wing Publishing

Los Altos, California

Seattle
8-5-15

Lark Wing Publishing
Los Altos, California

The intent of the author is only to offer information of a general nature to help you in your quest for emotional and spiritual well-being. In the event you use any of the information in this book for yourself, which is your constitutional right, the author and the publisher assume no responsibility for your actions or the consequences of your actions. Nonetheless, the author wishes you well on your journey to living a conscious life of meaning, purpose, and abundance.

ISBN 978-0-9905302-0-6

Cover design: Vikiana

Printed in the United States of America

For Bill, Lauri, and Patrick
I am forever grateful to you, who so wholeheartedly
inspire, support, and love me, as I do you.

When there is light in the soul, there will be beauty in the person.
When there is beauty in the person, there will be harmony in the house.
When there is harmony in the house, there will be order in the nation.
When there is order in the nation, there will be peace.

Chinese Proverb

Table of Contents

Where the Cards Are

Major Arcana

Minor Arcana Qualities

Where the Cards Are

Where the Cards Are

Family Cards

Don't spend your precious time seeking answers to who you are, but rather decide who you choose to be and create that person now.

Introduction

Happy, positive, self-fulfilling, resourceful people achieve greater success, accumulate more wealth, are healthier, more altruistic, and have more satisfying relationships than those who see life through the lens of pessimism and fear. People who follow their passions toward creating the lives of their dreams live seven to ten years longer than those who give up on themselves.

The basic components of a happy and satisfying life include the following elements:

- Paying attention to what you care most about.
- Noticing constantly what you are most grateful for.
- Fashioning your habits and goals consciously so that you're living a dynamic life of your own choosing.
- Investing in filling your treasure chest of life with love, happiness, enjoyable relationships, and the joy of being creatively expressive.

If you make these decisions, then this phenomenal life will not only bring you great satisfaction and joy, but you will likely excel in the areas of connection, playfulness, support, contribution, creative expression, and intimacy. In addition, living this life will have an enormous positive impact on the people around you and the planet as a whole.

Isn't this the very life you want for yourself, your loved ones, and all the people in the world?

While many books, programs, and teachers offer guidance on how to achieve happiness or how to be successful in business, in relationships, in career choice, and in health decisions, very few offer two key ingredients necessary to bringing all of this together. One key piece to the puzzle of how to be happy and successful is found by using inner wisdom, intuition, and creativity. The other piece is that all of this is more likely to be achieved with a little help from your friends.

James Wanless' *Voyager Tarot Deck* is the perfect vehicle for easily tapping into inner wisdom, intuition, and creativity. The *Voyager Tarot Deck* invites the use of the imagination to stimulate the intellect, emotions, body, and connection with soul to find clarity of purpose and to be confident of the direction in which to proceed, to feel happy about decisions made, and to experience the joy that comes from a life of inspired purpose. The reason Wanless' *Voyager* deck functions at such deep and profound levels is because of how thoughtfully and masterfully he has chosen and designed the images based on universal archetypal energies. These images animate energies that can be quickly and precisely focused on actions leading to insights, answers, and solutions.

The other piece of the puzzle that's not included in most guidance programs is the need for support. Rarely is anything accomplished in isolation. We're communal by nature and when we collaborate and support each other, amazing accomplishments occur. As is often noted, it takes a village to raise a child. In truth, we need that village throughout our lives to nourish and nurture our dreams, hopes, aspirations, and talents.

Another way to think about the journey to dream creation within the context of a group is that it is like having a staff of personal mentors, a covey of coaches, a passel of friends—each of whom wants you to be successful, each of whom has set the intention that you will be successful, just as you offer the same in return to the other group members.

Ready to start? If the answer is yes, you have the right book in your hands. You are exactly in the right place to begin a process guaranteed to produce profound and expansive alignment of your mind, body and soul, and the right place to experience the transformation and healing that comes when you connect with your authentic core. From this place of alignment, anything and everything is possible.

The Soul of Success offers the opportunity to commit to yourself and not feel alone. You'll discover yourself gently letting go of fear and opening to the freedom of liberated thinking. You'll find yourself creating a meaningful life for yourself, finding harmony in all of your relationships, and contributing in no small way to peace on the planet. And if you're concerned about where you will find the time to live this better, richer, more fabulous life of meaning, purpose, and abundance, the answer is that an opening almost always occurs. Interestingly, when you're aligned with your highest self, time appears to expand to meet your needs. When you act with integrity and possess clarity on what to do next, time no longer acts as a constraint. On the contrary, time becomes elastic, multidimensional, and accommodating. And if this isn't convincing enough, I will then ask the question: is there enough time left in your life not to make a commitment to creating the life you've always dreamed of?

The Soul of Success offers a way to think about the pieces of your life so that these pieces come together to create the life you want for yourself. When you make a commitment to yourself in front of a community of caring and supportive people, you will find yourself energized and passionate about both the big parts of your life and the ordinariness of daily life. You will find you have the clarity that guides you to make affirming decisions throughout your day with ease and joy.

The Soul of Success is a guide to tap into the innate inner wisdom common to everyone, in the company of fellow visionaries.

If you're ready to begin this exciting adventure to create your own life, if you're ready to assume the power you are capable of exercising—and that is the power to fashion your future, the power to live fully in the present, and the power to impact the future of the world—then I invite you to step into the circle that will support you. I invite you to gather with like-minded fellow travelers and begin the journey that will lead you into your Soul of Success.

Relax and have fun as you explore, discover, and connect with the more fulfilling, meaningful, and happier life that awaits you.

Get ready for an exciting journey into the future that begins now!

I also invite you to visit my website and blog for updates and additional guidance:
BettyDietz.com

Living your purpose means you're aware, awake, and appreciative of the wonders of life, which includes having fun while on the journey of self-discovery.

How to Use this Book

More than anything, I hope you have fun with your *Soul of Success* book. Coming from a background in education, literature, theatre, and psychology, I am well aware of the connection between learning and emotions. Emotional upheavals block your ability to take in and rationally process new information. If you are sad, stressed, depressed, irritable, enraged, head over heels in love, euphoric or ecstatic, you are not in a good learning mode and you shouldn't be making important decisions either. However, if you are happy, enjoying yourself, feeling secure and intellectually stimulated, you will be open to new ideas and will be able to use them in creative and advantageous ways. In other words, being playful is good for you!

T*he Soul of Success* explores systematic, intuitive, and purposeful opportunities for opening up a world of possibilities and showing you how to proceed on a conscious journey. I've used James Wanless' *Voyager Tarot Deck* as a guide because his tarot cards offer a thoughtful path in a beautiful design with the added benefit of fun and playfulness. And while I would encourage you to use the beautiful and deeply meaningful *Voyager Tarot Deck* as you journey through *The Soul of Success*, this book alone offers all you need for this adventure.

You also don't need any background in tarot cards before immersing yourself in your Soul of Success journey, but here's a sketch of tarot in general and *The Voyager Tarot Deck* in particular.

Tarot cards have influenced decision-making for over six centuries and likely began as a book of wisdom in Egypt, morphed into cards with numbers and pictures in the Middle Ages, and then evolved into playing cards. The playing card branch of the tarot is still used by many people as an oracle, but most of these decks are found on poker and blackjack tables around the world today. Tarot cards are now used everywhere; however, their variations are expressed in a multitude of ways. Some people design their own decks, drawing from their own imaginations to fashion the images and to name the energy of each card. The requirements for a tarot deck are to contain 78 cards divided into 22 major arcana numbered 0 to 21, and 56 minor arcana divided into four suits. The deck designer's inspiration takes over from there.

The general idea of the deck is that the twenty-two major arcana tell a story about a journey of self-discovery that moves from innocence to mastery. Joseph Campbell writes about this conscious path of growth through personal awareness as the mythical hero's journey. This journey begins when you decide to take a leap of faith to follow a dream or to realize a vision you only have some inkling of. At this stage, you know you must be on your way and that something is on the horizon for you to discover and when you do discover it, you will know a truth about yourself. You travel along, gathering allies and resources, facing demons and obstacles, leaving everything burdensome behind, and emerge with a deeper understanding of who you are. Because of this understanding, you are able to bring your gifts and talents into the world in the most beneficial way not only for yourself, but most importantly, also for the betterment of the whole world. When we express ourselves fully in positive ways, we connect with the needs of the world and become co-creators with the universe of a world of expansion, hope, and joy.

The reason the twenty-two cards can evoke a story this potent and relevant, is because they are based on universal archetypal energy. When using tarot cards, the possibility exists that you will get at what writer Vladimir Nabokov expresses about what it means to take a journey through story: "the telling shiver of truth" about your own life. This is the area where imagination and inspiration can guide you and shape your life. When you set out on a conscious journey to live a meaningful, purposeful, and empathetic life, you open up to the guidance and force of the mysteries at work within and without. A universe of possibilities becomes available. You are no longer buffeted by these energies, left wondering how to make sense of a life filled with dichotomy, paradox, and uncertainty. You are able to access the knowledge that these opposite energies are part of life and an important component to understanding yourself, others, and your relationship to the world.

James Wanless, who has devoted his career to expanding consciousness through the exploration of symbols for transformation, developed the revolutionary *Voyager Tarot Deck* with artist Ken Knutson in 1981. Together, they created a deck infused with images meant to stir the imagination and inspire the modern mind. These images are collages of symbols chosen to deepen a viewer's sensitivity to the energy of an individual archetype or of some aspect of one of the archetypes.

Because the *Voyager* deck holds the mystery, magic, and wonder of personal consciousness and its connection to the greater consciousness—what Carl Jung referred to as the collective unconscious—anything and everything about you and how you fit into the world is possible to learn from the *Voyager Tarot Deck*.

The Voyager Tarot Deck is both ordinary and extraordinary. The deck contains the typical number of 78 cards, 22 major arcana and 56 minor arcana found in all tarot decks. The 56 minor arcana are divided into four suits. In the *Voyager Tarot Deck*, these suits are called Crystals, Cups, Worlds, and Wands.

Crystals represent the mind and how we think.

Cups hold the energy of the heart and how we emotionally connect with our world and the people in our lives.

Worlds concentrate on the physical reality of our bodies and our environment.

Wands connect us with our higher selves, our best selves, and our divinity.

This brief background information gives you an idea of what the *Voyager Tarot Deck* is about, but whether you're an expert tarot reader or someone who has never seen a deck in your life, you can easily engage with the *Voyager Tarot* cards and this book with or without the cards. As I've said, you don't need a *Voyager Tarot Deck* to make the journey this book guides you on. However, having the deck to look at will greatly enhance the process.

The *Voyager Tarot Deck* is extraordinary in many ways. For one, the images on each card open us to the opportunity to explore who we are at deep and profound levels. Every word, number, and image on each card can be analyzed, felt, studied, and played with to give more and greater insights into what we can take from the card to better understand our question or intent when we turn to the *Voyager* deck for guidance.

Wanless' deck is also extraordinary because when you use his cards you are given the opportunity to experience your life from a new perspective that will provoke meaningful thought. The *Voyager* deck is meant to take you into your innermost sense of self, and out into your outermost expansive way of being part of the world. The *Voyager Tarot Deck* guides visionaries, like you, who are exploring the inner and outer realms of your personal, and our collective, universes.

The *Voyager* deck can be used an infinite number of ways. Turn the cards face down, choose a card, and see what that one says to you. Do set readings where each card means something because of its designated placement. Draw facedown cards randomly as you ask question after question. Have a reading with a professional, by yourself, with family and friends, with passersby. Have a reading with only one person or within a group where others offer insights and then determine for yourself what resonate with you. Choose cards face up and let your conscious mind guide you. Choose a card to use to look for synchronicities as you go about your day. Use them for journaling to help you understand a problem you're trying to work out or a decision you're contemplating. Use them to get a better idea of your life purpose. In other words, the *Voyager* deck is meant to be played with and used creatively. The cards are accessible, inviting and powerful.

I've been doing *Voyager* tarot readings with people for almost twenty years now and have done thousands of readings, and I have never found anyone who didn't experience a deeper understanding of themselves, their situation, or their concerns after interacting with the cards.

"Ahh, yes," and "Wow!" and "I get it!" are common responses to a reading with the *Voyager* cards.

When I began helping people find opportunities to creatively express their talents by doing workshops and teaching about being in the flow of life and stimulating creative problem solving, and helping people find opportunities to creatively express their talents, I always brought in the *Voyager* deck. People loved using the guidance so readily available through the images. You don't need to be trained as a tarot reader to use the *Voyager* deck. However, as with everything in life, the more you learn about the *Voyager* deck, the more helpful the cards can be.

This book, *The Soul of Success*, was written to share the ideas presented in and learned from those workshops and events. The *Voyager* deck is ideal to play with for inspiring, guiding, and deepening your understanding of how to create, reinvent, and discover the life you want to live, no matter what stage in life you are in. This guided voyage through Wanless' deck directs you toward self-exploration for deep personal growth, expansiveness, and clarity of perspective.

At the end of one voyage through the deck, you will likely discover that you are much happier, more fulfilled, and more excited about your life and that your life has gained greater meaning and purpose because you took the time, invested the energy, and made the connections to create at least a part of the life of your dreams. And you'll likely be ready for another voyage.

Equipment Needed

A sketch pad or journal, approximately nine inches by six inches works very well for keeping ideas in one place. A spiral-bound book will allow you to write comfortably because the pages open flat, and this size can easily be carried around so you're always ready when ideas pop up. I encourage you to write, as often as possible, those sudden insights or that information that seems to hold something for you even if you're not sure what it means, for these thoughts hold the potential for leading you to new connections or ways of seeing.

A recording device such as your cell phone can also be used to capture thoughts.

Colored pens, markers, and sketching pencils will give you opportunity to express yourself in brilliant, glorious color or thoughtful black and white.

Glue or tape are handy for adding things other than drawings or words to your notebook.

Note cards/index cards are excellent to use as reminders. They can be tucked into your pocket or bag, propped on a desk, taped to the dashboard of your car, tacked to a wall or cork board, or slipped into a drawer that you open on a regular basis.

The *Voyager Tarot Deck* is highly recommended, but again, is not necessary.

The Format

The Soul of Success is designed to guide you through a cycle of growth, wonder, and awareness so that you arrive at a specific destination invigorated and excited about the new possibilities that have opened for you because of the intentions you set and the directions you traveled.

Just as in the *Voyager Tarot Deck, The Soul of Success* builds on the awarenesses, strengths, and insights that arise from being inspired by the energy of each card.

Several cycles are contained within the full cycle of the 78 cards. This book focuses on the four major cycles of the deck. They are the four pillars on which your will build your dream.

Pillar One: See, Feel, Embody, and Align with Your Vision
In Pillar One, you will lay the foundation for growth and awareness. This would be like beginning a training program to participate in an athletic event. You get your muscles ready by slowly building up their strength. Major Arcana cards O through X and their corresponding Minor Arcana cards support you along the way.

Pillar Two: Subdue the Doubts and Banish the Gremlins
In Pillar Two, you move away from what holds you back, let go of what you no longer need, and face the parts of you that you chose not to acknowledge in the past. For the athlete in training, this would be when you give up unhealthy foods, late nights, and the other parts of your life that no longer support your goal to be a fine athlete.

Pillar Three: Stand Fully in Your Power
In Pillar Three, you bring yourself into alignment with who you are becoming on the mental, emotional, physical, and spiritual levels. For the athlete, this would be when the focus switches to an understanding of and a dedication to the knowledge that peak performance comes from being fit on all levels, the emotional, the mental, and the spiritual, as well as the physical.

Pillar Four: Claim Your Dream
In Pillar Four, you acknowledge that you are where you intend to be and that this moment is one of completeness. Eckart Tolle calls this the "power of now." The athlete uses competition for this, even though the finest athletes, even as they enter the Olympic stadium, are fully aware that they are out to show their best selves, that they are in competition more with their own top performance than against the nearest competitor.

As you end your journey, you can expect to experience satisfaction and joy as you acknowledge the challenges you've overcome and the support you've had to assist and guide you.

Again, think of the athlete who stands tall with grace and dignity, gold medal gleaming from the ribbon around his or her neck, relishing the joy and satisfaction of the moment, and who, at the same time, looks forward to returning to the training regime for the next journey.

All endings are also beginnings. Arriving at your destination means you've come to the place where your next journey begins.

The Process

For the purpose of initial exploration, I suggest you take your cue from the song and "start at the very beginning." Go on your Voyage to Success by starting with 0 Fool Child and ending with XXI Universe. Do at least one activity for each card. If you feel inspired or guided to do more than one per card, follow your instincts.

After one go around, you might want to play with the order for your next Voyage to Success. You could get a *Voyager Tarot Deck* and turn a card over and go to the page in the book that gives the information about the card you selected. Or, you could open the book to a random page and follow the guidance on the page.

No matter how you choose to Voyage to Success through the book, I suggest you always begin with the Fool Child. The Fool Child is where you claim your vision for your particular Voyage to Success. If you have your vision statement clearly in mind before you do any of the activities, you'll know where you hope to end up and the activities will make the most sense. As you move along, you might choose to change your vision statement, either wholly or in part, and that will work well, too. The point is to always have a vision statement as a focus as you play with the activities.

Trust yourself. Trust your instincts and intuition. Notice how your body reacts and responds to thoughts and actions as you Voyage along. These physical impulses are feedback meant to guide you. You know what's right for you. You know what you need to know and do to make your dreams come true. Your journey through the book allows you to uncover what's already inside of you and to be aware of and in tune with the opportunities that present themselves.

Fellow Travelers

Voyage with a group.

At the least, voyage with one other person.

Brené Brown, in her book, *The Gifts of Imperfection: Let Go of Who You Think You're Supposed to Be and Embrace Who You Are*, suggests that we are biologically driven to form connections to live our most fully realized destinies emotionally, physically, spiritually, and mentally. She adds that Daniel Goleman, in his book, *Social Intelligence: The New Science of Human Relationships*, shows how research into biology and neuroscience offers evidence that the human need for connection is part of our physiology.

I have been an educator for over thirty years and have learned, through classroom and other educational experiences, and by participating in educational research at Stanford University, that small groups are the most dynamic learning environments. Small learning groups consist of four to eight people. Much research supports this principle, but common sense also leads to this conclusion. Within this parameter, each person has the opportunity to participate, many ideas can be generated and talked through, contributions can be acknowledged, and all can feel they are accountable to the others in the group.

Whether you can form a group of four to eight—or even more—or not, I hope you can at least Voyage with one other person on a regular schedule. You will be more inclined to be proactive on your own behalf if you share your Voyages with at least one other person—and you'll likely be more stimulated to take part in your journey and be more excited to assist others in theirs. We all learn more in a group setting. As is often said, "There's magic and power in the gathering of people in a circle."

To Get Started

Connect with people who will make a commitment of six to twelve weeks. Time is needed in between meetings to integrate the energies and to play with the activities. Most of the activities can be performed, written about, and contemplated away from the meeting time. The meeting time can then be used for sharing what happened when experiencing the activities. Some activities, however, are intended to be done with at least one other person. These can be accomplished either during your meetings or before you arrive for your group interaction.

Set up a meeting schedule. Depending on the number of people in the group and the time allotted per meeting, several activities based on multiple *Voyager* tarot cards can be addressed during a given session. Two to three hours would be ideal for each session if you meet in person.

At the back of this book, you'll find an example of a Ninety-Day Curriculum that you can use, but I encourage you to go at the pace your group is most comfortable with.

Choose a leader or designate yourself as the leader. All groups need someone to shepherd participants through an agenda, to maintain the sacredness of time and place, and to occasionally and gently remind people of the intended purpose of the gathering. The leader, however, is not meant to be a "teacher" or "guru." The leader is very much part of the group. In time, the group will likely lead itself.

If a physical meeting time and place won't work, virtual connections are excellent, too. Simple emails can be the conduit, but social networking sites offer very good options as well.

Name your group. Decide on a name that suggests who you are and what you're about. I've been part of a group whose numbers have fluctuated between eight and ten for around twenty years now. We call ourselves the Joseph Campbell Group because in the beginning, we started our journey together by reading and watching videos by and about the adventurous mythologist. We used his teachings to guide us on our conscious "Hero's Journey," and have learned, through the power of myth, symbol, and story, of the role of the artist (we are all artists in need of creative self-expression), about the need for ritual and the regenerative energy found in higher consciousness. We have since used other guides for our many voyages. James Wanless and his *Voyager Tarot Deck*, for example, have been an important part of our group and individual journeys. No matter whose approach we are studying, we retain our name to remind us that we are on a conscious journey based on Campbell's principles.

While you go through *The Soul of Success*, I'll use Voyager Group as a group name, but I hope you give your group your own special name.

Whatever method you choose to connect with another or several Voyagers, I strongly urge you to find a way to be part of a group, no matter the size. There's power and magic in connections!

I hope you will find that this process of creating a life of purpose, meaning, and abundance becomes a constant for you and your family and friends. You, and the world, will be far richer, wiser, and happier for being a Voyager to Success.

Bon Voyage!

Chapter Zero

O Fool-Child Energies: Begin the Journey

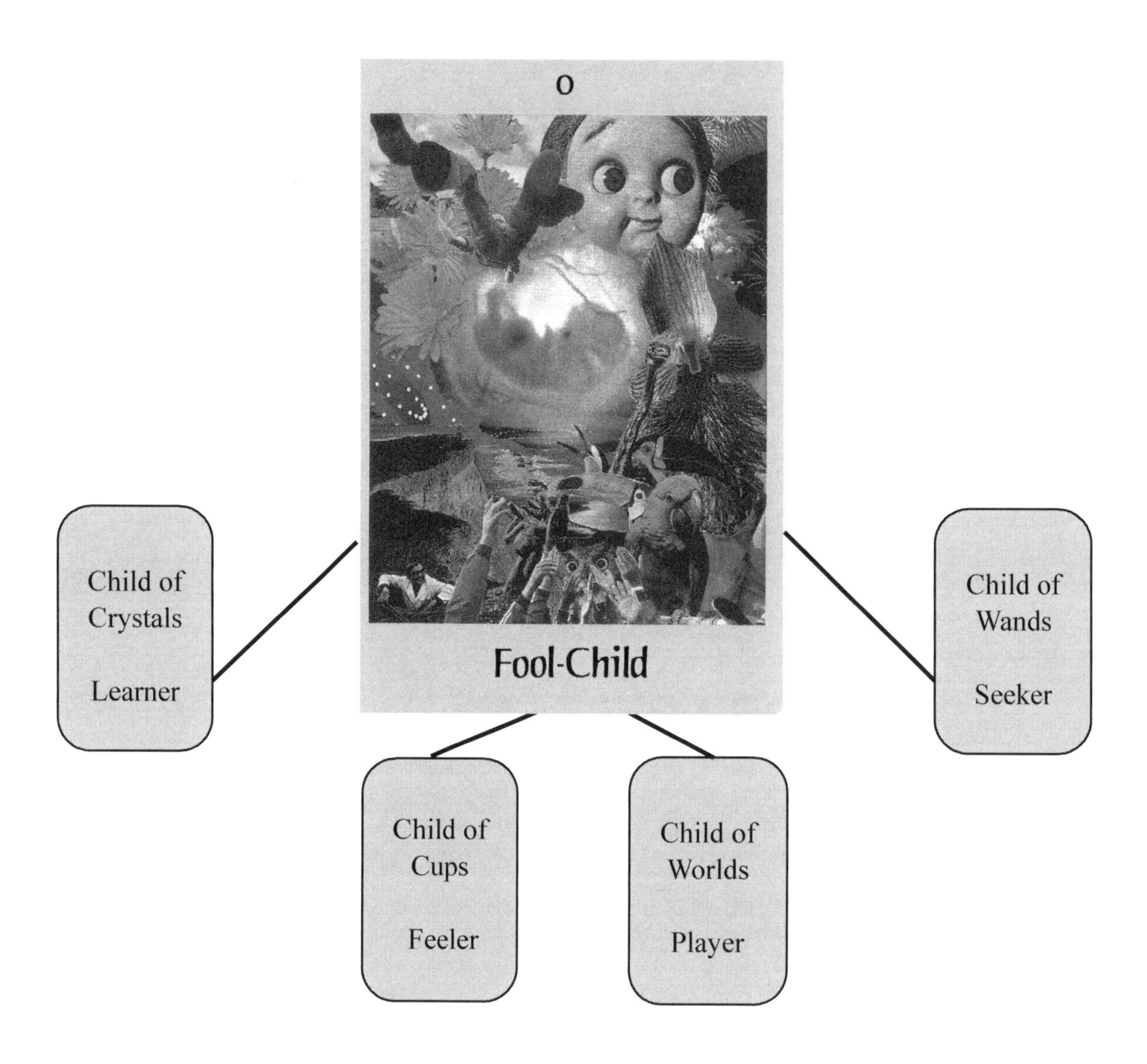

"It is something to be able to paint a particular picture, or to carve a statue, or so to make a few objects beautiful; but it is far more glorious to carve and paint the very atmosphere through which we look - to affect the quality of the day, that is the highest of the arts."

Henry David Thoreau, 1817-1862, author, poet and abolitionist

O Fool Child Plunge into the Adventure of Your Own Life.

You are a person of pure potential!

What do you need to prepare for the life of your dreams?

Everything you need to make this life possible is inside you. This *Soul of Success* book is merely a guide to help you get at what's already there.

Keep your whole self open—mind, body, heart, and spirit—and you will discover everything you need to create the life of your dreams.

Play with beginnings and endings.

Let go of any emotional attachments you may have to your dreams and goals.

Open yourself to life in unconventional ways.

Be the hero of your life.

Take that leap of faith and dance, walk, run, skip, ride, fly, twirl, and soar toward your dreams.

Robert Fulghum tells the following story in his article, "Everything I Need to Know, I Learned in Kindergarten":

When the frontiersmen in America left civilization for long adventures in unchartered territory, they had to carry everything with them as they rode on horseback.

Also, they knew they would eventually run out of supplies, so they came to carry what was commonly referred to as their "possibles." In a small leather bag hung around the neck was assembled, in a brass case, flint, steel, and tinder to make a fire. A knife, powder, shot, and a gun completed the list of basics, of their possibles.

Yet even when these spirited adventurers depleted, lost, or saw ruined the whole kit and caboodle, many survived.

They learned that the real bag of possibles was contained inside them.

Use this guidebook to set you on a path of creative evolutionary action that will put you into the mind of a new consciousness.

To Begin:

✱ **Write a vision statement** declaring your intention to create your new life. Now is the time to proclaim what it is that you are ready to bring into your life. What's out in the vast universe of unlimited potential that you are open to receiving?

A vision statement is a simple declaration that may sound something like one of these statements:

I, Betty Dietz, commit to writing a book with the intention to inspire creative visionaries to reach their highest potential, benefitting themselves in all areas of their lives while also having a positive, powerful, and long-lasting affect on the world.

I, (name), commit to educating children about global warming.

I, (name), commit to writing a play about how to find peaceful ways to solve conflicts.

I, (name), commit to easing the pain of people suffering from depression.

I, (name), commit to resolving my issues with my abusive family.

I, (name), commit to discovering a stimulating, interesting, creative career that will pay well.

I, (name), commit to resolving the tension between my partner and me.

I, (name), commit to eating a healthy diet and exercising regularly.

Write your vision statement based on whatever you want to focus on.

✱ **Announce this intention to your group**. If you don't have a group, find at least three people willing to hear what you are up to and tell them the vision you have for yourself now. Don't elaborate on the details. You don't know them yet. This is your leap of faith.

✱ **If anyone offers you ideas or contacts**, write down these thoughts and names and act on their inspirations when the appropriate time arrives. Now may or may not be the time, but soon an idea that may have seemed too "out there" at this stage of your commitment might appear easy and just the right thing to do.

✱ **Practice saying your vision statement in a way that communicates what you are doing so anytime anyone asks about what's up in your life, you're ready to spread the word.** The more people you tell, the more opportunities will open up to help you along your path. Make this statement short and clear. This might sound something like: You know how some people want to live more meaningful lives? I'm writing a book with over 200 activities to show how to live a soul-inspired life.

Learner/Child of Crystals
Activate your curious mind.

Use the Energy of Child of Crystals to:

Be like a child: open, inquisitive, and curious.

Examine how your beliefs and attitudes create your reality.

Look to the future with optimism and a sense of wonder.

See the big picture and how things are connected.

Caution: Don't fall back on old ways of thinking just because that's what you were taught as a child.

Play with these activities for exploring your learner's mind:

✱ **Write down some positive, healthy beliefs you hold as part of your core belief system.**

✱ **Write a list of beliefs you would like to claim but don't feel ready to own yet.** This is your wish list.

✱ **Choose one belief from your wish list.** Write this out on several index cards. Place these cards in places where you'll see them as you go about your day to remind you of the qualities you are getting ready to own. Change them out when you feel ready to move the wished-for belief to your list of core beliefs.

✱ **What beliefs and behaviors are you holding onto that you haven't examined lately?** These may be beliefs or attitudes that you haven't looked at ever, but you accepted because you were told to. These would be the things that you do because you've always done them or because everyone in your family believes this or votes this way or reads these authors or watches or listens to this news station or goes to or has gone to these schools, stores, vacation spots, places of worship.

✱ **Make a list and examine these beliefs.**

✱ **Eliminate the attitudes, beliefs, and behaviors that no longer suit you.**

Here are some examples of belief statements. You may choose to use some of these, but be sure to make up your own statements, too.

- I am a caring, loving person.
- I know I make valuable contributions to my family, my job, my community, my friends.
- I am outstanding and effective.
- I am intuitive and sensitive.
- I express my creativity in positive, engaging ways.
- I am intelligent and perceptive.
- People can rely on me.
- I work hard at making the world better in big ways and small ways.
- I am active and healthy.
- I am perfect just the way I am.
- I am well loved.
- I receive love with an open heart.
- I receive compliments with grace and ease.

Share some of your responses with your Voyager Group.

Life is process. We go through stages, awarenesses, and understandings of our world views. To hold to any one state is a kind of death to the soul. The soul pushes toward growth.

Feeler/Child of Cups
Be sensitive, open, and trusting.

Use the Energy of Child of Cups to:

Let your feelings guide you to discover the world in new ways.

Express your feelings fully and exuberantly. Be animated!

Allow your feelings to flow by quickly.

Express yourself and then move on.

Caution: Don't repress your feelings. Don't hold onto any one emotion. Be in the moment with your emotions.

Play with these activities for exploring your emotional state:

✱ **Hug someone you care about every day for at least a week.**

✱ **Smile at people as often as possible—in passing, at the check out counter, when boarding a bus, a train, a plane, at the dog park, when picking up your child from a friend's house.** Make a concentrated effort to offer a smile as often as possible everyday for a week.

✱ **Honestly express your feelings to let others see more of who you are.** This might look something like this:
When a friend asks about your job search, you might respond with a quick, "Going well. I'm sure something will come up for me."

Or, you could respond more honestly by relating how you feel and saying: "I feel good about my interviews. I work hard to prepare for them. But I'm surprised at how how long this process is taking. I sometimes worry I'll never get another job."

Be honest about your feelings and allow others to be honest with you, too.

✱ **Everyday for seven days, tell someone a dream you have for yourself.** Or tell each person a different dream you have. Let each person know you're telling him or her about your dream because you trust he or she will be supportive of you and your goals.

✱ **Make a collage that celebrates you.** Use photos, drawings, words, phrases, poems, or anything else that speaks to you about what a great person you are. Have this out for at least a week. Longer would be better.

✱ **Write a poem, a short story, or an essay about something that moves you.** Spend the whole week, or even longer, on one of these projects. Or you may choose to write seven different pieces. Continue if your writing muse takes up residence.

✱ **Write a note telling someone you care about how you're feeling about them right now**. Repeat this for seven days and seven different people. Short and sweet is good.

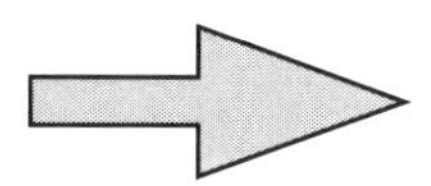

Write your responses to these activities in your journal.

Share some of your responses with your Voyager Group.

Player/Child of Worlds
Create a playful mindset.

Use the Energy of Child of Worlds to:

Make your life fun. Lighten up!

Create the life you want to live by first seeing this new way of being in the world in your imagination, fantasies, and daydreams.

Play at being who you want to be.

Seek excitement, and enjoy what you do.

Caution: Don't get stuck in the fantasy world. Use the dream to reach your goals.

Play with these activities for exploring playful ways of being in the world:

* **Seek out something novel to do.**

* **Read Jane McGonigal's *Reality is Broken,* or go to her website and play one or more of the games she recommends.** Whether you use McGonigal's book for this exercise or not, I highly recommend *Reality is Broken*. She suggests, after much research and with great enthusiasm, that gamers will solve the world's biggest problems and that we can all be gamers.

* **Choose one of your senses and totally immerse yourself into concentrating on just that sensation for sixty seconds.** For example, while eating, close your eyes and for sixty seconds notice how your food tastes as you chew. Pay attention to which part of your tongue lights up with the flavor sensations you are experiencing. Examine the texture and assess how much you like, or don't appreciate, how the food feels in your mouth.

Write your responses to these activities in your journal.

Share some of your responses with your Voyager Group.

* **Play a game by yourself.** Play a game with another person. Play a game with a team. Make up a game to play.

* **Act out a scene from a play or a movie by yourself or with others.**

* **Daydream for ten minutes.** Set a timer and stay with your daydream the full ten minutes. This is also called lucid dreaming and can be used to tap into your subconscious to give you insights you already know but haven't given yourself opportunity to bring to the surface yet. Write down what you thought about. Write about the daydream. Think about, explore, and seek input from others about the images that came to you.

Friedrich Kekule reported that he discovered the ring shape of the benzene molecule after having a reverie or daydream of a snake seizing its own tail. The vision came to the organic chemist after years of studying the nature of carbon-carbon bonds, so he took the time to contemplate this mythical symbol that appeared to him in light of the problem he was attempting to solve, and he was able to connect with the answer.

Seeker/Child of Wands
Discover yourself.

Use the Energy of Child of Wands to:

Seek out eternal truths by looking closely at the world around you.

Connect with everything you see.

Trust yourself and your inner knowing.

Be sincere, attentive, and uninhibited in your quest for transformation.

Question authority! (Especially your own inner critic.)

Caution: Don't get so "grown up" that you lose your curiosity about life.

Play with these activities to explore how to connect to ~~your~~ yourself, your world, your divine nature:

✱ **Think about something you want to make happen to promote your dream, and then think about a person who could help you make even a small step toward achieving your goal.** Now call that person and tell him or her about your dream for yourself. See what happens next. If nothing, let the experience of making the call be the gift. If this person offers a suggestion, follow up on what's been offered.

✱ **Write a note to someone who has been influential in your life, and thank this person for what he or she gave you and explain what you gained from this person's influence.**

✱ **Send the note!**

✱ **Take a walk in nature or in your own garden, and find a tree to stand near or sit under.** Ask for guidance on how to take the next step toward your dream for yourself. Be still for as long as feels comfortable and see what comes to you. Acting on what you "hear" or "see" or "feel" or "know" is the next step. Don't second-guess yourself. Trust what comes to you and act on this inspiration.

✱ **Invite someone to lunch or dinner at your home and prepare a healthy and delicious meal.** Have a conversation. Ask about this person's life. Enjoy the time you spend together.

✱ **Watch a movie that invites provocative thought, that inspires you to think about something differently, or that moves you to want to take action against some injustice.** Write down what you want to do or see happen. Take one step to make this happen. If you can do this with one or more other people who are interested in taking action to positively affect the world, that would be even better. The power in numbers, great or small, should not be underestimated.

✱ **Light a candle and watch the flame burn for ten or fifteen minutes.** Write whatever comes to you after the ten or fifteen minutes elapse. Are you inspired to do something new? Take a step in that direction.

✱ **Go outside or look outside or thumb through a picture book or magazine and notice what bird or animal attracts your attention.** What qualities does the animal have? Claim these qualities as your own.

Ask your animal or bird friend what message you're being given. Listen to what you hear in your head and heart. Take advantage and do what you can to follow the guidance of this creature.

✱ **Use an oracle deck for intuitive messages.** Some decks that I recommend are John Holland's, Angeles Arrien's, Steven Farmer's, and, of course, James Wanless'. This list isn't exhaustive. Use whatever deck speaks to you.

Make a practice of writing in your Voyager Journal everyday, recording responses, reactions, thoughts, and ideas that come from any of the exercises you do as you make your Voyager journey.

Sometimes just having a record of your thoughts will inspire you to do something new in the future. Writing in your journal about your meditations and activities as an everyday practice can help you sort through all of those innovative and exciting ideas that are brewing within you.

Through writing, you can discover what you're awakening to.

When you are in the flow of life and doing your best—oftentimes most amazing—work, you are likely living instinctually. To live instinctually means trusting that each next movement is the right one to take and unhesitatingly taking that step.

Athletes who push themselves to excel often speak about getting to a place where they "know" what to do next: where the next safe toehold is on the sheer face of the granite; how to lean into the next curve for maximum speed without wiping out; what bend of the knee will make the jump that much higher.

Artists often speak about channeling their muse: whole books are written as if on their own, and the writer nothing more than a conduit between inspiration and form; clay forms itself into the perfect shape; dance movements follow the music precisely; colors on a canvas seem to appear from somewhere beyond the artist's palette.

Share your thoughts, actions, and musings with your Voyager Group.

"Youth is not a time of life--it is a state of mind. It is a temper of the will; a quality of the imagination; a vigor of the emotions; it is a freshness of the deep springs of life. Youth means a temperamental predominance of courage over timidity, of the appetite for adventure over a life of ease... Nobody grows old by merely living a number of years; people grow old by deserting their ideals."

Samuel Ullman, 1840-1924, businessman and poet

Chapter One
I Magician Energies: Express Your Personal Power

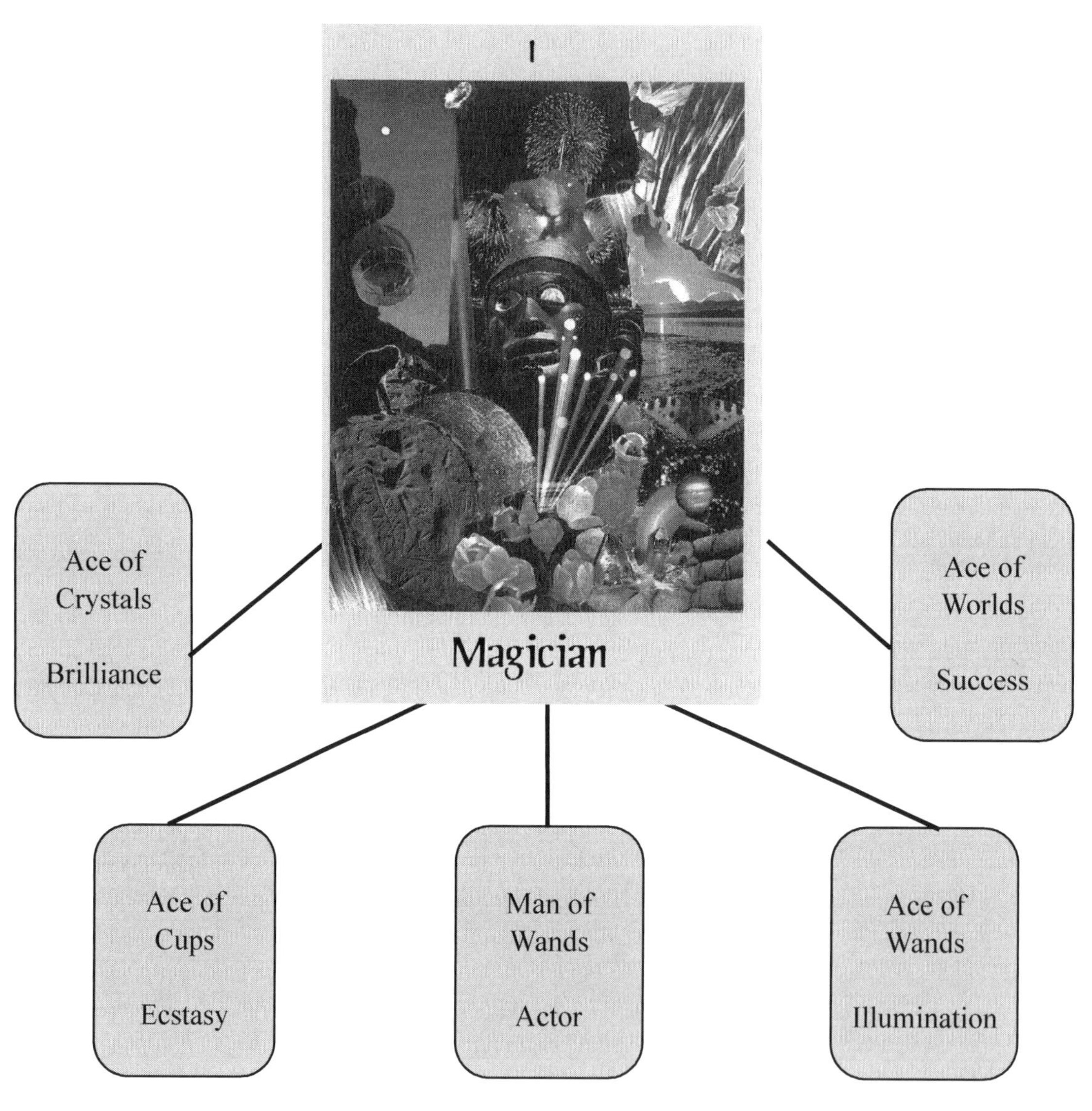

"Magic is believing in yourself. If you can do that, you can make anything happen."
Johann Wolfgang von Goethe 1749-1832, poet, novelist, and philosopher

I Magician Make it Happen!

Let your imagination run wild! Excite your senses! Be ecstatic! Feel your power!

Make up your own story and tell the world who you are and where you're going. Then open yourself up to getting the support you need to make your dreams come true.

✱ See yourself as you want to be in five years, ten years, twenty years. Then write the script. Name yourself—are you a doctor, singer, dancer, drummer in a rock band, MacArthur recipient, healer, writer of best selling books? Tell what you accomplish. Mention the obstacles you overcome and the allies you meet along the way. Remember, this is the story you're making up as you prepare to live the life of your dreams. Let your imagination run wild!

Read your story to your Voyager Group.

Write Your Own Story

Once there was a _______(name who you expect to be in your ideal future—"writer," "creative holistic entrepreneur," "a third grade teacher" or ??),

who _________ (state your accomplishment, such as "wrote a novel about the impact of war on the family of a vet," or "inspired thousands of people to start businesses," or "helped third graders to be successful in school and in their lives," or ??).

This happened in spite of these many outside challenges: _______(list a few things that might keep you from your goal).

This was accomplished because of the support of mentors, teachers, guides, and helpers such as _________(include people you know as well as some you'd like to have appear in your life.)

This was accomplished because _______ (your name) was able to overcome inner obstacles that included __________. (Name some inner blocks to your success. This could be poor self esteem, lack of energy, pessimism, fear of failure, fear of success in your chosen dream arena, a penchant for putting other people's dreams and needs ahead of your own or ??)

This was accomplished because ______ (your name) had these strengths, talents, and abilities: ___________. (Include attributes and talents you now claim and those that you feel you'll need to reach your dreams.)

✱ Michael Larsen, of Michael Larsen-Elizabeth Pomada Literary Agency, offered a Holiday Wish List for perfect days in his blog in December, 2011.

Michael imagined his perfect days would begin by waking up feeling inspired to do work he was passionate about. He then offered a list of activities and ways of being and thinking which included such things as the kind of food he would eat, how he would take care of his body, where his time would most productively be spent, what his environment would look like, and where he'd invest his thoughts.

Taking a cue from Michael, here's my imperfect list of possibilities for perfect days:

Waking up feeling grateful for the restful, satisfying sleep I had and feeling ready to invest my day in pursuits I'm passionate about.

Realizing that this day holds everything for me and resolving to enjoy and savor the good things that come my way and to let go of what doesn't support or nurture me and my dreams.

Delighting in the home I've created that's filled with light, books, art, views of nature, music, and opportunities for people to gather in joy, sorrow, celebration, spiritual renewal, companionship, and stimulating conversation.

Having time with my supportive, loving, fun, encouraging, inspiring and inspirational family and community of friends.

Communicating with my husband and children about their lives, hopes, dreams, and concerns.

Eating nutritious, delicious, and healthy meals from food grown and produced locally.

Feeling both challenged and inspired by my creative projects.

Investing several hours in my writing projects.

Celebrating an accomplishment.

Hearing loving words expressed by the people I care about and speaking loving words to them.

Supporting others in the pursuit of their dreams.

Being patient with my own and others' shortcomings.

Taking small steps toward big goals regularly, consistently, and mindfully throughout the day.

Exercising by walking, stretching, doing energetic movements, and playing tennis.

Taking care of my financial obligations to be debt-free, mindful of where I'm spending money, and not spending money on the frivolous or unaffordable.

Reading stimulating, well-written, and thought provoking materials.

Enjoying a movie, play, concert, or art.

Using sparingly and appreciating abundantly our precious natural resources.

Noticing how amazing and wonderful the world is as I walk in a natural environment.

Experiencing the warmth, energy, and tenderness of touching another person, animal, or plant.

Ending the day with a kiss and a hug from someone I love and who I know loves me.

Make your own list of what your perfect days would include.

Brilliance/Ace of Crystals
Energize your brilliant ideas.

Use the Energy of Ace of Crystals to:

Be aware of flashes of insight and to not let them slip away.

Organize and act on your ideas. Write down your thoughts before they're lost.

Refine your ideas so they appeal to others. Use them for your own success and for the betterment of the lives of others.

Trust your intuition to guide you in positive, helpful ways.

Caution: Don't be dismissive of the flashes of brilliance that come to you. They'll go elsewhere if you don't capture and nurture them.

Play with these activities to explore your brilliance:

✱ **Use your dreams for inspiration.** Write down your dreams and see what they're telling you. Share them with your group, and see if you get any "aha's" from what others see in your dream. Just remember that we all offer our own projections, that is we talk about what the images or scenes mean to us when we comment on other people's dreams (and lives).

For help with dreams, check out Jeremy Taylor's books and website at Jeremytaylor.com, or James O'Hara's website at archetypeworld.net.They both offer tips and insights into how to work with dreams. For example, they both suggest using the phrase: "In my version of your dream . . ." when giving feedback to someone who has shared a dream. This phrasing creates more openness for accepting the insights that are meaningful to the one who shared the dream and for not taking on anything that's a projection on the part of the commenter. However, just because a statement is a projection, doesn't mean the feedback can't be helpful.

✱ **Keep a people journal.** Write down a statement about the people who have come into your life throughout the day. These people may be people you meet or speak with, but they can also be people on TV, in movies, on the radio, or someone you read about. They can also be fictional characters. Daily, weekly, monthly, read what you've written and see what comes to you.

✱ **Make a list of what you want to contribute to the world.** Add to the list as often as new ideas come to you.

✱ **Keep an intuition journal.** Write down thoughts that seem to be important, but that you're not sure what to do with. At the end of every week, read what you've written for the past week, for the past month. What comes to you now?

✱ **Pay attention to synchronicities as you go through your day.** What is in front of you? What is off in the distance? How can you use these images as metaphors to gain clarity? Make up something to fit the image to your question or issue. Be wildly imaginative! Note your brilliant insights.

✱ **Use your own deck of whatever cards are meaningful to you to pick a card a day.**

✱ **Read a line, a paragraph, or a page from any book and see what "message" rises from the passage.** Do this everyday for at least two weeks.

Share your responses/reactions to some of your activities with your Voyager Group.

Ecstasy/Ace of Cups
Feel your way to success.

Use the Energy of Ace of Cups to:

Live in ecstasy by loving and revering all of life.

Completely express your emotions—the full range of your feelings, from dark to light, happy to sad, energetic to boring—everything!

Be emotionally expansive. Explore all of your feelings.

Express all of your feelings in a positive, constructive, and exuberant way.

Caution: Don't suppress "bad" or "negative" or "nasty" feelings.

Play with these activities to explore your ecstatic emotional state:

✱ **Play the Silly Faces Game.** Look into a mirror and make faces that express a wide range of feelings.

✱ **Make a set of index cards describing different emotions based on something concrete, and pick several at random.** Facially express each emotion.

Show an emotion that reflects each of the following circumstances:

- happy that you won a prize
- ecstatic to see someone you care deeply about
- delighted to hear from someone who lives far away
- pleased that you finished an assignment
- sad because you feel lonely
- scared because you might lose your house
- upset because you can't find your keys
- worried about the results of a biopsy
- concerned over debt
- disappointed because someone stood you up

✱ **Play the Silly Faces Game with a partner.** Each person makes a face mimicking the other's reaction to an emotion. To do this, say or read the trigger phrase, such as "annoyed because the dog pooped in the house." One person makes an appropriate facial reaction. The other person responds in kind.

At some point, switch who goes first and who does the mimicking.

When you've both completed the exercise, talk about how this felt. Which "face" did you feel most comfortable doing? Which were hard to get into? Any thoughts on why you had these reactions?

✱ **Hug someone! Hug lots of people!**

✱ **After reading an article that moves you, write a letter to the editor, the blogger, or the essayist and begin by expressing an emotion.** You might start your letter by saying, "I was angry to learn that . . ." or "I am delighted that you . . ." Explain why you are feeling the way you are in a positive, constructive way.

← **Send the letter.** →

Write in your Voyager Journal about what you did and how you felt doing the activities.

Share these responses with your Voyager Group.

Success/Ace of Worlds
Recognize yourself as an achiever.

Use the Energy of Ace of Worlds to:

Establish yourself as a success in the world.

Confidently and with determination move toward your dream.

Expand your material success.

Create the world you want to live in. Do whatever you need to make this happen.

Dream and envision.

Caution: Don't attach yourself to your success. Success happens to you, but it isn't you.

Play with these activities to explore what it's like to be successful:

✱ **See yourself as accomplishing whatever you want to accomplish.** Dress the part as often as you can.

✱ **Make a list of the awards you'd love to win.** This list is meant to acknowledge the accomplishments you'd like to make and the legacies you'd like to leave, so the "awards" aren't necessarily real awards. They might be something like "the Tony for being the best reader of the most exciting stories in the children's hospital cancer ward."

✱ **Write a to do list of ten steps you can take that will move you toward accomplishing what you want to achieve.** Everyday, do at least one thing on that list. Do more when you can. Add to the list as often as you think of things.

✱ **For your next Voyager Group meeting, have a "dress the part" day: wear the clothing and accessories and bring the accouterments of who you hope to become.**

✱ **Contact people who are successful in the field you are preparing for.** Write or call them and tell them how much you admire what they've accomplished and ask for one specific piece of advice. For example, if you hope to be a published author, write to one of your favorite writers and ask what they did to get their first book contract.

✱ **Make a visual aid that acknowledges your success and put it up in your office or home.** Jack Canfield wanted to be a successful author, so he had a mock *New York Times Best Seller's* list printed with his name and the title of his book, *Chicken Soup for the Soul,* at the top spot. He placed this in a prominent place in his office and, as they say, the rest (his multi-million dollar "chicken soup" industry) is history.

✱ **Record an acceptance speech for the award you'd like to win for your accomplishment and listen to it everyday.** Add a sound track of applause.

Get together the clothing you would wear if you achieved your goal. Maybe you want to be a successful musician in an orchestra. Buy an outfit that makes you look like you could step into the first chair at the symphony. Practice your instrument several days a week wearing this attire. Visualize yourself playing with the whole symphony to a packed house at the symphony hall of your dreams.

✱ **Everyday, spend five or ten minutes sitting quietly and visualizing yourself in the life you want to live.** Be imaginative. Add people you want in your life, add material objects you'd love to surround yourself with. Include images of the work you'll be doing and see the people who will benefit from what you're doing.

Conclude your meditation by taking in a deep breath and exhaling slowly. With that in and out breath think the thought: everything in my life is here as an answer to my deep desire to stand in my integrity.

Do this visualization with your Voyager Group as well as making it a daily practice. Sharing an experience and allowing others to "bear witness" to our process creates powerful energetic support without a word being spoken.

Take another deep breath in and again exhale slowly. With this in and out breath think the thought: I stand in my integrity.

When you open your eyes, allow yourself to live with the thought: I stand in my integrity.

Share an activity or some of your responses to an activity with your Voyager Group.

Look at everyone you meet and see them as a VIP. Ask yourself what you could do or say to make that person know how important he or she is. Sometimes, all it takes to make someone feel special is making eye contact.

Illumination/Ace of Wands
Acknowledge that you are enlightened.

Use the Energy of Ace of Wands to:

Know whatever you need to know. All knowledge is available to you.

Grow with ease and grace. Whatever you need for growth will be readily accessible.

Act with courage to create a new, more conscious, and more energized life for yourself.

Be alive to who you are.

Trust yourself to be authentic, truthful, and honorable with others and with yourself.

Caution: Don't burn up or out by being too intense or by pushing yourself too hard.

Play with these activities to illuminate your connection to your highest self:

✱ **Follow your intuitions and dream messages.** Constantly take action on any "hit" of inspiration that you get. When something doesn't work out, move on. Be very active once you get an idea. See it through. Follow the threads of inspiration.

When you're inspired, you'll likely feel energized, almost electric. Put yourself into the zone of action when you feel the buzz. This may take courage, but the rewards are great if you follow the inklings and tinglings in your body.

✱ **Take action even when you don't know exactly where you're going to end up.** The power of creation is in the process. You may change course many times, but if you're not doing something, nothing is going to happen.

- What's one action you could take right now to get you closer to achieving your dream?
- What's one action you could take tomorrow to get you closer to achieving your dream?
- What's one action you could take next week that will get you closer to achieving your dream?
- Commit to eliminating any source of negativity or any blockages that keep you from the truth of who you are and where you are going.

Did you take any of these actions? ←

Trust in process, bring awareness to your intentions, have the courage to act, and you'll achieve what's in your highest good.

Write your responses to these activities in your journal.

Share some of your responses with your Voyager Group.

Actor/Man of Wands
Know that you can make good things happen.

Use the Energy of Man of Wands to:

Be a shaman and explore all of life by taking on the essence of what's around you.

Know that you have the power to influence and transform anything to make your dreams come true.

Act out what you want to achieve. Make your own meaning.

Trust your inspirations and act on your inspired creativity.

Caution: Don't be unnecessarily cautious, defensive, or self-conscious.

Play with these activities to act the part of being connected to your highest self:

The best actors embody their parts. Be who you want to become. Name and claim how you see yourself when your dreams come true.

William Ball, artistic director and founder of San Francisco's American Conservatory Theatre, writes in *A Sense of Direction: Some Observations on the Art of Directing* that all actions follow desire. People want something, so they take some action to obtain what they want for themselves, for others, or even to change the world. Ball writes that the essence of life, and therefore, acting, is about taking action. If you know your objective, you can infuse your life with actions to get what you want.

Objective
To write a book I can be proud of.

My actions: I set aside time at least five days a week to write for one, two, or more hours a day. I show up, and I write. I do not read email or surf the web.

Jonathan Franzen, best selling award winning author of *Freedom* and *The Corrections*, writes on a computer that isn't connected to the internet and doesn't have any games on it. When he needs to do research, he sets aside time for research. But his writing time is only for writing.

✱ **State your objective and the actions that show how you can do what you hope to accomplish.** Your objective is a step you can take to get closer to your bigger goal of achieving your dream as stated in your intention statement.

Your objective and scenario might look like these examples:

Objective
To get the bank to lend me money for my business.

My actions: I dress the part and wear clothes to impress the loan officer. I prepare my business plan. I prepare my speech to convince the loan officer I'm worth investing in and my business is a winning concept. I make an appointment to speak with the loan officer. If this one says no, I repeat the process until one says yes, always taking in and seeking out feedback to refine my actions.

Take those actions!

Objective
To impress someone that I'd be a good life coach for him or her.

My actions: I offer a free coaching consultation. If it's in person, I dress nicely. I smile often. I make eye contact when I speak. I ask the person some questions about his or her goals, give feedback, offer suggestions, and offer encouragement to show what a coaching session is like. I end the session by asking if she would like to sign up for a series of five sessions at a special rate. If she hesitates or expresses concerns, I address each issue she raises.

If the problem she has is about money, I ask what she would lose or what she would miss out on if she didn't achieve her goals. I assure her I will be with her, supporting her, on this most important journey she has expressed a need to commit to.

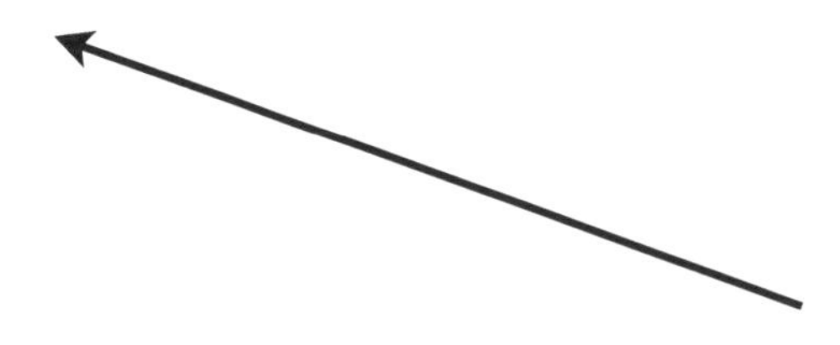

Take those actions!

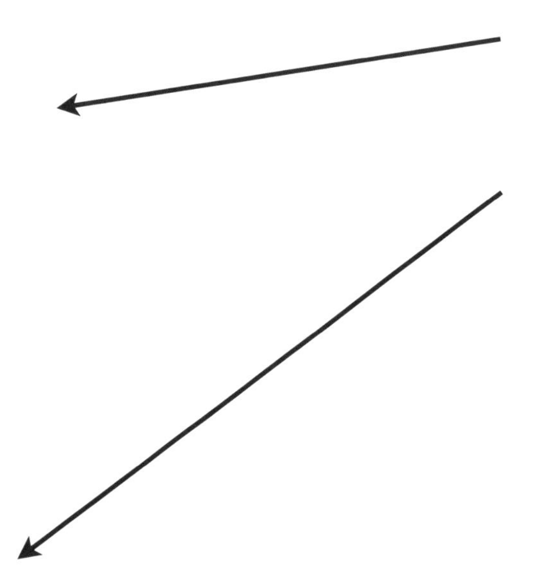

In your Voyager Journal, write several objectives and actions you can take that will get you closer to fulfilling your dreams.

Share these with your Voyager Group. Share what actions you've taken. If you haven't taken any actions, share your thoughts as to why you haven't. What help do you need to take these actions?

Chapter Two

II Priestess Energies: Use Your Inherent Wisdom

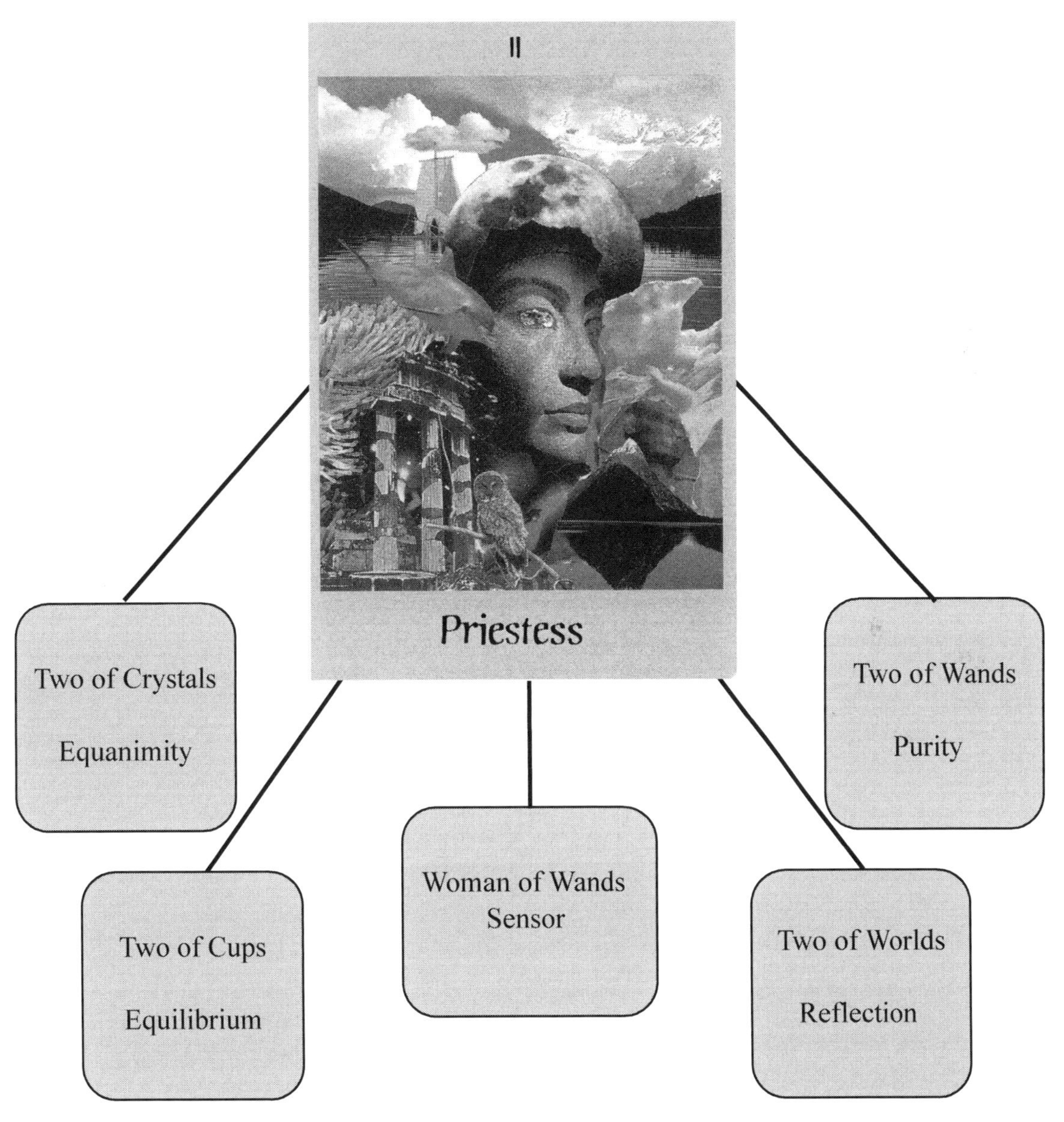

"Write down the thoughts of the moment. Those that come unsought for are commonly the most valuable."

Francis Bacon 1561-1626
philosopher, statesman, scientist, and author

II Priestess
Trust Your Intuition.

Tap into your subconscious for all the answers you need.

Be still and sink into your own inner wisdom.

Be calm and let your mind be still.

Meditate.

Trust your intuition to lead you to the truth of what you need to know.

Act on intuitive hits.

Tap into your own wisdom and trust in yourself.

Find a place and time in your day, everyday, for stillness and contemplation.

Caution: Beware of inaction.

Elias Howe had been working unsuccessfully to invent the sewing machine. One night, he dreamed he was being attacked by fierce African tribesmen. He awoke in a sweat from the nightmare, and as he recalled the dream, he noticed that the spears that repeatedly poked at him in his dream all had a single hole in the pointed end of the spear. Because he had been struggling with how to mechanize sewing, he understood the answer was being given to him in this dream.

Larry Page grew up surrounded by computers. Both his parents were computer scientists. Page says that he knew from the time he was twelve that he wanted to be an entrepreneur. When he and Serge Brinn connected and became friends at Standford, both were writing their PhD dissertations and playing off each other's ideas. Page was interested in how to link millions of webpages. Brinn liked algorithms. Ultimately, Page is said to have gotten the message about mining data in a dream, and eventually Google was founded.

Many artists say they write, paint, dance, and sing in an almost trance-like state where they allow the words, melodies, images, and movements to come to them. They open themselves to receiving inspiration. When they give up the struggle to "find" something, they discover the creative juices flow almost effortlessly.

Know what problem you're attempting to resolve or solve. Know where you want to get to. Know what you want for yourself, and your world. Work toward the resolution. Take the time to be still and pay attention to what surfaces in your mind's eye, what you seem to hear that comes from within, what your heart tells you, what your body seems to be saying. Write down the images and thoughts that seemingly emerge out of nowhere. Keep a journal of these thoughts for at least two weeks and see what messages await you. Better yet, make this kind of journaling a lifestyle practice.

Listen to a visualization recording and when you "come back," write down what rises to consciousness. Don't censor anything. Don't worry if the thoughts don't make sense. Write until you feel you've written enough. Wait a week or two and then read what you wrote. Share what you've written with your group or at least with one other person.

✱ Write a response to what you've written after one of your visualization meditations.

✱ Listen to a recording or watch a video about something that interests you, and doodle as you listen.

✱ To understand the messages that come to you, prepare yourself for who you want to be, what you want to know, do, and understand.

- Take classes.
- Get coaching.
- Read up on your field of interest.
- Seek out the stars in your arena.
- Find a mentor.
- Teach what you want to learn.
- Create a Voyager Success Circle.
- Talk to someone everyday about your vision for yourself and for the world you want to create.

✱ Pay attention to the inspirations that arise from within, write them down and act on them at the appropriate time.

Don't hesitate to express yourself in new and unfamiliar ways! Be bold and daring as you explore your inner guidance.

Share some of your responses with your Voyager Group.

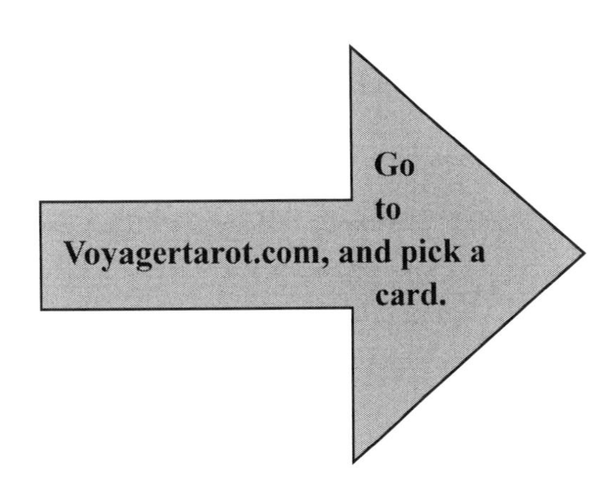

Equanimity/Two of Crystals
Seek a heightened state of balanced awareness.

Use the Energy of Two of Crystals to:

See without judging what you are noticing.

Think in terms of proportion, beauty, and balance. Stay centered.

Be positive and optimistic.

Enjoy the peacefulness and serenity that comes with thoughtful and balanced awareness.

Caution: Don't get fixated on perfection. Think about the best possible plan, not the one and only best plan.

Play with these activities to explore how to be in your equanimous mind:

* **Go someplace in nature that is quiet and peaceful.** Find something that you can look at for at least five minutes. This might be a single leaf, a flower, a tree, a mountain off in the distance, water flowing in a stream, or a meadow with deer grazing. Notice how you feel as you sit in the presence of the beauty around you.

* **Go to an art exhibit or museum, preferably one where they have chairs or benches so you can sit and enjoy the art.** Don't rush through the exhibit or museum. Instead, choose one gallery or section that has a few pieces of art that appeal to you. Sit and enjoy them. You may be inspired to write about the piece or write something inspired by the piece. You may feel like drawing. Or you may just feel like soaking in the beauty or feeling the power of what's in front of you.

* **Find a photo of yourself when you were a child glowing with the innocence, joy, and wonder of yourself and the world**. This child still exists within you. Nurture this part of yourself. Carry the photo around with you and look at it often. Remind the child she or he is loved by you. Offer today's wisdom, knowledge, and loving thoughts to the child you were to keep her joy alive for you now.

* **Entertain positive thoughts.** When a negative or self-defeating thought comes to you, say the words to yourself, "cancel, cancel," and replace the non-productive thought with a positive one.

Monitor what you think, and only allow thoughts that will be most beneficial to you and to your goal of achieving your dreams.

Choose a painting that you're attracted to and sit in front of it for at least five minutes. Time yourself, so that you really stay with the image in front of you.

Focus on the lines, the colors, the forms, and the textures.

Think about how proportion, beauty, and balance have been achieved in the painting.

Notice how you feel as you sit in the presence of something you find beautiful.

To practice being non-judgmental about yourself, use the journalist's approach. Think of a belief you'd like to adopt or an issue you're trying to resolve or a goal you're attempting to reach. Now write about it as if it has already happened, and you're reporting on what occurred by using the five w's of objective reporting: who, what, when, where, and why.

Who is it about?
Describe yourself objectively.
An example might sound like this: Mary, a woman in her forties, wants to find something exciting and worthwhile to do that will bring in as much or more income than she is making as a tech writer. Mary is single and has no one else but herself to rely on for support. Mary is responsible in how she handles money and makes sure she not only makes enough to live on comfortably but also contributes to a monthly savings plan.

Mary loves photography. She takes her camera with her everywhere.

(Say as much as you want. Explore many areas of your life or only a few.)

This is straight forward reporting. ("Just the facts, Ma'am.") No judgments about yourself!

What was the problem?
Explain the problem, state the belief you'd like to change, or describe the goal you'd like to reach as if you've already achieved what you want.

An example might sound like this: The problem was that Mary wanted to do something more creative, but she didn't think her art was good enough to support her.

Mary realized this thought was not serving her well, so she claimed a more meaningful statement for herself. She affirmed that she could continue working as a tech writer, do her art, and explore ways to make art part of her livelihood.

When was this problem resolved?
Be imaginative here. See yourself as if your dream has come true.

For example: Everyday for the past year, Mary spent half an hour finding ways to market her photography. She checked sites online, called and wrote to other photographers, read articles and books about marketing photography, visited cafes and asked about putting up her work for sale, talked to people in co-op galleries, contacted magazines, offered the use of her images to non-profits, created a website for her work, and created a Voyager Group for support.

Her work started to sell well enough that Mary could switch to part-time as a tech writer.

Where did this success happen?
Remember, this is all made up, so think of a way this could happen.

For example, Mary sold, and continues to sell, the most work from home through her website and through a co-op gallery she now belongs to.

Why did this happen?
Make up what you believe could motivate you to change your belief and to embrace the concept that you can make your life work for you in a way that nourishes your creativity and feeds your soul as well as your body.

For example: Mary has always been a perfectionist, but when she chose to include art into her life, she realized the creative process could be very messy.

The checks don't come in on a regular, consistent basis. The image doesn't always turn out the way she intended. The attendees at a gallery showing sometimes are fewer than hoped for. Mary realized that she would have to give up expectations of how things are "supposed" to be and embrace how things are. Mary traded perfectionism for persistence.

Mary adopted the mantra: "And that's the way it is."

Try using Mary's mantra throughout your day. How does using the phrase: "And that's the way it is," make you feel?

Write your responses to these activities in your journal.

Share some of your responses with your Voyager Group.

Many lists have been made about regrets people report having as they approach their own deaths. Some of the offerings I've heard that belong on this turn-back-the-clock wish list include:

To find my own true north and not live the life I thought others expected me to live.

To take work less seriously and to spend more time with the people who enjoyed being with me.

To be more open and loving with all the people I cared about.

To be more optimistic about how things would turn out.

Equilibrium/Two of Cups
Experience emotional balance.

Use the Energy of Two of Cups to:

Be emotionally expressive. Ride the waves of emotional turmoil and return to balance and calm.

Transform negative feelings into positive, constructive vibrations so that even when you don't feel great, you're always moving back to an easygoing emotional state.

Express love that shows you are nurturing, creative, inspirational, clear, and in an equally fulfilling relationship.

Caution: When you find yourself being unfeeling, uncaring, emotionally repressed, or cold, stop yourself. Don't allow yourself to stay in negative spaces.

Play with these activities to explore your emotional state of equilibrium:

✱ **Move to get yourself back in sync after an upsetting encounter.**

Jog, swim, take a walk, shoot some baskets, play tennis, play soccer, go for a bike ride.

Do something that gets you moving. And don't run the unpleasant scenario through your brain while you're doing this. Think positive thoughts, and focus on the activity at hand.

Chi Gong and Tai Chi exercises and yoga poses are also excellent.

✱ **Do energy exercises.** Go to Donna Eden's website, www.innersource.net, for free tips and exercises that are easy to do. Her books and DVDs are also helpful.

Here are some tips I've learned from her and use regularly:

Tap on energy points, tapping from five to ten times on each point: with your four fingers of both hands, tap on the top of your head, tap above your eyebrows, tap under your eyes, tap under your nose, tap on your chin, tap on the pinky finger side of one hand and then the other.

Stand and march in place. As you lift your right leg, tap the kneecap with your left hand. As you lift your left leg, tap that kneecap with your right hand. Do this for about two minutes.

Massage your fingers. Start at the tips of one hand. Gently press the tip of your thumb between the thumb and index finger of the other hand. Move to the index finger and continue on until you've massaged the tips of all ten fingers. Move along slowly as you massage. Then move to the middle joint, then to the third joint. Massage your palms and the backs of your hands. Shake your hands gently.

Massage your scalp. Using your middle fingers, make tiny circles at the base of your scalp. Start near your ears and work toward the center of the base of your scalp. Make your way back to your ears along the same route using those same tiny circles.

Write your responses to these activities in your journal.

Share some of your responses with your Voyager Group.

"Do you have the patience to wait until the mud settles and the water is clear? Can you remain unmoving until the right action arises by itself?"

Lao Tzu, 570-490 BC
founder of Taoism

Reflection/Two of Worlds
Evaluate, contemplate, envision.

Use the Energy of Two of Worlds to:

Go inward to find answers.

Be receptive to your intuitive hunches and act on them in a positive way.

Be self-reflective and honor what you learn about yourself.

Take time out to relax, rest, and regenerate so that you can tap into your inner wisdom.

Go to places in nature where you can be quiet and undistracted.

Caution: Avoid being so passive you aren't able to take appropriate actions.

Play with these activities to explore how to be calm and contemplative:

✱ **Meditate.** Even short periods of meditation on a regular basis can offer extraordinary benefits.

✱ **Simply stop and calm yourself.** Take five deep connected breaths, and then be aware of any insights that come to you.

✱ **Walk, swim, or jog.** These physical activities can be calming and can put the mind into a meditative state.

✱ **Do a repetitive task such as knitting, embroidering, or cross stitching which can be meditative and mind calming.**

Much has been written about the wisdom of the body. To learn to trust yourself and the information available to you that comes from within is to act on what you know or on what you have a feeling is right to do and see what happens next.

Over time, you'll accept that you know what's right, that you don't need a "reason" to justify the action.

Remember, often when we take this kind of action and our lives simply go along just fine, we don't know what we avoided. Trust that you know what's right for yourself.

"To the mind that is still, the world surrenders."
Lao Tzu, 570-490 BC, founder of Taoism

I have a friend who thought she needed a yearly mammogram once she turned forty years old. She had one when she was forty and another when she was forty-one and she made the appointment for her next one for two days after her annual check up when she was forty-two. During the appointment with her doctor, she was told she didn't need a mammogram every year and she should wait until the following year to get it. There was no history of breast cancer in her family, and she had no lumps, bumps or complaints along those lines. Nonetheless, she decided to go ahead with the mammogram, and what turned out to be a cancerous and fast growing tumor was detected and quickly removed. She received chemo and radiation therapy and is a cancer survivor. She acted on her intuition and she believes this saved her life.

Write your responses to these activities and this story in your journal.

Share some of your responses with your Voyager Group.

Purity/Two of Wands
Be wise and be your authentic best self.

Use the Energy of Two of Wands to:

Be honest with yourself about who you are now and where you are now on your journey of consciousness.

Be tolerant of your shortcomings.

Be authentic and true to yourself without falsity or artificiality.

Use your inner power to move in any direction that best serves you and the world.

Caution: Don't allow yourself to be limited by false or outdated beliefs that no longer ring true for you.

Play with these activities to explore how to be pure in your connection with your highest self:

* **Eliminate outdated thoughts and beliefs:**
Make a list of things you think, say, or believe that could be followed by the phrase, "because that's the way I was raised," or "because it's true; it's a fact," or "because I've always known that," or some variation on the theme.

Revise them to reflect either what you currently believe or what you'd prefer to believe. Beliefs, after all, are formed based on choices we make about them.

* **As a group, share belief statements.** Each person reads a few of the statements on his or her list. Go around the group and have everyone offer contradictory perspectives to each statement. Pass no judgments on any of the statements. The idea of the activity is to bring to consciousness the many ways to see "the truth."

Share some of your responses with your Voyager Group.

The practice of Zen martial arts includes learning to be clear headed by being in a state of "no-mindedness," called Mushin. This freedom from thought comes from letting go of all feelings, including worries, fears, joy, accomplishment, or failure. The Mushin mind is one with the Universe and totally present.

* **EFT (Emotional Freedom Technique), The Sedona Method, PsychK, and Byron Katie's The Work are good ways to both evaluate and release old, outdated, and limiting beliefs.** More information on these modalities can be found online.

To eliminate outdated thoughts or beliefs, consider the following exercise:

You might hold the belief that "life is hard" or "money is hard to come by" or "the rich get richer and the poor get children" or "anything worth doing is worth doing well."

Now take each one of your statements and write another one or two that changes or contradicts the one you hold.

For example, if you hold the belief that "anything worth doing is worth doing well," you could write: "anything worth doing is worth doing poorly until you get it right," or "anything worth doing is worth starting and seeing where you wind up."

Reflect on what you've written.

Is there another way to consider your belief that would serve you better and better enable you to achieve your dreams?

Sensor/Woman of Wands: Fire up your sensitivity to the unseen world.

Use the Energy of Woman of Wands to:

Use your physical senses to alert and reveal messages that will guide you and others.

Allow yourself to tap into your psychic and intuitive abilities.

Dance and perform ceremonial rituals.

Be enlightened and an enlightener, awakened and an awakener, a creator, and an empowerer. Awaken to the deepest essence of who you are.

Caution: Avoid being manipulative and controlling.

Play with these activities to explore how your woman's sensor way can connect you to your highest self:

* **Throughout the next week look at situations that cause pain or discomfort as opportunities for growth by discovering the gift within each challenge.** So often, when something unpleasant occurs in our lives, we ask, "Why did this happen?" Instead, transform the query. Seek guidance by asking what can be learned that will be helpful or comforting, or that will offer encouragement to continue on life's journey of meaning and purpose. Take time to be still and to hear the answer.

I know a programmer who developed high blood pressure and was a regular in his dermatologist's office where he was getting new lotions and potions to try to alleviate his rashes. He lost his job when his company's funding dried up. Now, he's a high school math and science teacher, reveling in the creativity of his students and of his job, and he hasn't had the need to purchase any skin ointments in months, and he's being weaned ~~him~~ off his meds.

* **Review your week. What gifts were offered in the guise of a challenge?**

Intuitive people look for opportunity in all challenges, and they assume the opportunity exists and that they just have to trust they will uncover the gifts awaiting them.

We all know people who suffer stress related health issues because of their jobs, their relationships, or their personal life challenges. But I also know people, and you likely do, too, who have turned trauma into opportunity and have regained their good health.

I have a friend who was a tech writer with numerous health issues. When she was sixty years old, she sold everything but her house, rented that out, moved to Mexico, established a B & B, and put her heart and soul into her art projects. Her health complaints are now minimal, and she barely notices flare-ups. Before, she felt almost lifeless, lethargic, and was in constant pain. Depression was a constant companion. Now, she fills her day with activities that enliven her. She was part of a dance company for a festival; she takes Spanish lessons; she's making new friends and being included in their family celebrations; she takes art classes and works on small and large sculptures pain free; she's lost weight; she's gained male companionship.

* **Who do you know or who have you read about who has turned obstacles into opportunities?**

Write your responses in your Voyager Journal and share them with your group.

Chapter Three

III Empress Energies: Use Love to Heal

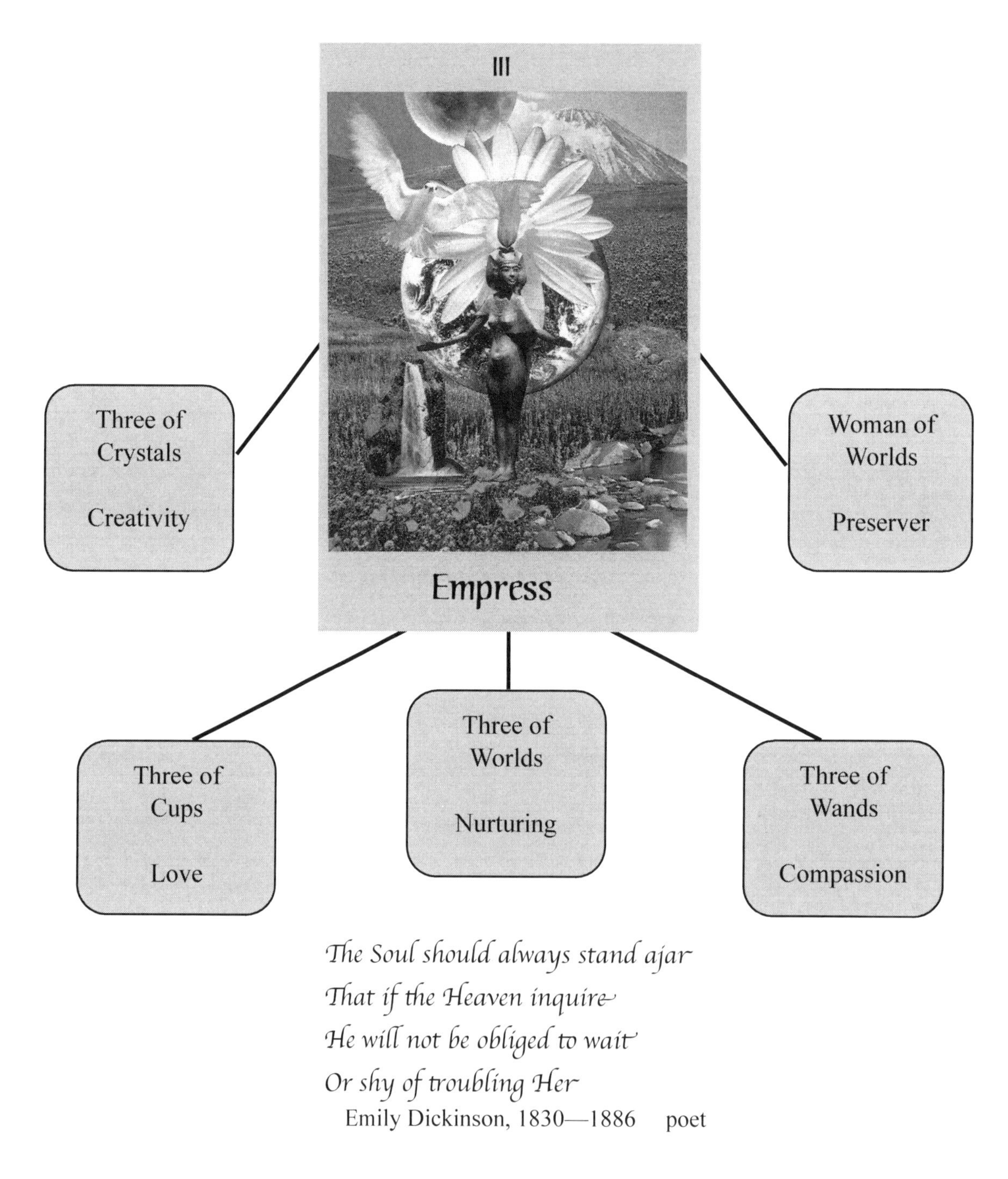

The Soul should always stand ajar
That if the Heaven inquire
He will not be obliged to wait
Or shy of troubling Her

Emily Dickinson, 1830—1886 poet

III Empress
Love, Create, Inspire

Creativity, fertility, and fecundity are stimulated with this Earth Mother archetype.

Support and nurture whatever you bring into the world—children, art, books, a business, a home, a good-will project—and let them develop into their own best selves.

Fulfill your spirit's yearning to bring something new into the world.

Access the healing power of love that is nurturing, supportive, and comforting.

Liberate your potential.

Transform your everyday life into a life of extraordinary beauty.

Be compassionate towards yourself, as well as towards others.

Nurture and care for your dream everyday. Early in the morning is usually the best time to invest in creative projects such as painting, writing, and composing because you're still so close to your unconscious, your dream, your intuitive state of mind.

Picture Julia Roberts as Erin Brockovich, the single, down and out mother barely holding her life together but doing the best she can for her children. The screen image presents her as the Venus/earth mother archetype of beauty and large breasts. And look what she does! Almost solely on her own, she saves the earth from further despoiling by a giant power company in California. A true story, too!

Access Empress energy, take on global warming Monday morning, see results before the week is out!

But don't forget, Joan Crawford in *Mommy Dearest* was also ruled by Empress energy. Don't let the issue of control take you down!

Write your statement of intention again—this is the one you wrote to activate your Fool Child energy by making a commitment to do something big, wonderful, creative, and inspirational!

Now add this statement: I commit to working on my project _____ hours a day, ______ days a week. I will set aside ________ as the hours I will devote to my project. These are the times you plan to use to create your dream. The same time everyday may not be available to you, so write what works.

Add your creativity times to your calendar. Treat these blocks of time as sacred. Many famous people are known to have said that showing up is the most important component to success.

Think of your project as something that needs you to nurture and care for it. If you adopted a kitty or a puppy, you wouldn't feed them when you got around to it. When you plant a garden, you don't water and weed when "inspiration" strikes. You don't change a baby when you feel like it. You don't go to work when the mood hits you. This project is your dream life and is very important.

Share your intentions with your group.

"Our life is the canvas, our intention the brush strokes, our emotions the paint. Do masterful artists let paintings that they have painted long ago decide how they will look at their life upon waking up each morning? Do the master artists use their creative energy and spend time repainting the same picture over and over because they have decided that the previous copies aren't masterpieces yet? I see master artists painting new pictures everyday knowing that each one is unique and will speak to and inspire people regardless of how it is viewed. Once a painting is done, does the artist sit in the gallery where it is displayed in order to gauge the reaction, feelings and thoughts that others take away when viewing it? While sitting there, is the artist apologizing to those who don't like it, reasoning with those who are angered by it, or smiling with those whose heart was opened by it? I see the artist doing what they do best, what they are here to do, regardless of what others say or think. Do what you do best, what you are here to do."

Jefferey Jaxen, open source researcher and writer

websites: www.jeffereyjaxen.com & www.awakeandempoweredexpo.com

Creativity/Three of Crystals
Express yourself fully.

Use the Energy of Three of Crystals to:

Be imaginative, innovative, and generative. Bring something new into the world.

Grow by entertaining new ideas.

Think about new ways to do things, new ways to see things, and new ways to get your ideas into concrete form.

Release old patterns, especially family patterns, that stifle your creativity.

Caution: Don't let your ideas wither and die from inactivity.

Play with these activities to explore your creative mind:

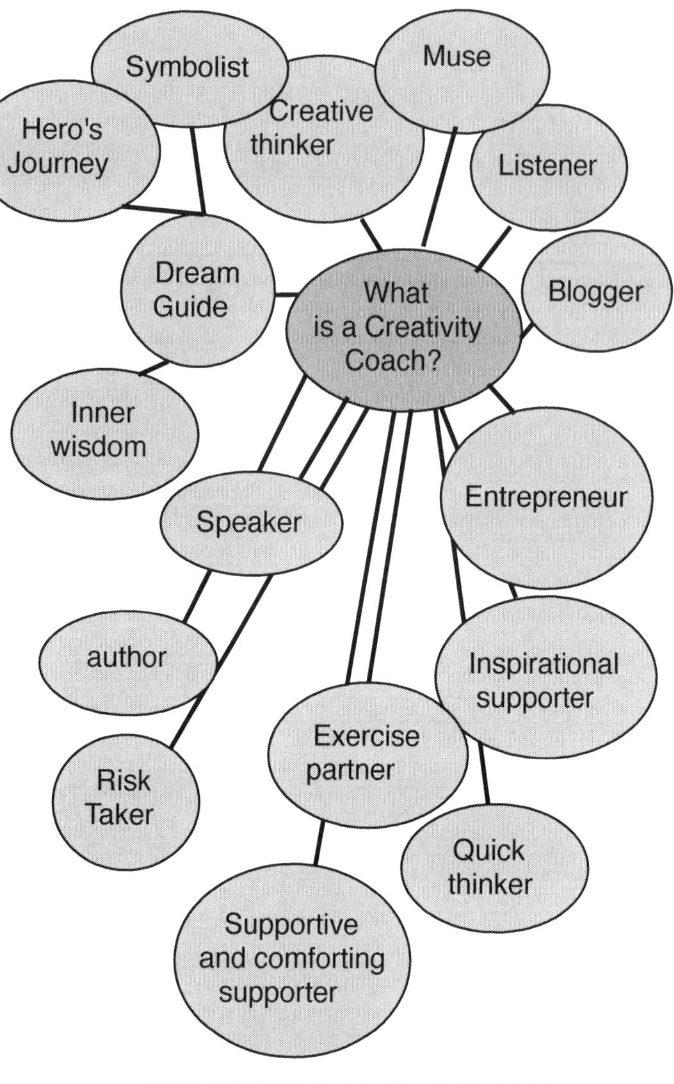

✱ Use the circle method of brainstorming:

Use many colors of ink and a large sheet of paper for this exercise.

In the middle of the paper, write "What (or Who) is a ________" (fill in the blank with one word or a short phrase to name who you will be when you achieve your goal of making your dreams come true). Circle the word or phrase.

Draw lines out from this circle with all the thoughts that come to you that describe who or what this means to you.

Don't worry how the words "fit." This is meant to awaken possibilities.

Use different colors for the words.

Take off from words/phrases that strike you as interesting and draw circles from these.

Continue brainstorming with any phrases that grab your attention.

✱ Be open and curious when brainstorming. As an exercise, think of a list of at least twenty things someone could do to get a job. Be outrageous! Be clever! Be wise! Be practical! Be impractical! Be quick about putting this list together!

Write a poem about being in the job you want. Run naked down a busy sidewalk with your "privates" covered with cardboard with your job plea and phone number written on it. Put up a video on line of you singing your praises. Juggle on a street corner in front of a sign pointing to a pile of your resumes. Take a class.

✱ Play the "I Can Do One More" game. Either alone or with a group, take an ordinary object and come up with a list of between twenty-five and one hundred ways to use it.

For example: a CD is the object.

Possible uses for it include: listen to music, listen to a lecture, listen to a meditation, look at photos, store a book, documents, accounts, photos, play frisbee, use as a coaster, twirl it around a finger, use as an ice or snow scraper, use as scraper for pots and pans, put in the garden to scare away birds and rabbits, add beads, glitter, streamers and use to decorate outdoor trees, set candles on them (great reflections), prop upright on your desk shiny side facing you for good feng shui, or set upright next to your computer to see when your boss comes into your cube, drill holes and use for earring holder, cut into small pieces and use for making mosaics, use as a mirror, take with you backpacking to use as reflector or distress signal device, write party invitation on it, use for a greeting card, spin on its side and entertain your kids and yourself, use as a bookmark, put lots of them together to make blinds or room partitions, let the kids color on them while waiting at restaurants, use them as reflectors for blind driveways, use them as wheels for a toy.

✱ Write a six-word autobiography or a biography of someone you know.

Here are some examples:

Lauri: Vibrant, thoughtful, focused, compassionate. Collaborative leader.

Patrick: Playwright, playful, movie-making karate instructor.

Mark: Intuitive, thoughtful, observant, passionate, persistent. Novelist.

Susan: Dedicated, determined, passionate. Director. Teacher. Writer.

Darrien: Moved. Cried. Got it together. Celebrated.

Share or do these activities with your group.

Write your responses to these activities in your journal.

Share some of your responses with your Voyager Group.

Being open to criticism and to hearing probing questions creates better results than only soliciting or entertaining positive opinions about our ideas and creative and innovative projects.

Love/Three of Cups
Open your heart and express what's inside you.

Use the Energy of Three of Cups to:

Share yourself through the creative arts.

Use your healing power of touch to show your love.

Transform any situation with love.

Reach out with open arms and embrace the love and the life that's around you.

Express your love by nurturing your own dreams for yourself.

Caution: Avoid being overbearing or being judgmental of others, yourself, or your art.

Play with these activities to explore your emotional state of love:

✱ **Paint, draw, or sketch everyday for seven days**. Again, if the muse continues to hang out with you, don't send an eviction notice. Whether you believe you can paint, draw, or sketch well, do this in the spirit of being in love with or curious about what's in front of you. Don't judge the result.

✱ **Design a garden.** Design one that is large. Design one that is tiny. Everyday for seven days either work on the one design or do several sketches.

✱ **Speak kindly to everyone you communicate with.**

✱**Send kind thoughts to everyone you meet up with who looks sad, upset, or down and out.**

✱ **Smile and wave (with an open hand) at drivers who cut you off.**

✱**Be as outrageously kind, loving, and thoughtful as possible for one whole day**. Repeat often.

✱ **Take photos of trees, flowers, plants, clouds, weeds, and insects**. Do this everyday for seven days. On the seventh day, find a way to show them off. Facebook? YouTube? Slideshow sent to friends and family? Be sure to bring the photos to your Voyager Group.

✱ **Take photos of smiles.** Again, find a way to show them off at the end of the week and bring the compilation to your Voyager Group.

✱ **See a romantic movie with someone you love.** Let the emotional feelings well up. Hold hands. Snuggle. Relax into the emotional communication.

✱ **Volunteer.** Giving your time to another is one of the deepest expressions of love we can offer.

Write your responses to these activities in your journal.

Share some of your responses with your Voyager Group.

A friend in his eighties was asked the secret to his happy life. "Find a woman you love," he said, "and everyday tell her one thing that you love about her. Makes for a good marriage and a great life." He and his wife have now been married for sixty years and they both are usually cheerful and very happy.

Nurturing/Three of Worlds
Be supportive, responsible, caring.

Use the Energy of Three of Worlds to:

Love what you have created.

Care for what you bring into the world until what you've created can stand on his, her, or its own.

Provide an environment of growth and support for everything you create.

Treat the art you are making and the artist that you are with respect.

Caution: Avoid smothering what you've created with too much attention or too many restrictions or by imposing too many conditions.

Play with these activities to explore your natural nurturing way of being in the world:

✱ **Do you have a relationship you haven't given much attention to lately?** Dedicate some time on a regular basis for the next month (or longer) to engage with this person. Maybe this means talking on the phone once a week or writing a long, thoughtful letter or email every week or taking a walk or sharing a meal at least once a week with this person.

✱ **Plant a garden.** Enjoy some part of the process everyday for a week. This project will, of course, require a longer commitment once begun.

✱ **Do you have an unfinished project you haven't worked on in weeks, months, or years?** Take out one of these abandoned babies and stay with it until it is completed.

Nurture the artist within!

✱ **Do you have some creative project that's completed but that no one but you or maybe you and your partner or parent have seen?** Get this project into the world in some way.

Are you a writer? If you've written a novel, find an editor or book doctor or mentor to go over the novel with you, tightening and expanding and cleaning up where needed.

When you're satisfied with your work, start sending out queries to agents or consider self-publishing.

If you are you a photographer and have photographs hidden away, put some images together to create a series, mount them, frame them, and take them to a cafe, a civic center, a restaurant, a bank, a business, or some public place and convince someone at your choice of venue to let you hang your show.

Are you a dancer, musician, or singer? Make a short film and put yourself on your Facebook page or on YouTube or somewhere else where others can enjoy your creative offering.

Write your responses to these activities in your journal.

Share some of your responses with your Voyager Group.

"Believe in yourself and there will come a day when others will have no choice but to believe with you."

Oscar Wilde, 1854-1900

writer and poet

Preserver/Woman of Worlds
Generate your creative impulses.

Use the Energy of Woman of Worlds to:

Manifest tangible, physical products that represent your creative self.

Take your time with your projects. Allow yourself time to rest.

Measure, design, outline, revise, review, rethink, reanalyze, and reframe until your finished project is ready for the world.

Infuse the creative process with joy.

Caution: Don't rush the creative process. Allow for generative periods of growth.

Play with these activities to explore your woman's preservationist way of being in the world:

✱ **Protect your creative projects until they're ready for the world.** Don't send something out too soon. You wouldn't send a kindergartner to college. Don't send your creative projects out in the world prematurely either. Revise, redo, adjust, get feedback, and then, when you feel your project is mature enough, let it walk on its own two feet into the world.

✱ **Nourish yourself with healthy food.**

✱ **Exercise daily.**

✱ **Get outside in nature everyday.**

✱ **Let the sun shine on your face everyday you can.**

Your body is the source of your creativity and needs to be nurtured and cared for, too.

Eric Maisel is one of the great creativity gurus who has written numerous books, blogs, newsletters, articles, and curricula on creativity and who has coached individuals and led workshops large and small on how to get past lethargy and fear and move into action on whatever dream one harbors. In *The Creativity Book*, he writes of the advantages and needs of being creative no matter who you are or what you do.

Maisel has concluded that a basic human task in life is to become an "everyday creative person." He suggests that when we mine the richness of our creative intelligence, amazing results become the norm. We are better able to think more deeply and profoundly, as well as more fantastically, so we can discover more opportunities for resolving issues and making needed changes. We can become more confident and more aware of our external and internal influences and motivations, so we can act more quickly and more authentically. We more readily notice the abundance around us, so we can draw on resources more quickly, easily, and frequently.

For the "everyday creative person" life just keeps getting better, richer, and more amazingly brilliant.

✱ **Find a project that you can enjoy and work hard at.** Set aside time at least five days a week to involve yourself in the process of creating something new. Work to completion, even if you don't think you like the results. The task at hand is to enjoy the process of creativity rather than stand in judgment of the result of the process.

I went to a special exhibit at the Van Gogh Museum in Amsterdam many years ago, and they had on display some of the thousands of sketches Van Gogh had made in preparation for his paintings. He would sketch a hand hundreds of times before he decided he was ready to have that be the hand for his man with a yellow hat. He did the same for feet, bends in arms, and folds in material.

Many now famous authors who have had their first books become great successes will tell you that the best seller wasn't really their first book. It was the first book they were able to get published, but they had written one, two, five, ten books that never left the house. All part of the process.

✱ **Do something to help someone else bring their ideas or work into the world.** Teaching, coaching, guiding, or showing someone else how to do something brings out great creativity in yourself.

✱ **Buddy with one other person who shares your creative genre or type of goal you have for yourself.** Set up a schedule for communicating with each other. Try speaking twice a week for ten or twenty minutes. Use this time to encourage each other. Try to get together for at least an hour once a month to check in and show off what you've accomplished with your art or your goal.

Write your responses to these activities in your journal.

Share some of your responses with your Voyager Group.

Georgia O'Keeffe's art demands that we slow down and take notice. A flower is no longer just a flower. In O'Keeffe's hands, that pansy asserts a sense of wonder, passion, and intimacy that keeps us transfixed and present.

Compassion/Three of Wands
Understand and love.

Use the Energy of Three of Wands to:

Understand and be tolerant of the human condition, which includes frailty and suffering.

Be aware of the needs of others. Be empathetic.

Reach out to help others. Use your gentle touch to show you care.

Heal with the power of love.

Caution: Don't allow yourself to be taken advantage of. Don't give more than you are capable of receiving.

Play with these activities to explore your way of connecting to your highest self through compassion:

* **Do you know someone who is suffering from loss, from poor health, or from depression?** Offer to do something for or with this person such as Reiki, a massage, some healing modality that you're familiar with, or include this person in an activity with you such as walking, hiking, biking, swimming.

Or take this person out for a cup of tea or lunch or bring something to him or her that would be cheering.

* **Go on a double date.** Find something to do together as two couples and end your time together in some quiet place where you can relax and enjoy a conversation. When you go out with others, you're not only having a good time in the moment, but you're also building memories to draw on when you want to recall warm feelings about your life or the people you shared the experience with.

If you are not part of a couple, ask out someone you enjoy being with. This doesn't have to be a romantic date. Hearts are meant to be opened whether we're in a relationship or not. You could do a parent-child double date or a four friends double date.

* **Volunteer for a few hours at an animal shelter and interact with one of the animals in need of companionship.**

* **Do what Martin Seligman recommends in his book *Authentic Happiness*:** Write a one page letter of gratitude to someone who has been important in your life. Laminate the letter. Call the person and make an appointment to see him or her. When you meet up, tell this special person that you are grateful for what he or she did for you and explain you've written a letter and you'd like to read this to him or her.

Read the letter and give it to your special person.

* **Be an active and non-judgmental listener.** Allow the people in your life to feel, think, and act as they do in their most authentic way. For example, notice when you try to control people's feelings by saying something like, "You shouldn't feel that way," or "Try not to feel so bad. This will get better." Instead, tell about a time when you, too, felt this way.

* **Notice who you are noticing.** When someone or some animal grabs your attention, check in with yourself to understand what about the person or animal is speaking to you. Are you connecting with their courage, strength of character, limited perceptions?

Part of the hero's journey is making that leap in consciousness that gets us to act on behalf of the greater good of others individually and collectively.

✱ Another opportunity from Seligman's *Authentic Happiness* book can be accomplished either within your Voyager Group or in a family or friendship circle.

Each person invites someone to be part of the group on a given night—Gratitude Night.

Those extending the invitations simply request the invitee's presence without offering more information.

Those extending invitations prepare a speech, a poem, a song, or some other artistic representation that acknowledges the gratitude felt because the person they are inviting to Gratitude Night is in their lives.

The evening might include some snacks and drinks, too.

When everyone has gathered, sit in a circle.

One person from the group that did the inviting, explains what will happen next: Each invitee will introduce their guest one at a time and give a short explanation of why this person means so much to them.

Those who have done the inviting, introduce their guests one at a time and present their short explanation in whatever form the one doing the honoring has chosen.

Some people may give brilliantly thought-out speeches, but brevity and charm touch the soul, too.

As Seligman suggests, other ways to express gratitude might be through poetry.

(With apologies to Dr. Seuss)

If I hear you have troubles
No matter what kind,
They might be from the right,
Or come from behind,

Don't worry, Molly,
I'll be right here by your side.

And I won't be leaving by train
or by car,
I won't be traveling from you very
far.
I won't be riding off to the west
Or flying to places to sun and to
rest.

No, I'll be right here!

I care about you, Molly
Have I made that clear?

Write your responses to these activities in your journal. Share some of your responses or the activity with your Voyager Group.

Chapter Four

IV Emperor Energies: Create Your World

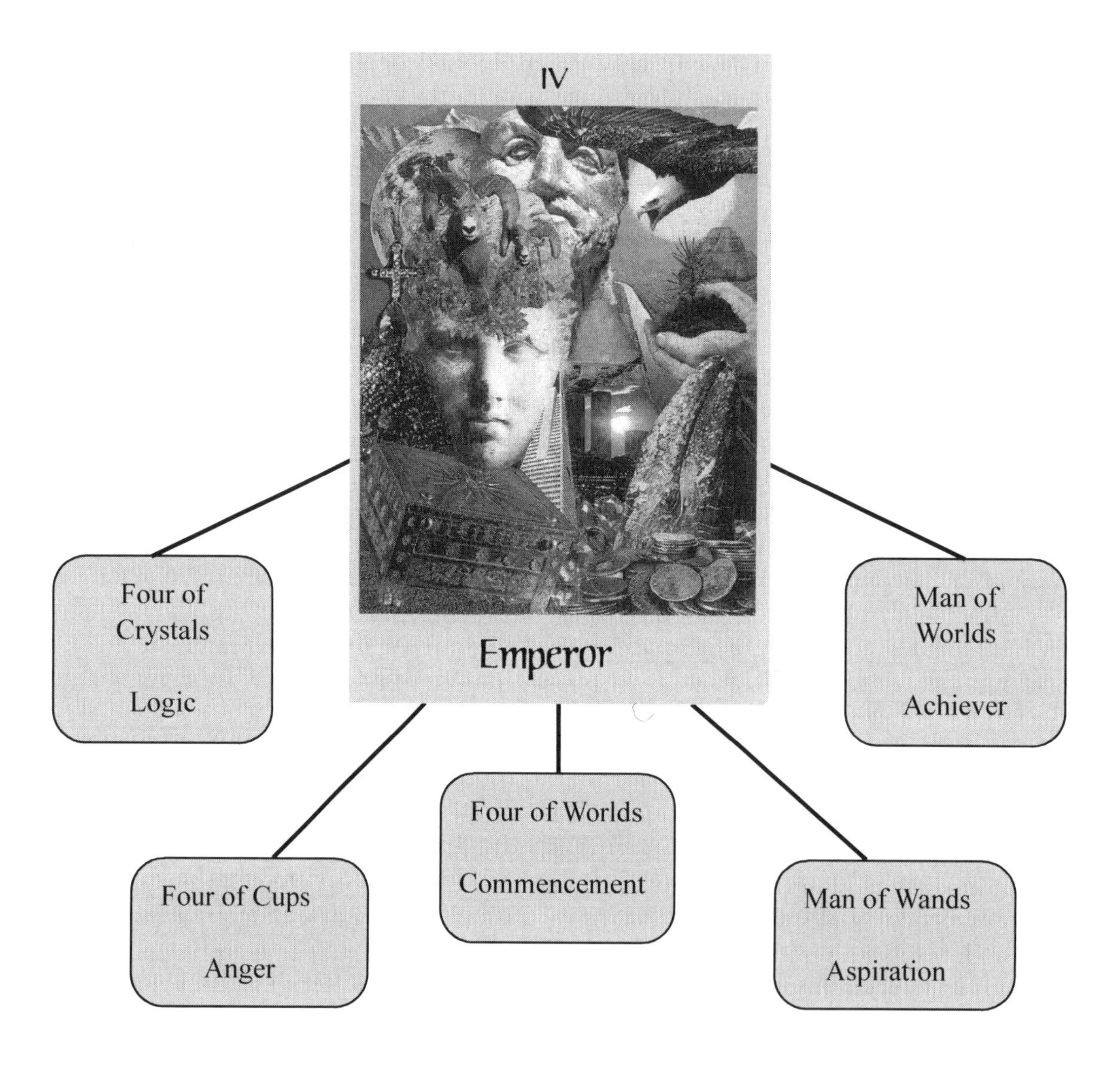

"Only put off until tomorrow what you're willing to die having left undone."

Pablo Picasso, 1881 to 1973
Spanish painter, sculptor, printmaker, ceramicist, stage designer, and one of the most influential artists of the 20th century

IV Emperor
Have a vision; make a plan.

Act on your goals.

Be logical, analytical, and organized.

Be determined and resolute.

Think like an entrepreneur and make your vision a reality that generates income.

Leave a legacy that will help make the world a better place for successive generations.

Think big and act with daring.

No matter what your dreams are, be heroic and courageous in your efforts to create something innovative and helpful for yourself and others.

Caution: As successes come, beware of the urge to be overly competitive, headstrong, ruthless, or power hungry.

Play with these activities to explore your way of connecting with your vision:

✱ **Have a vision.** Everything starts in the mind. If you can see what you want, you can create what you see. What do you see for yourself?

✱ **Get with a partner.** Set a timer for ninety-seconds and during that time tell your partner how great you are. Talk about your accomplishments, talents, personality traits, and abilities. Really elaborate on how great you are. At the end of the time, switch and listen to your partner tell you about how great he or she is for ninety-seconds. Notice how you feel as both speaker and listener.

✱ **Revisit your statement of intention**. Can you see yourself in your vision statement? Can you picture yourself creating this opportunity for yourself?

✱ **Picture yourself as if your dream has come true.** Now have a dialogue with that person you will become. Ask your future self any questions you might have about how you got there and how you feel now that you have achieved this big goal.

✱ **Answer yourself.** Write out your responses or speak this dialogue with your future self into a recording device.

When you're finished, read or listen to this "conversation" with your future self.

✱ **Revisit your initial statement of intention made with Fool-Child energy.** Do you want to revise your statement of intention in any way? Revise if you feel the need to.

Consider the titans gathered around the dinner table at the home of Silicon Valley venture capitalist John Doerr and his wife, Ann, when President Obama came to the small town of Woodside, CA in 2011: Apple Chairman and CEO Steve Jobs; Facebook founder and CEO Mark Zuckerberg; Carol Bartz, president and CEO of Yahoo; Cisco Systems' CEO John Chambers; Twitter CEO Dick Costolo; Oracle CEO Larry Ellison; Netflix CEO Reed Hastings; Stanford University President John Hennessy; Genentech Chairman and former CEO Art Levinson; Google CEO Eric Schmidt; and former state controller and venture capitalist Steve Westly.

Emperors every one! People who think big, act with daring on their visions, and grow from what they learn from their failures. And yes, they have all experienced major failures, too. Steve Jobs, if you recall, was fired from the company he founded, and he thought he was finished, a failure, when he was thirty years old.

Other, less obvious, and most extraordinary titans include Mahatma Gandhi, Mother Teresa, Dorothy Day, Martin Luther King, Jr., Elizabeth Cady Stanton, Desmond Tutu, Nelson Mandela, and Rosa Parks.

✱ **Make a list of the titans you admire because of their accomplishments.** They don't have to be famous. As you list the people, for each one, include a list of what it is that you admire about them.

Whatever we can see in others, we can claim for our own.

Each of the qualities you wrote down are qualities that are in you.

Use these qualities! They are yours!

Write your responses to these activities in your journal.

Share some of your responses with your Voyager Group.

Logic/Four of Crystals
Imagine the world you want to create for yourself.

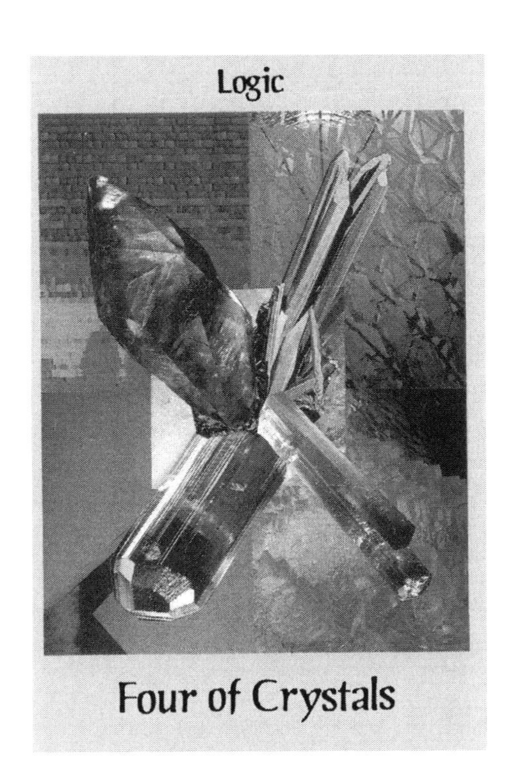

Use the Energy of Four of Crystals to:

Think and plan so you know where you're going.

Pay attention to structures and patterns so you can use what's relevant and helpful.

See the big picture and how the details fit into your dreams.

Think. Organize. Plan. Make decisions.

If you can visualize something, you can make it happen.

Caution: Don't forget to also accept randomness, chance, and mystery as part of the world.

Play with these activities to explore your logical mind:

✱ **Really, deeply, and in great detail imagine what you want.** Write this scene in your journal.

Picture yourself being the person you are dreaming you will be. Use as many sensate details as possible.

Where are you? Are you a speaker with a message for health and healing that you want to get out to a large audience? Then picture yourself standing on a stage. See the size of the stage and the set up. Flowers? A podium? Chairs? Notice what you're wearing (the fit, the colors, the material, the shoes). Picture the people you're speaking to. How many people are in the audience? What sounds are you hearing? Imagine that you can hear what people are saying about you as they anticipate your speech. Maybe many have seen you speak before. Hear the excitement in their voices as they speak about how much they're looking forward to hearing what you have to say. Breathe in the scents, the aromas, and the fragrances around you. Feel the energy pulsating.

Experience the excitement, the contentment, the serenity, and the joy that accomplishing your goal has brought you.

Try to feel those emotions now. Really get into the scene you've created.

✱ **Pay attention to what you're thinking.** We have upwards of seventy-thousand thoughts a day, and most of them skew negatively toward ourselves. Negative thoughts, no matter where they come from, have powerful adverse effects on our bodies, our minds, and our emotions. Don't let your own negativity control you and your destiny.

For any thought you notice, ask the Buddhists' questions:
Is it true?
Is it necessary?
Is it kind?

✱ **Eliminate negative thoughts.** Transform negative thoughts into ones that are true, necessary, and kind.

For example, if you hear yourself saying your dream is too big, change that to a loving message that's supportive. Tell yourself you deserve to get what you want. Remind yourself of how much you've already accomplished and reassure yourself that this big dream can be achieved, too. Tell yourself that you can take one step at time. Take that step!

"Seeing is believing, but feeling is God's own truth." an old Irish saying

Share your vision for yourself with your Voyager Group.

Anger/Four of Cups
Be productive. Turn anger into positive action.

Use the Energy of Four of Cups to:

Channel your anger into activism that benefits the world.

Make something good happen even when you are hurting.

Feel your anger, but don't remain angry. Allow the emotion to pass through you.

Act on your anger in a positive, constructive way.

Inspire you to do something productive.

Caution: Don't be controlled by hatred or despair when you've been hurt.

Play with these activities to explore how anger can help you be positive, productive, and pro-active:

✱ **Get a pack of index cards, or use your favorite electronic device for this activity.**

On each card, write a word, a phrase, or a sentence or two about something or someone that makes you angry. This can be from any part of your life. Write up as many cards as you'd like.

- Start with a word or phrase such as injustice, war, greed, pain, homelessness, poverty, the stigma of mental illness, or a physical or mental illness that you or someone you love has. Or name the person or group that really pushes your buttons.

- Explain what this word or phrase means to you. Be concise. This exercise is meant to remind you of your values and not become a dissertation on how you came to this conclusion.

  Ex: Greed means excessive materialism.

  Ex: MS means a slow, painful death.

- Give one example of how this word is represented in your life and in your world.

  Ex: Wall Street's getting richer while unemployment soars.

  Ex: Sue has MS and she needs help with every part of her life.

✱ **Prioritize your concerns.** Stack the cards in the order of relative importance to you.

✱ **Sensitize yourself to the issue expressed on the top card.** Read up on the problem, write notes to yourself about the issue. Talk to people about this issue. Get as much information as you can.

✱ **Go back to your cards and choose one issue you feel the need to address in some way.** You don't have to know what you want to do just yet, you just need to be aware that you have a desire to do something because of how angry you get when you see, hear about, or think about anything to do with this problem.

Anger exhibits itself in the body. Noticing when your heart races or your shoulder muscles tense or your jaw or fists clench will be good clues that seeing, hearing about, or thinking about an issue makes you angry.

Research suggests that when you repress anger or repeatedly act out in hostility, homocysteine builds up in your blood, and this chemical has been associated with heart disease.

✱ When you decide on the issue you would like to take on, brainstorm to help settle on how you want to make a difference and ease the suffering that results from this issue.

At this point, these productive outlets don't have to be practical or realistic.

- Write each idea down in a word, phrase, or short sentence. Use one index card for each idea.
- After you've written as many possible ideas as you feel you can, set the cards aside for a day or two.
- After a few days, revisit your index cards by going through each one.
- Anytime you realize there's no juice and no energy in working with this issue in the way stated on the card, take the card out of the pile and discard or recycle it.
- When you find something that excites you, put your anger to work and make a difference in your life and the lives of others.

Some examples of how to brainstorm about how to help people with MS:

- Write a novel that shows this theme.
- Interview people who are doing something to help people with MS and post these interviews on your social media site, or in blog posts, or on your website.
- Write a book that includes interviews of people who have MS.
- Start a charitable organization to raise money for research for finding a cure.
- Start an awareness group of how MS affects MS patients, their families, and society as a whole.
- Do something to help someone with MS whether it's a family member, a friend, or a stranger.
- Join a group of activists who are already doing something about the problem.
- Join or start a bike ride, a marathon, a walkathon, or some other physical activity to raise awareness and money for research.
- Speak to congressional representatives about health care reform.

"It is now long ago that I resolved that I would permit no man, no matter what his colour might be, to narrow and degrade my soul by making me hate him."

Booker T. Washington, 1856-1915
educator and author

Jaycee Dugard, who was kidnapped at age eleven and held captive and raped for eighteen years, founded ~~the~~ The JAYC Foundation which provides support and services for families recovering from abduction and the aftermath of other traumatic experiences.

Candy Lightner, a mother whose thirteen year old daughter was killed by a drunk driver, created the now world-wide organization, MADD.

Megan's Law, named after a child who was assaulted and killed by a neighbor, allows people to know where registered sex offenders live.

Leymak Gbowee, 2011 Nobel Peace Prize winner, helped stop the civil war in Liberia by leading women in a protest because she chose not to feel helpless in the face of abuse any longer.

Elie Wiesel, author, scholar, Nobel Laureate, peace activist, and Holocaust survivor, was fifteen years old when he and his entire town were sent to Auschwitz by the Gestapo. Horrors surrounded him. He suffered starvation, torture, disease, and unimaginable losses, including the deaths of his father, mother, and sister. Somehow, through great determination, wisdom, and personal insights, he has lived a productive, creative, generous, and loving life. "The anger here is in me—hate is not," Elie Wiesel has stated. "I write and I teach, and therefore, I believe anger must be a catalyst."

A father whose twelve-year-old daughter was kidnapped from her home and murdered established the Polly Klaas foundation to help parents whose children are the victims of a kidnapper.

Write your responses to these activities in your journal.

Share some of your responses with your Voyager Group.

Commencement/Four of Worlds
Set your plans in motion to create your world.

Use the Energy of Four of Worlds to:

Be determined and resolute and follow your enthusiasm for your projects.

Assert yourself in a positive way.

Keep the naysayers from holding you back from achieving your goals.

Argue, state clearly, and respond with determination for what you truly believe can empower and energize you.

Think things through and strive for completion.

Caution: Don't take irresponsible actions just to act.

Play with these activities to explore how to begin to get your vital energy into the world:

✱ Identify who you are right now by writing a mini-memoir based on each of the following questions:

Where do you live? What type of structure do you live in? Who do you share your home with?

What do you do to earn your livelihood? What did you do ten years ago to earn your livelihood?

Why are you now interested in starting something new? Can you identify a turning point either recently or anytime in your life?

What do you know a lot about? What skills would you identify as your strengths?

What is one skill that you would most like to develop over the next year?

Who do you know? What groups do you belong to? What organizations are you involved with? How do you interact with these groups?

Who are the friends and relatives who most support, encourage, or inspire you? How do they support, encourage, or inspire you?

✱ Make a summary statement of your mini-bio that includes your vision statement.

Stepping into your role as a creator means moving away from the comfortable, predictable, safe, and familiar. Committing to a project pushes you into a world where the unexpected is the norm, and when you do, seemingly out of nowhere, ideas, people, events, and experiences pop up to assist and support you. Yet the outcome is certainly not a sure thing. Although embarking on a creative project is exciting, compelling, and invigorating, the process can also produce anxiety and stress.

✱ Remind yourself of your vision statement by either copying it or rewriting it to reflect new ideas and thoughts you now have.

Share your mini bio with your Voyager Group.

"People say, 'What is the sense of our small effort?' They cannot see that we must lay one brick at a time, take one step at a time."

Dorothy Day, 1897-1980
co-founder of The Catholic Worker Movement, journalist, and social justice activist

Achiever/Man of Worlds
Put your drive to succeed in high gear.

Use the Energy of Four of Worlds to:

Set measurable and achievable goals.

Network, build a team, synergize.

Clearly see the great vision you have and the steps you need to work toward your vision.

Be disciplined, diligent, and persistent in your pursuit of your goals.

Caution: Don't be unprincipled and don't wear yourself out. Work towards your goal with determination and integrity.

Play with these activities to explore how to succeed in the world:

✱ **Write your intention on an index card or on your electronic device that you carry with you.** Read your intention often throughout the day.

✱ **Every night before you go to bed, write down five things you can do to move toward your goal of making your intention your reality.**

- These five items don't have to be big. They should be actions that are reasonable, easy, and that can be accomplished soon.
- Carry over the ones not completed. Keep carrying them over until you do them.

✱ **Everyday, do those five things.**

✱ **Create a virtual support group.** Make a vision board with pictures of from ten to twenty people or fictional characters who have qualities you admire and want to have more of in your life.

Choose people for a variety of reasons. Here are some examples:

- People with whom you share personality traits.
- People with whom you have obvious connections, such as those in the field you are interested in or because they come from a similar background as you.
- People you think are amazing beyond belief because of what they've achieved.
- People who have stumbled, fallen, and gotten back up again.
- People who have inspired others to achieve worthwhile goals.
- People who have been kind to you.
- People who have been supportive of you.

✱ **In your journal, write a sentence or two explaining why you chose each person.**

✱ **Hang the vision board in a place where you can spend time alone.**

✱ **Take time everyday to look at your virtual support team.**

✱ **Whenever you feel stuck or uncertain about something, choose one or more of your virtual teammates and hold a conversation with them.** Do this out loud or write the dialogue out in your journal.

Write your responses to these activities in your journal and share some of your responses with your Voyager Group.

Whatever you can identify in another is present in yourself. This energy is readily available to you.

Aspiration/Four of Wands
Focus your attention on attainment.

Use the Energy of Four of Wands to:

Use your willpower and concentrate on your goal.

Aspire to fulfill your highest intentions.

Let your spirit soar.

Think of yourself as a revolutionary in the forefront of thought and creativity.

Make things happen!

Caution: Don't be impatient or unnecessarily forceful.

Play with these activities to connect with your aspirations:

✱ **Create a vision window.** Similar to a vision board, the vision window is more focused and is meant to be hung on a wall or placed on a bookshelf where you can look at it often and be reminded of your dream. By using the symbol of a window, you are seeing what's just on the other side of where you are now. You get to gaze upon your dream and the more you can see the reality of your dream, the more likely you are to make the dream come true.

Take time to focus on what you want to aspire to and on who you want to become. Reread your vision statement for yourself. Really see yourself in your new role. What do you look like? Who is around you? How do you feel (what emotions are you expressing as the person you've become)? Get into the experience of what your life will be like when you have attained what you aspire to be.

Be open to allowing new thoughts, ideas, and aspirations to come to you.

Doing this project with others is also a bonus because the energy of creativity sparks each person to think more wildly and expansively.

The structure of your vision window can be as simple as a drawing of a window on a piece of paper, but I would encourage you to go multidimensional. Use a picture frame, a shadow box, a shirt box, a real window, or something you've constructed yourself as your container.

Glue or tie or in some way affix the objects to a background board or poster board or set them into the window frame on shelves. Use as many or as few objects as artistically appeal to you.

Paint your frame. Here are some ways to think about color symbolically:
Red stimulates positive action.
Deep pink is for passion.
Orange boosts confidence and stimulates creativity.
Yellow expresses hope and joy.
Green suggests harmony, healing, and vibrancy.
Blue promotes honesty, truth, peace, and relaxation.
Purple exudes power and attracts prosperity.
Turquoise calms, heals, and gives a great feeling of psychic safety.

Hang your window to your future self in a prominent place where you are constantly reminded of your aspiration for yourself.

✱ Go to the TED lectures website or the one for the Commonwealth Club or some other place where you can find an expert speaking on your topic of concern. How does this lecture inspire you to get started on a project? What is one step that you can take now? Take it!

✱ Think of a project with global impact that you would love to bring to life. Create a list of people you would like to work with on this project. Make this a dream list of people you know, people you know of, and people who are famous. Choose one, two, or more of the people on the list to contact with a general proposal and see what kind of response you get.

Richard Branson, visionary extraordinaire, has, among many projects, helped found the Elders, a group focused on human rights and most recently, OceanElders, created to give the oceans a loud and focused voice. Some of the people he gathered for the ocean project include CNN founder Ted Turner, oceanographer Sylvia Earle, Jackson Browne, Rita Colwell, Jean-Michel Cousteau, Graeme Kelleher, Sven Linblad, retired Navy Capt. Don Walsh, and Neil Young.

Share some of your responses with your Voyager Group.

According to research psychologist and author, Sonja Lyubomirsky, if you have an unfulfilled dream at any age, you would be wise to find a way to pursue this goal. You may need to refocus the actual goal, even as you keep the passion alive, but research suggests greater happiness is found when we have something we believe in to work toward. As it turns out, the accomplishment takes second place to the actual investment of ourselves into the project. Our spirits yearn to be filled with the wonder of the journey.

From *The Myths of Happiness* by Sonja Lyubomirsky

Whatever the problem you face, the answer might show itself more clearly if you make a systemic change rather than continuing to patch the holes in the current flawed structure.

Chapter Five
V Hierophant Energies: Commit to Personal Growth

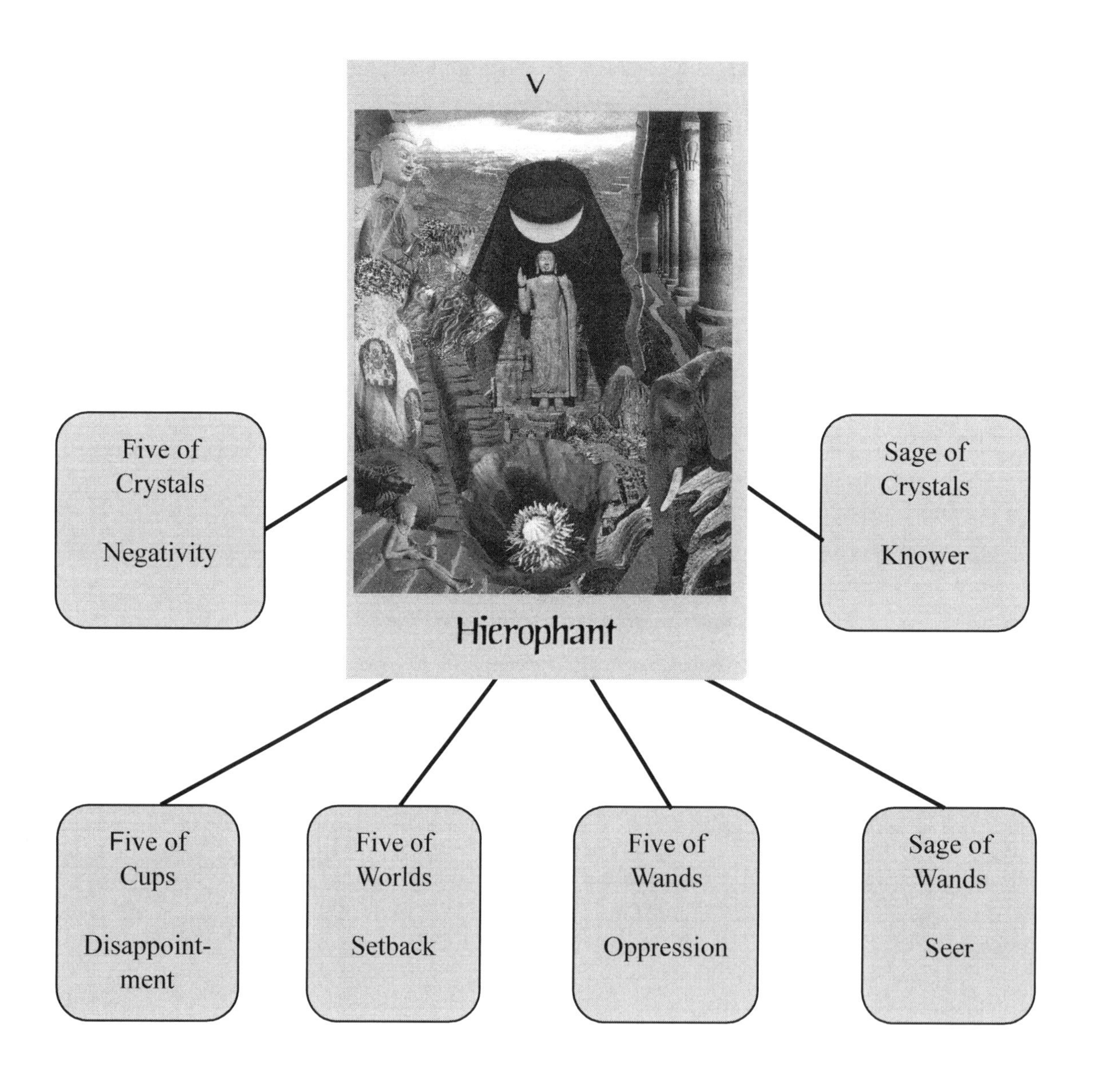

"Far better to live your own path imperfectly than to live another's perfectly."

from the *Bhagavad Gita*

V Hierophant: Walk the mystical path in sensible shoes.

Activate the Hierophant archetype, and you're on the fast track of personal growth.

The hero's journey, your quest for self-actualization, for enlightenment, is the basic struggle between good and evil embarked on so that you can develop into a mature, emotionally healthy, conscious adult.

When you overcome the obstacles in your life, you allow yourself to trust that you are capable of enjoying an abundant, prosperous, and happy life.

In Carl Jung's terms, "the essential function of the heroic myth is the development of the individual's ego-consciousness—his awareness of his own strengths and weaknesses—in a manner that will equip him for the arduous tasks with which life confronts him."

As you work with Hierophant energy, always remind yourself: There are no mistakes, only lessons.

The Hierophant archetype plays out in the realm of the hero's journey.

It is the energy told through the stories of Odysseus, Beowulf, Percival, Buddha, and Christ.

Today, the hero's tale is told through the adventures of Dorothy, Luke Skywalker, and Frodo, among others.

✱ As a journal entry, write about a couple of examples of "mistakes" you made.

What lessons were there for you?

Do you think you learned these lessons?

What makes you think you have or haven't learned the lessons from these "mistakes"?

Share some of your responses with your Voyager Group.

Poet T.S.Eliot reminds us that after all our of our inner and outer adventures, when we find ourselves back where we began our journeys, this place that was once so familiar to us is now unknown territory. Once transformed, we can no longer see with our old perspectives. This is Hierophant energy.

I was at a business seminar for spiritual entrepreneurs, and an attendee I'll call Amy told this story of something she had initially thought of as a big mistake:

Amy was working on learning the template we had been given for how to offer a program to a potential client when she booked an appointment with the director of a hospice center. This method of presentation was new to her, yet, concerned she'd appear unprofessional, she carried no notes into her meeting. Nonetheless, she felt confident because the template was simple, and she had practiced before she left home. Everything was moving along perfectly, and finally, she stepped up and made her offer. But instead of an acceptance, the hospice director said he wasn't sure if this would work after all. Amy's brain froze. She felt empty-headed. At the bottom of the template left on her desk at home, she knew there was something written about what to do when the potential client said he had some concerns, but nothing came to her. She stared at the man in front of her. What were the words she was supposed to say now? What would Jesse, the seminar leader, say? Still nothing came to her. Finally, she remembered one word printed at the bottom of that form and she blurted out, "Would you dance with me?"

Stunned by the request, the center manager, perhaps used to strange requests from the people in hospice, agreed to dance with her. He stood and walked around his desk. She got up from her chair and, without any music to accompany them, they danced. She hummed to give them a beat and let herself melt into the experience almost giggling at how silly they must look. She, as short as he was tall, had her head facing into his chest and could feel the vibration of her humming reverberating onto her cheek.

Finally, this generous man asked, "And why are we dancing?"

"Because I want to dance with your concerns," she replied, finally remembering the words printed on the form left on her desk at home. They both burst out laughing, she, while blushing from the tip of her blonde-haired head to the bottom of her sandaled-feet, or so it felt to her.

As embarrassed as Amy was, she continued the conversation about what she could offer the center, and the director made sure she had the opportunity to tell his clients about her program. Nine people signed up for what I am sure is a creative, intuitive, and inspired program.

Who could resist someone this delightful? Who, other than she, would even see this dance as a "mistake"?

Negativity/Five of Crystals
Negate defeatist thinking.

Use the Energy of Five of Crystals to:

Face the reality of what has gone awry or of what might go wrong, and accept the challenges you're given.

Realize that everything you think is only your interpretation.

Accept that all great successes have included great challenges.

Know that you can change a negative thought into a positive one at will. It's your choice.

Caution: Don't give in to negativity. Negativity creates confusion, stress, and conflict.

Play with these activities to explore how to defeat negative thoughts:

Remember that if you can name it, you can claim it. And following on this old adage, if you claim it, you can use it anyway you choose.

✱ **Bring something to awareness that has been keeping you from accomplishing a dream in any area of your life.**

You might say, I'm not writing my novel because the chances of my work getting published are slim to none. Now think about this statement. How is it serving you? If you're not writing your novel because you hold this belief, then it's not serving you well, and you would be wise to reframe this thought into something that supports you and your dreams.

✱ **Look at the negative statement you made and write a positive statement that supports your dream.** Following on the example about writing, you might remind yourself that writing your novel is important to you. Or that writing brings you closer to who you are as a thinking, feeling, creative person. Or that writing puts you in a good mood or makes you feel productive.

✱ **Do this reframing exercise with any negative statements that crop up in your mind throughout your day.**

Even if you don't write down these negative thoughts, changing them as you think them will be very beneficial. You could also say "cancel, cancel," whenever you notice a negative thought, and then follow up with one, two, or three positive statements to counter what popped into your mind.

The creative process has many components, and you will learn something helpful from every step of the way. But you must be acting on your own best interests if you're to learn anything. Being negative is not in your best interest. Being positive supports you.

Share some of your responses with your Voyager Group.

→ Being negative is a choice. As is being positive. ←

You can blame your circumstances and bemoan your fate, or you can seek out, or better yet, create the situations that will make your life better and celebrate your good fortune.

Knower/Sage of Crystals
Expand your consciousness.

Use the Energy of Sage of Crystals to:

See the synchronicity of all phenomena.

Recognize the oneness of the universe, yet acknowledge its diversity, too.

Allow yourself to be open to having a big vision. Use your innate wisdom to observe with detachment.

Bring forth your revolutionary ideas to share with humankind for the benefit and evolution of all.

Caution: Don't forget that you are a microcosm of the macrocosm. You are the universe.

Play with these activities to explore ways to expand your consciousness:

✱ **Commit! Commit to something big, ungainly, risky, unusual, uncertain, unprecedented, and/or challenging.**

Write down what you're noticing when you make your commitment. Is your heart pounding? Are you palms sweaty? Do you need to see what the noise on the street in front of your house is all about? Do you need to answer that text message now? What are you going to do for dinner? Are you all of a sudden hungry? Tired? In need of exercise? In need of FB, a tweet?

These are all distractions!

✱ **Write down what you are committing to.** Tell someone about what you are committing to.

✱ **If you can begin your commitment right now, do so, and pay attention to what happens in your mind, body, heart, and soul as you begin.** If you can't begin right now, notice what happens when you do make this choice to take action on your creative project, on your dream for yourself.

✱ **Recommit to your project and remind yourself that your commitment is vital to your well-being.** Only you can create your project. Your project is important because you are important.

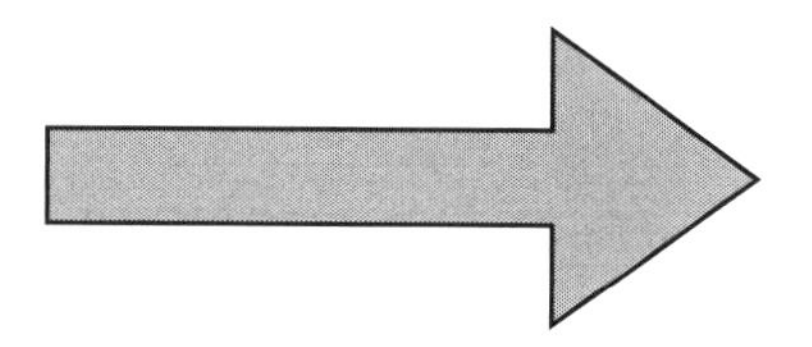

Eric Maisel, one of the foremost authorities on creativity as a way of life, insists that meaning exists only when we make it. You have to infuse your project with meaning because you are the creator. You have to keep distractions and detractions, especially negative thoughts, out of your way because your project, whether this means the project of creating your life or the project of creating an expression of your inner self, is only important when you guide, nurture, support, love, obsess over, think about, and in all ways, prioritize your creative instincts, time, and energy.

✱ **Now are you ready to dive into this big, beautiful, messy, extraordinary creative project?** Do one thing right now that will get you closer to your goal.

Share some of your responses with your Voyager Group.

Disappointment/Five of Cups
Reassess your attachment to results.

Use the Energy of Five of Cups to:

Set your goal while remaining flexible enough to reevaluate and move in other directions when needed.

Be grounded in the present reality, not in the way you want or expect things to be.

Accept the fleeting and impermanent nature of beauty and perfection.

Release old disappointments connected with family, extended family, or close friends.

Caution: Don't let a dashed dream hold you back. Learn what you can from the situation and move on.

Play with these activities to explore how to let go of expectations:

* **Make a list of people who make you angry, annoy you, irritate you, or in some way upset you.**

* **Note the things about these irritating people that upset you**.

* **Claim each of these faults as aspects of yourself.** Ouch! That's a tough one, isn't it? But do it as an exercise.

* **Take some time to simply notice when you exhibit these traits you're not fond of seeing in other people.**

* **One at a time, commit to eliminating each fault or annoyance.**

* **Show yourself some affection.** Give yourself a hug. Rub your arms and tell yourself how wonderful you know you are. Be overly dramatic in your show of affection. Kiss the back of your hand. Enjoy the feeling of being filled with love.

Take 100% responsibility for learning the truth about who you are and how you can improve your life so that you're happy, healthy, wealthy, and wise. Then, let go, and trust the process.

If someone annoys you because she talks too much, spend a week being especially conscious of when you dominate conversations.

If someone upsets you because he acts out violently, notice where you act out of rage in a destructive way. While you likely don't hurt people to the same degree that a person who physically harms another does, allow this observation to remind you of where you are unkind or manipulative in your own way.

Share some of your responses with your Voyager Group.

Disappointment, the word, sounds like it's saying you have an "appointment" with "dis." (As in "dis is the way it's supposed ta be, ya know.")

"Once you replace negative thoughts with positive ones, you'll start having positive results."
Willie Nelson, singer and songwriter

Action is required to make your dreams come true.

First you have to have a dream. You know this. As the "Happy Talk" song says, “If you don’t have a dream, how you gonna have a dream come true?” This dream also needs to be concrete. You have to be able to visualize the outcome you seek in great detail by including all of your senses when you imagine what you want. You need to positively and productively obsess over your dream. You must put in the time to make your dream come true. Sitting on your hands in your room in expectant solitude won’t magically bring a book to fruition or a meaningful career into your life or a partner into your heart.

Additionally, you have to pay attention to the opportunities that present themselves. Some may be those you’ve perfectly calculated to help you get to where you want to go. Others may be serendipitous encounters that project you into exactly where you hoped to find yourself. Paying attention and being conscious of your dream as you live your everyday life means that you’ve let go of the need to create the exact path TO your dream even as you take somewhat calculated steps toward your dream.

Along the way of this eclectic, usually nonlinear route, opportunities will likely present themselves that may be even better possibilities than you had imagined. We’ve all heard many people who have achieved brilliant success, exclaim, "This is even better than I had imagined." Or, "I never believed I’d make it this far." Or, "I went in a completely different direction and found more satisfaction than I’ve ever imagined possible." I’m sure you are aware of many other versions of the “Wow!” story.

However, if you only want results your way in your time frame, you are likely setting yourself up for disappointment. Often, when we get what we wanted, we find ourselves unfulfilled in other ways. We may not have included some important pieces in our imaginings. The beautiful blonde turns out to be more interested in and distracted by her career and less interested in building and exploring a relationship with you. The money may pour in, but you may find you have neglected your health or your relationships as a result.

The ubiquitous saying, "let go and trust the process," sums up Disappointment. Yet, as simple as this phrase appears, the action needed to both let go and trust can keep you from achieving your dreams.

Setback/Five of Worlds
Open yourself up to new possibilities.

Use the Energy of Five of Worlds to:

Learn from what hasn't worked.

Review, retreat, regroup, realign, and redirect your thoughts, energies, and goals whenever you experience a setback.

Concentrate on how to move forward with the new information you acquire through your setback.

Be prepared to experience setbacks. They are a part of life.

Caution: Don't focus on the setback. Learn from what set you back.

Play with these activities to explore what can help move you forward in spite of setbacks:

✱ **Where have you failed recently?** Who can you speak to about how to succeed where you have failed?

✱ **Make a word collage of times when you have been set back.**

Use a large piece of paper for this activity—the bigger, the better.

Use colored markers or pens.

In no particular order, write a phrase or sentence to express setbacks in your life.

Change the colors, sizes, and shapes of the fonts as you write each statement. When you're finished, read through the statements you've made.

Don't judge the statements.

✱ **Make another word collage on another sheet of paper.** Again, use varying colors, sizes and shapes of the font. This time, write phrases and sentences that capture successes that you remember were sparked by the setbacks you listed.

Let this be a very random recollection. Write what comes to mind rather than writing what directly resulted from a setback.

Again, don't judge, just write.

✱ **On a third piece of paper, write a word collage of where you see yourself next year.**

Anyone who has succeeded has also failed.

For example, if you've self-published a book and don't know how to get an audience for the book, find people who have self-published successfully and speak to them about what they did.

Look for models.

Gather information.

Stories abound of people who have overcome and triumphed over setbacks. Karin Volo relates how she was imprisoned for almost four years before being let go without being charged for anything. She was separated from her family, including her young children, and everything she held dear. After the first week of incarceration, she began a yoga practice, studying from a book in the library. Shortly after that, she taught yoga to fellow inmates. Throughout her period of confinement, she studied positive philosophies and held to the principle that this nightmare, too, would pass. After her release, she created a business to help others in dire situations.

Processing and accepting setback invigorates the spirit because you're reminded that life touches you in many different ways.

Steve Jobs, the founder of Apple, was fired from his own company when he was still in his twenties. Convinced that Silicon Valley was finished for him, he felt angry, depressed, defeated, betrayed.

But he didn't sit and stew in what he saw as a void. He realized he had to find a way to make his life, his career, his dreams work. One thing that he did, was he sought out other pioneers in the computer world and every one of them spoke about defeat as a catalyst.

History now shows he was catapulted from this place of major setback into what he claims was greater success than he could ever have achieved without this early defeat.

Take out your iPhone, iPad, or use your Mac (your PC will work just fine, too, of course) to check out his Stanford University Commencement Address from 2005 to get a glimmer into how he has used other setbacks to create opportunities for himself. And, at the same time, change the world! Or for a fuller picture of the late genius entrepreneur, read his authorized biography by Walter Isaacson.

Share your word collages with your Voyager Group.

Write journal entries responding to the process of making and sharing your word collages.

Positive psychology research points to the need for cultivating positive thoughts, positive emotions, and positive behaviors even when the struggle to do this feels almost impossible. When we change our minds from a negative belief to having a self supportive perspective, we can make our lives and the lives of those who matter to us much more rewarding, fulfilling, engaging, and fun. The struggle to push through is well worth the effort.

Oppression/Five of Wands
Liberate your potential.

Use the Energy of Five of Wands to:

Understand that oppression is always self-created.

Know that lack of energy, low or no creative urges, a sense of heaviness or feelings of despair come to remind you that you can revitalize your spirit.

Find a source of inspiration, seek out help, and connect with others who can inspire you.

Know that feeling oppressed means you are meant to look for a way to liberate yourself.

Caution: Don't get caught up in your oppression. You can liberate yourself. You have many resources both within yourself and out in the world.

Play with this activity to explore how being aware of what or who oppresses you can lead you to connecting to your highest self:

Forgiveness must become a way of life for peace to reign in the heart and in the world.

✱ **Throughout your day, say the Ho'oponopono Prayer of Surrender:**
I love you. I'm sorry. Please forgive me. Thank you.

This simple Ho'oponopono Prayer: ***"I love you. I'm sorry. Please forgive me. Thank you,"*** is a powerful way to help you move away from whatever is oppressing you, no matter the source of the oppression. Here's a brief explanation of each phrase:

The prayer is being addressed to the divinity that you are and that connects you to all of life, all of the world, all of the universe. This is the place where unconditional love resides. The "I" is you and it is not you. The "I" is the divine that is greater and more loving than any individual can be. "I love you" acknowledges that you are loved and that the love in you embraces the divine within you, too.

"I'm sorry" acknowledges that you take responsibility for resolving this issue. You are not necessarily at fault for having the problem, but it is your responsibility to take care of the issue. To take care of the issue means you find peace within yourself no matter what goes on around you. Whenever you notice you are in a state of serenity, you know you have taken care of the issue for that moment. Sometimes, the best that can be done is to find this peaceful state for a few seconds. Think of this as a process, not as goal that is achieved or that is resolved once and for all.

When you say, "Please forgive me," you are asking for absolution, for liberation from the oppression you feel because you've been carrying this misperception that has been holding you back from living a full, vital, vibrant, loving and joyful life. The misperception is that you are inadequate in some way and that you are not fully and completely lovable right now. The truth is you are perfect and perfectly lovable.

"Thank you" expresses your gratitude. All healing begins when you are in a state of gratitude. You have to be clear about your awareness that your old, outdated, unhealthy perception is leaving and you are surrendering to the new, clearer perception of yourself that is now open to joy.

Say the Ho'oponopono Prayer of Surrender for yourself, not for the person who is being difficult. The longing is what oppresses you, not the words or behaviors of another. You long for a different relationship (maybe even for a different person to be related to!).

Your goal is to surrender to what is. Another way to express this is to find the beauty in the messiness of this relationship. The creative imagination can be helpful in many, many ways!

When you have a specific issue you want to address, focus the prayer on the issue. If you are facing a health challenge, then focus on the problem as you say the prayer. You could even put your hands on the area of the body where the issue is or you could simply place your hands on your heart chakra. If you are dealing with a problem in a relationship, then focus on the issue you have with this other person. Always think in terms of yourself. For example, if your sister is saying you are selfish, think of this as your problem. Not that you are selfish but that you are allowing her words to hurt you.

With focus comes clarity. With clarity comes inspiration. With inspiration comes positive action that leads to joy. When you have clarity, you'll know what actions you need to take to relieve the pain you've nurtured inside yourself.

In an abusive relationship, focus on yourself and on why you have chosen to continue to engage with this person. Sometimes you have no choice but to be with this person who seeks out every opportunity to dig her metaphorical claws into your skin. Yet you have the choice of how or if you will respond. In other words, when the dragon's circling, ask yourself if you're going to "feed the dragon" or keep her hungry.

Just focus on this. Bring the thought to consciousness as you say the quick prayer. Don't attempt to analyze or resolve anything.

Take appropriate action. The sooner you do whatever is needed to make a change, the more likely you'll find yourself calm and joyful for longer periods of time—even in the presence of the dragon, no matter what shape she chooses to assume.

Do this exercise in your Voyager Group even if you've done it elsewhere. Discuss how you are responding to the Ho'oponopono Prayer.

Seer/Sage of Wands
Be alive with passion and power.

Use the Energy of Sage of Wands to:

See yourself as being on the leading edge, in the vanguard of understanding and experiencing your full human potential.

Strive for self-realization through connection with your "higher self."

Have the courage to be yourself.

Be fully energized by your personal power.

Caution: Don't become a visionary who cannot be of service to the world. Use your wisdom wisely.

Play with these activities to explore how being alive with passion and fully energized can connect you to your higher self:

✱ **Write your legacy now.** This isn't the great American novel or your speech for receiving the Nobel Prize for peace. What I'm suggesting here is that you create a written document similar to Randy Pausch's *The Last Lecture.*

Professor Pausch was forty-seven years old, and he knew he was dying, so he presented what was to be his last lecture to his students. In this one-hour lecture, he inspirationally captured his thoughts on what he valued. He spoke about how he chose to live a life worth cherishing without regard to the time he had or didn't have.

✱ **When your legacy is written or recorded, share your insights with the intended recipient or recipients.**

✱ **Watch Randy Pausch deliver his lecture on YouTube.**

✱ **Watch Brené Brown's TED lecture on how she came to understand and embrace the value of imperfection.**

✱ **Watch any of the TED lectures.** The speakers show what it looks like to live a life of personal power energized by passion and connected to their higher selves.

- Decide on who will be the recipient of your written legacy. A large circle of family and friends? One very special person? A few specific people in your life such as your children or your closest friends? A wider audience of people you interact with socially or professionally?

- The format can be anything that suits you: a series of poems, a short compilation of essays or letters with each one meant for a specifically named individual, a straightforward speech, or any other form you might choose.

- The most powerful written or oral legacy will include what you value, what motivated you, what convictions led to very specific actions, and what hopes and dreams drove you to create the life you lived.

- Give yourself a time frame to complete this legacy. I suggest one week because if it goes on too long, you'll find yourself writing a tome.

- Begin by thinking of three values that you hold dear. For each value, think of an action, an event, or a choice you made that was based on this value.

You may find yourself changing your legacy as your priorities and values change. Readjusting your ethical compass is an important way to navigate the world. As you learn more about yourself, you learn better how to be the person you are and want to be.

About Values

You might find values' clarification an interesting topic to explore with your family and friends. As a family or group, make a top ten or top twenty list of values you hold as a family or group.

Individually, rank this list. On the top of the list, place the value most honored and proceed in descending order.

Discuss, talk about, explain, write about, and keep the conversation going for the next several months at various intervals. Notice how your values play out in your life by the choices you make. Notice how the values of those in your family or group play out.

Notice where values come in conflict with each other. For example, getting good grades might conflict with being healthy because a student has to study hard and loses sleep and doesn't eat well.

Or being honest could conflict with having a huge income if some of that money comes from cheating on taxes or being in collusion with stock traders.

A Very Limited List of Values to Live By (To Get You Started)

being healthy
being charitable
having peace of mind
being contemplative
being resourceful
being open to new ideas
honoring traditions
tithing
getting good grades in school
being artistically expressive
focusing on natural gifts
focusing on being well balanced
focusing on developing the less obvious talents one has
being respectful of authority
always questioning authority
internal peace
external peace
kindness
beauty
earning a modest salary
having a huge income
being able to retire by a certain age (30, 40, 50, 60, 70 years old?)
being independent
living in community/with family
being honest and trustworthy

Write your responses to these activities in your journal.

Share some of your responses with your Voyager Group.

"To thine own self be true, and it must follow, as the night the day, thou canst not then be false to any man."

from *Hamlet* by William Shakespeare

Chapter Six

VI Lovers Energies: Integrate Opposing Energies

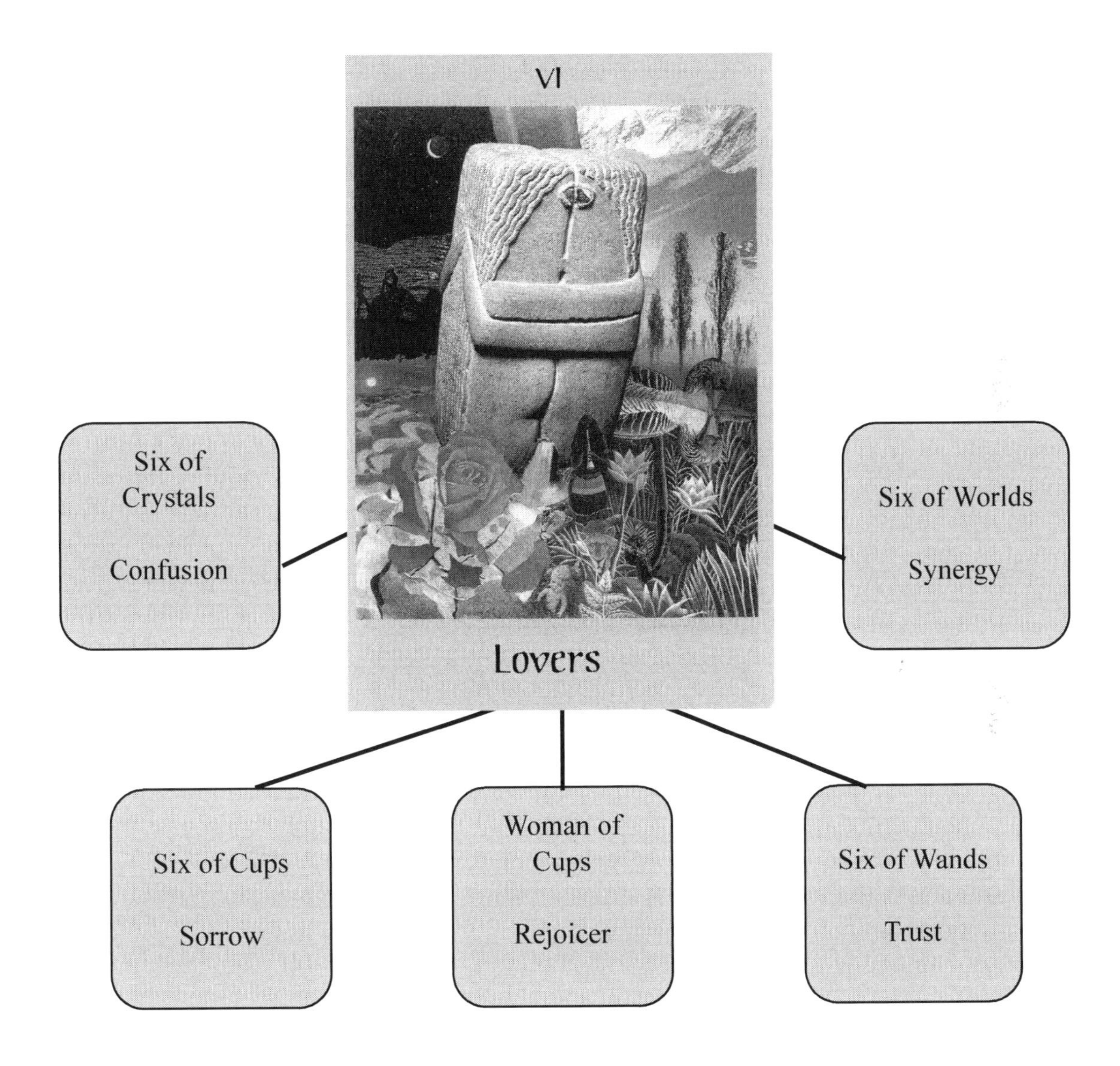

When you choose to live in the present, you are embracing the precious moment that is now, that is all that there is, and you are saying yes to being alive.

VI Lovers: Integrate, synthesize, synergize.

Lovers energy promotes love for yourself, a partner, family, friends, community, and the world through empathy, compassion, faith, and trust.

Relate to yourself, your beloved, your family, friends, and community with an open heart.

Be joyful and playful.

Emotional expression of all kinds connects you to yourself and others.

Create community.

✱ **Everyday, choose to take at least one action to express an emotion in a positive and authentic way to help connect you to others and the world.**

In your journal, write about any actions you took to be authentically expressive. Write about your responses and reactions to doing this activity and to how people responded and reacted to you.

Share some of your responses with your Voyager Group.

The archetypal energy of the Lovers' card is integration.

First, integrate the opposites within yourself. Embrace the unwanted parts of yourself, both the aspects of yourself you consider "bad" as well as the gifts you have but don't claim or act on.

Next, acknowledge the projections you make on people you are most intimate with. For example, you may choose to not develop social skills because you've come to rely on your partner or best friend to take care of this part of your life. Instead of letting this piece of yourself wither, strengthen your ability to interact in social situations by learning how to set a plan in place for a group or how to fully and completely express yourself in a group by learning these skills from your partner or friend.

Actively learn these skills. Observe them, speak about them, and read about how to use these skills. Do whatever it takes to make these skills your own so that you can use them with ease.

Finally, take your skills and talents into the world where they can be shared for the betterment of others.

Confusion/Six of Crystals
Entertain competing ideas and points of view.

Use the Energy of Six of Crystals to:

Be confused. Confusion is the state of extreme mental activity and agitation where great ideas are born.

Play with opposing concepts, and brainstorm numerous ways to accomplish your dreams.

Allow old beliefs, old forms, and old structures to break down to make way for a new way to live your dreams.

Caution: Prevent a breakdown. Allow your mind to bend to new ideas during times of stress.

Play with these activities to help you move beyond analysis paralysis:

✱ **To integrate your most creative ideas into your physical reality, use the power of synchronicity.** Make connections. Make up connections. Let the power of symbols lead you to your next step on your path to creating the life you want to live, to moving you in the direction of making your dreams come true, to guiding you to take the next step toward achieving whatever you have set out to do.

Taoist philosophy teaches that yin and yang are the fundamental creative principles at work in the universe. Constantly flowing one into the other, these complementary opposites include dark and light, feminine and masculine, right and left brain energies, among others.

However, when you allow your mind to entertain opposing ideas, you may find yourself agitated, confused, and irritated. You may become anxious, even depressed, and unable to get on with your life. You may find yourself organizing, planning, developing new plans and dropping them before they're finished because you can't think them through to the end.

During this time of agitation, allow time to let really good ideas come to the surface. Get comfortable with confusion, for this is the place where inspiration swims.

Creativity and chaos are cohorts.

✱ **Notice an animal, a bird, a lizard, or an insect that presents itself to you today.** This creature might appear in front of you in real life, in a book, in a movie, in a conversation, or on TV. What are this animal's special characteristics? What does this animal mean to you? What more do you know about this animal? Imagine the animal has come to give you a message. What is the message you can imagine yourself hearing? Go online or look in a book to get more insights into what this animal represents. How do these insights shed light on the question you've been pondering or the project you are working on?

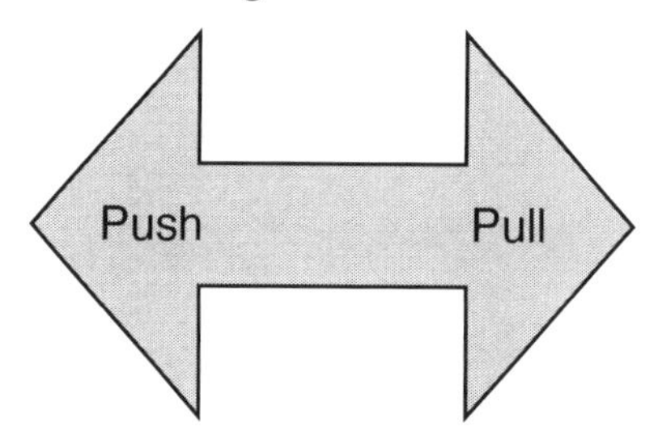

Jonas Salk is said to have regularly walked along the beach seeking signs for guidance in his work or with a problem he was attempting to solve. He'd look around and notice a gull flying, a rope twisted a certain way, a shell, kelp clumped in a specific pattern, the foamy bubbles the waves leave as they recede. He'd then let his mind make connections to how the one item he focused on could tell him something about a specific issue he sought insight into.

The Voyager Tarot cards are perfect for using symbols to guide you out of confusion.

✱ **Think of a problem and draw a card facedown.** Turn the card over. Notice what immediately attracts your attention. How can that word, number, or image guide you? Make up something. Choose another word, image, or number, then another, always asking yourself how each image can tell you something. Don't censor yourself as ideas pop into your head. Let the images speak to you. Finally, scrutinize the card and look for something you did not notice until you checked out the card closely. This image, number, or word could be telling you what you're overlooking or what you don't want to "see" in terms of the question or problem of the moment.

✱ **If you choose a card with other people around, get their input, too.** What do these images mean to them? Their insights can give you even more ideas.

✱ **Get a reading from a professional Voyager tarot card reader.**

Write your responses to these activities in your journal.

Share some of your responses with your Voyager Group.

Do a reading for yourself to answer a specific question or to address a specific problem. A helpful three card reading has you choose a card that represents how things are now, a second card that represents the path you're on based on the question you asked, and a third card that tells you what will likely be the outcome of being on this path.

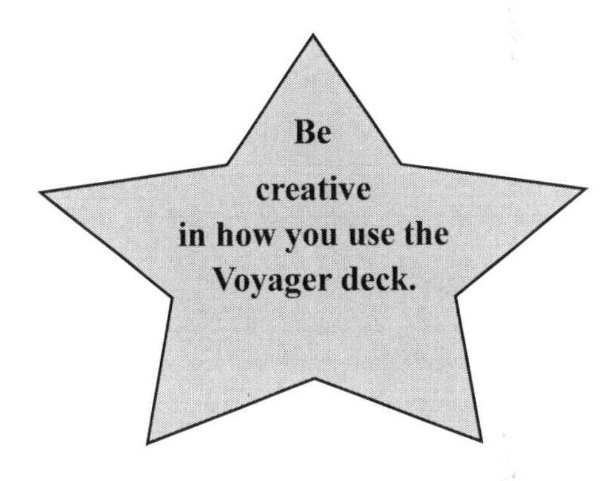

Confusion can overwhelm you and sabotage your dreams or you can allow yourself to sift through the plethora of ideas until the brilliant thoughts that will assist you shine like stars in a dark sky: clear, radiant, and powerful.

"Risk! Risk anything! Care no more for the opinions of others, for those voices. Do the hardest thing on earth for you. Act for yourself. Face the truth."

Katherine Mansfield, 1888-1923 author

Sorrow/Six of Cups
Feel, and then release your sadness or grief.

Use the Energy of Six of Cups to:

Cry when you're sad or grief-stricken.

Revitalize yourself through catharsis.

Release the pain of sadness and grief.

Experience life at the deepest levels of feeling.

Liberate your feelings by expressing yourself fully, and you will lift your spirits.

Caution: Continued depression needs to be addressed with professional assistance.

Play with these activities to explore how to experience and release sadness:

✱ **Watch a "tear jerker" movie with a big box of tissues next to you.** Cry. Crying releases toxins in the body and stimulates the immune system.

✱**Write a "pity" letter to yourself.** Include specific incidents that make you sad. Cry as you write. Let the tears flow freely. Set the letter aside for a day or two.

Reread the letter. Include anything else you've thought about that makes you sad. Set this letter aside for another day or two. Reread the letter. Are you still crying?

This exercise is usually enough to get the tears out and feelings to pass even when the situation or situations that have made you sad haven't changed.

✱ **Take your "pity" letter—if you wrote it on the computer, print it out and then delete the file—crumple the paper and hold this ball of pain in your hand.** Say something out loud that acknowledges you are ready to release your sadness. This may sound something like: "Even though my heart felt broken when these things happened, I now release myself from the pain and grief I have experienced. I am whole, I am loved, I am loving."

✱ **Next, find a safe place to burn this letter and then take the ashes and bury them in soil around or near your home.** As you do this, repeat your mantra. The one I've used is the one above. Thank the earth for receiving your offering and for helping you release your grief. Tell the universe you are now ready for something wonderful to come into your life. Say your vision statement out loud.

The reason the simple release of feelings in a controlled environment helps is because you are consciously deciding to accept the situation without accepting the emotional upheaval that the problem has caused.

You are feeling the feelings, which is important. You are acknowledging fully and completely the pain of the sorrow. Now you can release this energy, feel the next emotion that arises, and release that emotion, too.

Respond to these activities in your journal. Share some of your responses with your Voyager Group.

"A hero is an ordinary individual who finds the strength to persevere and endure in spite of overwhelming obstacles." Christopher Reeve, 1952-2004 actor, director, producer, and paraplegic

Rejoicer/Woman of Cups
Energize yourself. Feel the joy and bliss.

Use the Energy of Woman of Cups to:

Allow your love for the beauty of life to bubble up.

Be aware of the beauty inside yourself. Allow yourself to feel your joy throughout your body and be sensuously joyful.

Fully express your joy at being in touch with the wonders of life.

Accept and forgive.

Caution: Don't get overwhelmed by the emotional expressions of others. Don't take on the intense feelings of others as if they were your own. Empathize but discriminate.

Play with these activities to energize your sense of joy and bliss:

✱ Huddle with fellow employees or fellow volunteers at the end of each week to share accomplishments, victories, and great moments of the past week. Use this time to acknowledge that you are all on the same team, all working toward excellence, and all doing your best.

✱Find a way to celebrate success, both yours and that of others. You can do this in your family by declaring one day a week or two days a month, Family Celebration Day.

Each person shares his or her accomplishments, victories, and great moments of the previous week or two. Make it a party and serve dessert. Wear party hats. Make a special meal together. Celebrate the joy of sharing the joy.

✱Decide on a quick service project you can accomplish with very little effort either by yourself or with a few friends. Don't over think this project. Simple is beautiful, too. Taking ten minutes to have a conversation with a homeless person would work for this activity. Bringing some homemade sandwiches to an area where homeless people congregate and handing out the food along with a few smiles is simple, yet profound. Or you might gather materials for schools, jails, shelters, or hospitals and deliver them. Think both big and small.

Jon Gordon, author and inspirational speaker, teaches that happiness isn't something to be sought after. Instead, he says, "share your strengths and decide to work with passion and purpose and happiness will find you."

The research on happiness and positive psychology support his belief, showing that people who use their talents, gifts, and strengths to create something in service to others, are the happiest, most invigorated, most grounded people who don't easily get upset when things go wrong.

Write your responses to these activities in your journal.

Share some of your responses with your Voyager Group.

"Appreciation is a wonderful thing: It makes what is excellent in others belong to us as well."

Voltaire, 1694-1778

French Enlightenment philosopher, novelist, playwright, poet, and historical writer

Synergy/Six of Worlds
Bring resources together. Create alliances for success.

Use the Energy of Six of Worlds to:

Combine energies so that the whole is greater than the sum of each of its parts.

Have emotional courage and physical vitality.

Be energetically expansive.

Take risks to make your dreams come true.

Weave your talents and inner and outer resources into a brilliant design for success.

Caution: Avoid being defensive or contrarian.

Play with these activities to explore how to use the power of synergy to get your work into the world:

✱ **Find or form a teaching-learning community based on something you're passionate about.** Gather a group of people, large or small, who are all interested in doing something creative or entrepreneurial or service oriented but don't know where to put their energy or how to proceed. Work together to decide what to do. Get one or several projects going.

✱ **Create a Mastermind Group,** a small group of supportive people who are interested in being a sounding board and support team for you as you create your new life or pursue your new project.

This group should include five to seven people who are willing to dedicate a specific amount of time on a regular basis to support each other as each participant pursues a personal, professional, or creative project.

This is another way to use synergy to get big results after you've completed your time with your Voyager Group. But remember that you can also go on the Voyager Soul of Success journey multiple times. And both a Voyager Group and a Mastermind group can be in place simultaneously.

Write your responses to these activities in your journal.

Share some of your responses with your Voyager Group.

Jean Houston, the noted cultural historian, reports that Margaret Mead, on her deathbed, told her to forget everything Mead had been teaching about working with governments and bureaucracies. Instead, the famous anthropologist said she'd reconsidered her whole approach and had come to realize that "if we're going to grow and green our time, it's a question of people getting together, gathering together, in teaching-learning communities."

Meet either in person or on the phone weekly, biweekly, or monthly. Keep meetings short.

To begin, everyone checks in for five minutes stating what has been done since the last meeting to move toward their goals. After each person speaks, every member of the group offers this person something supportive, asks a question, makes a suggestion, or comments on the person's project or process. The person who has checked in commits to a specific action.

In between meetings, everyone has a call pal, a person from the group with whom they connect at their discretion. This might be once or twice in between meetings. These call pals rotate after each meeting.

Trust/Six of Wands
Believe in yourself. Know you are supported.

Use the Energy of Six of Wands to:

Have faith in yourself and the courage to seek out opportunities to realize your dreams.

Trust in the goodness and positive support of the universe.

Trust your own instincts and intuitions to guide you away from those who aren't trustworthy.

Trust in change for everything changes. Be open and vulnerable.

Caution: Don't hold on too tightly to anything.

Play with these activities to explore how to let go and trust:

✱ **Think about something you once longed for and eventually attained.** This may be receiving a prize, finding a partner, having a baby, achieving a business success, or completing a personal challenge. Or something else that meant a lot to you when you knew you had reached your goal or that your dream had come true. Remember how euphoric you felt when you knew you were successful. Close your eyes now and bring that moment to consciousness. Try to feel the happiness of that distant pleasure.

The memory may warm you or possibly dishearten you. You may have divorced that partner, the business may have eventually gone south, the muscles you built up for the marathon may have turned to fat. No matter where you are today, however, the accomplishment of the past served you and continues to serve you well. You now know you can do whatever it was that you achieved and you also know that it was only a part of your journey. Also, even if you set the same goal for yourself, the journey would be different for you now.

✱ **Close your eyes again and imagine what achieving the same goal would look like for you today.** If you wanted a baby today and you're a woman in your fifties, how would you go about bringing a child into your life? If you're now suffering from "fat limitations" and you were once a prize-winning swimmer, what would you need to do to achieve another blue ribbon for the breaststroke? Let your imagination weave as many scenarios as possible to show you an updated version of how to accomplish something you once attained.

The process would be very different, wouldn't it? The feeling of accomplishment would also likely offer you other sensations than those experienced the first time you held your prize.

Sometimes we forget that the process is the important piece. We think the medal or the acclaim or the "moment" of achievement is what we're after. But that's never the case. The baby you had may be thirty years old today and you'd never trade all the wonderful days and years of that relationship to keep your child as a newborn.

Life is about process and having faith that the conscious journey, the path of self-awareness where you assume full responsibility for your own actions, choices, and thoughts, is your right life's journey. And then trusting that forces greater than yourself are part of that journey, knowing that you will receive guidance, support, comfort, and love along the way.

Process is the only part of life that is constant. Process opens you to love, joy, gratitude, appreciation, and hope.

✱ **With a Voyager tarot deck, do a three-card reading either with someone else or by yourself about what to expect over the next six months.** If you don't have a deck, go to voyagertarot.com and choose each card from the card a day. Or use cards from another oracle deck you are familiar with. Choose the cards either face up (consciously) or face down, and let your unconscious guide you.

Card One will represent who you are now.

Card Two will represent the path you'll be on over the next six months.

Card Three will represent the probable outcome of being on this path.

Trust any intuitive hits you get.

Look for inspiration in the reading for an action you can now take that will move you even one small step toward making the next six months easier and better for you.

If you want more clarification for any card chosen, choose another card for more insights.

If the probable outcome card feels too negative or not "right" for you, choose another card and see what that one offers.

Take the action and trust the process.

Share some of your responses with your Voyager Group.

Write your responses to these activities in your journal.

"Twenty years from now you will be more disappointed by the things you didn't do than by the ones you did do. So throw off the bowlines, sail away from the safe harbor. Catch the trade winds in your sails. Explore. Dream. Discover."

Mark Twain, 1835-1910
writer and humorist

Dustin Hoffman has a great story about how he was propelled toward a different path than the one he had imagined for himself when he was given an internal and external shove to audition for his role in *The Graduate*, the movie that made him an unlikely movie star.

Hoffman was a stage actor. He felt he was all wrong for the movies, and even after he was up on the big screen, many people agreed with him. He was short, slight, had a big nose, a slumping posture, and an over all Jewish look. Hollywood was not keen on casting someone swarthy in romantic lead roles, and Hoffman never sought out movies as a career choice.

Nonetheless, Mike Nichols, who wrote and produced *The Graduate*, saw Hoffman and knew he was "Mr. Right." The extraordinary moment of recognition came when Nichols saw Hoffman in a play in New York. The play was *Harry, Noon, and Night.* The role Hoffman had that so impressed Nichols was that of a German transvestite fishwife!

Hoffman had to be convinced to audition for *The Graduate*. He felt panicky during the scene he had to do with the beautiful and talented Katherine Ross and almost everyone involved couldn't believe that Nichols could make this work—including Hoffman and Ross.

The part was meant to go to Robert Redford, and here was Hoffman, the opposite in appearance, but fortunately equal in talent, needing to be convinced every step of the way that he should have the lead role in a major motion picture.

But Hoffman did take that leap of faith, and he has been sailing along in the energy stream ever since. Think about what the world would have lost out on if he had been too reticent, too unimaginative, and too untrusting to put himself in a role totally outside of his image of who he was before this opportunity presented itself.

Some of Dustin Hoffman's films: *The Graduate; Midnight Cowboy; Little Big Man; Soloway; Who Is Harry Kellerman and Why Is He Saying Those Terrible Things About Me?; Straw Dogs; Lenny; Papillon; Alfredo; All the President's Men; Marathon Man; Straight Time; Agatha; Kramer vs Kramer; Tootsie; Ishtar; Rain Man; Family Business; Dick Tracy; Billy Bathgate; Hook; Hero; Sleepers; American Buffalo; Wag the Dog; Runaway Jury; Finding Neverland; I Heart Huckabees; Meet the Fockers; Lemony Snicket's A Series of Unfortunate Events; Stranger Than Fiction; Mr. Megrim's Wonder Emporium; Little Fockers; Kung Fu Panda; Belonging*

Chapter Seven
VII Chariot Energies: Commit to Your Own Success

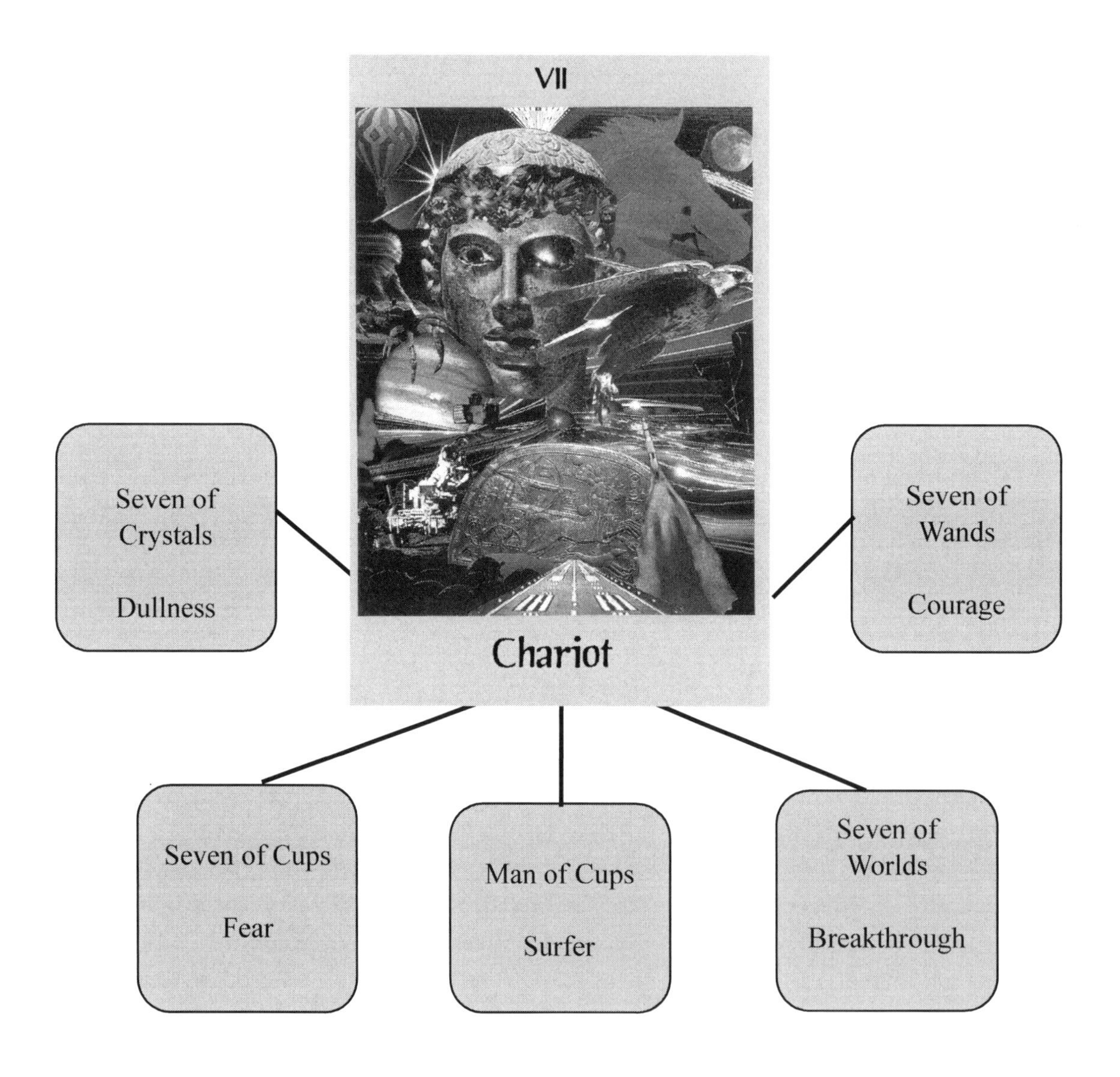

"Do just once what others say you can't do, and you will never pay attention to their limitations again."

James R. Cook. 1728-1779
Naval explorer

VII Chariot: Push yourself forward on your hero's journey toward enlightenment.

Chariot energy gets you through all setbacks and obstacles through your commitment, determination, and the emotional investment you make in your dreams.

Be a warrior in service to your gifts, talents, and potential.

Take risks to move forward.

Initiate new paths, new directions.

Be decisive. Be goal directed.

Get tangible results.

Rest before exhaustion sets in.

"Your time is limited, so don't waste it living someone else's life. Don't be trapped by dogma-- which is living with the results of other people's thinking. Don't let the noise of other's opinions drown out your own inner voice. And most important, have the courage to follow your heart and intuition. They somehow already know what you truly want to become. Everything else is secondary."

Steve Jobs 1955-2011
Co-Founder of Apple Computer

* **Don't forget your dreams.**
* **Reread your vision statement.**

Joseph Campbell, the mythologist, explains the hero's journey as having many obstacles that must be overcome before integration is possible.

Dorothy encountered the forces of evil and her own perceived weaknesses in Oz. Luke Skywalker fought battles with evil and with himself. Frodo faced orcs, ents, elves, spiders, dark riders, Gollum, Smaug, mountains, rivers, as well as his own temptations.

These heroes held to their goals to keep them going. Dorothy wanted desperately to return home; Luke felt the call to save the galaxy; Frodo was determined to restore peace to Middle Earth.

Write a response to Steve Jobs' statement.
Share your response with your Voyager Group.

Dullness/Seven of Crystals
Calm yourself during times of mental agitation.

Use the Energy of Seven of Crystals to:

Take a break from too much thinking.

Rest your mind through meditation, relaxation, and exercise.

Reevaluate your beliefs and bring them up to date with who you are now.

Be on the look out for new opportunities to make your dreams come true.

Caution: Don't fall victim to boredom. Rest your mind, but remain curious, imaginative, and open-minded.

Play with these activities to explore how to calm yourself when you're feeling overwhelmed:

✱ **Do Dr. Judith Orloff's Three Minute Meditation to help you revitalize yourself throughout the day whenever you feel overwhelmed.**

✱ **Take a long walk every morning for two weeks straight.** Better yet, make this part of your daily program.

✱ **Find a beach, a stream, or river to sit near**. Pay attention to the sounds of the water.

✱ **Sit in a quiet setting and go through all the major muscle groups by first contracting the muscles, then relaxing the muscles.** This process reminds your body to relax.

✱ **Listen to a visualization recording that takes you into a state of deep relaxation.**

✱ **Take a nap.** Research suggests a fifteen to twenty minute nap not only refreshes the brain and body, but accounts for greater longevity, too.

✱ **Camp and hike in nature.**

✱ **Using markers, colored pencils, paints, or charcoal, fill a page of paper with color.** Do this very slowly, very meditatively.

✱ **Walk a labyrinth.** If you don't have access to one, find an expanse of open space and imagine one as you walk slowly, meditatively.

Find a place where you can be alone for three minutes. Even a stall in a public bathroom will work.

Take a deep breath. Close your eyes.

Place your hand somewhere in the middle of your chest—this is where your heart chakra is.

Picture a place where you would feel relaxed and at peace. This could be anywhere, real or imagined. Maybe your place for serenity is out in nature. Maybe you have a special room in mind. Or you might think of a building, such as a meditation center where you've found peace in the past.

Visualize this place. See the details, feel the air around you, smell the soothing scents that waft by, and hear the gentle sounds that are part of the special ambiance of this private sanctuary.

Notice the warmth of the area under your hand. Maybe you get a sense of expansiveness, or you might feel waves of energy. Observe what you feel, open your eyes, take another breath, and continue with your day.

This exercise is meant to take only about three minutes. You can do it many times throughout the day to help get you past "brain buzz" and to a place of creativity and thoughtful action.

Fear/Seven of Cups
Face your fears.

Use the Energy of Seven of Cups to:

Feel the fear and push onward toward your goals.

Be courageous in spite of what appears daunting.

Take on the biggest issues one small piece at a time.

Stop and reflect on what's really going on when you're afraid. Decide if this is the time to be prudent and redirect yourself or if this is the time to push onward.

Caution: Don't give in to worry, anxiety, and terror. This only makes you defensive, timid, insecure, and closed up.

Play with these activities to explore your emotional state of fear:

✱ **To overcome fear, face yourself in some extraordinary way.** Many people on paths of personal growth set themselves yearly challenges: do a Ropes Course, skydive, solo backpack in the wilderness for a week, run a marathon, compete in a triathlon, fire walk, bike through the Rockies, and on and on. If taking on an extreme physical challenge is possible for you to do, pick a physical activity that would challenge you and go for it. The rewards are tremendous.

If taking on an extreme physical challenge isn't possible, write yourself a letter and explain why you aren't able to do anything too strenuous.

✱**A good way to learn what's holding you back and to get beyond blockages is to use Tapping or EFT (Emotional Freedom Technique).** You can start learning about this technique on Gary Craig's website www.emofree.com. Opportunities abound for discovering this technique. Search the Internet and see which teacher appeals to you.

✱ **Release yourself energetically from old wounds that continue to hold you back.** Maybe you were in a bad relationship and are now afraid to enter into another intimate relationship. Sit quietly and imagine your ex is standing in front of you. Forgive this person and send this person off to be on his or her own path. Forgive yourself unconditionally for feeling bad, sad, guilty, or whatever residual feelings hang on. Let go of these feelings and this relationship.

Many programs are based on overcoming fears in everyday life by providing opportunities to face survival issues in a more threatening, and usually an outdoor environment.

Outward Bound and scouting programs are examples of how young people can face challenges and realize how much they are capable of.

To become a Masai warrior in Kenya and Tanzania, a young teenaged boy must kill a lion with a spear.

A program established to help the widows of US soldiers brings them to Alaska where the women do such courageous feats such as rappelling down sheer granite mountainsides.

Ed Catmull, co-founder of Pixar, speaks about the need for, and the dangers of, facing fears and challenges. Failure in the outside world can be devastating and brutal, so he says they try to keep their failures in the studio. Ideas are ruthlessly challenged, reworked, and challenged again so they can grow from their mistakes and revise and sharpen until the movie is as good as is possible. Then they release the final version.

Fear can also be thought of as places where we have conflicts. We want one thing, but something else keeps us from getting what we want. For example, you may want to write a novel, but you have a list of "reasons" why you can't take the time for this project on a regular basis.

✱ **To get at the core of your fear, write your vision statement at the top of a page.** Now list all the reasons why you can't get to this today, tomorrow, and everyday for the next three months. Be as exhaustive as possible in naming the reasons for lack of action on your part. For example, your list for the conflicts you have for getting your novel written on a steady, regular schedule might look something like this: no time, need to do more research, need to think more about the project, might be a waste of time. Who will publish anything I write? Who will read what I write? How do I begin? What will my family think of me if I write what I want to write?

✱ **Look at your list.** Cross out the conflicts that have eased and cause no more concerns. Sometimes just looking at something squarely will dissipate the tension.

✱ **Look at what's left on your list**. For each one that's left, write a rebuttal to the statement.

✱ **Revise each statement that's left in the form of a declaration of what is possible.** For example, to the question "Who will publish what I write?" you might state: My book may not get published, but it will get written. I am a writer, and I will write because that's what I find meaningful.

Naming the demon is an important and necessary first step.

Face whatever you have acknowledged as your demon, fully prepared to find its weakness so you can find your own strength.

Be fearless pursuing your dreams for yourself.

Don't die with your words, your music, your love, your talents, or your dreams still hidden away inside yourself.

Write your responses to these activities in your journal.

Share some of your responses with your Voyager Group.

Surfer/Man of Cups
Negotiate emotional upheavals.

Use the Energy of Man of Cups to:

Ride emotional highs and lows with equal balance.

Have the courage to explore and express your deepest feelings.

Be an emotional risk taker.

Go with the flow of life and emotionally connect with both life's pleasures and life's challenges.

Caution: Notice and experience even upsetting feelings, but don't hold on to them. Move on to the next emotion, always being in the flow.

Play with these activities to explore and express your wide range of feelings:

✱ These activities are adapted from one suggested by author and life coach Scott Catalanis. This exercise needs to be done with another person. Two variations are offered here, but the possibilities are endless. Play with them in any way that sounds interesting to you.

Variation One: Do this exercise with someone with whom you can find a statement or belief about which you disagree. To get at this, begin by writing a list of ten statements that you either totally agree with or totally disagree with. These should be statements that bring up an emotional response.

Your list might look something like this:
I love to read mysteries. I love the Colbert Report. I hate backpacking. I'll never go snow camping. I love spending long, lazy afternoons at the modern art museum. I can't ever imagine going skydiving. I love flying. *Hamlet* is my favorite play. I think Woody Allen is a brilliant director. I think Hilary Clinton would make a great president. Going to church is for sissies.

Look at both lists, and pick one statement off of either list where you disagree.

With that statement in mind, do these steps one at a time:
Clearly state the point of disagreement:

Person A: *I love spending long, lazy afternoons at the modern art museum.*

Person B: *I hate modern art museums.*

When you connect with another in an authentic, deeply respectful way, you open up to what's at the core of your humanity: your ability to be clear, compassionate, honest, and direct.

As you play with these exercises, keep these thoughts in mind:

You are not your thoughts. You are not your feelings. Thoughts and feelings are vehicles that can be used to connect your experiences with the outer world to your inner realm.

If you want to be understood, you need to communicate your thoughts and feelings clearly.

Everyone you communicate with also wants to be understood.

Being in clear, honest, and open communication with another means that you are not always in agreement with each other.

Accepting that your perspective is only one possible and valid point of view opens the doorway to peace, happiness, fulfillment, joy, and abundance on all levels of your life.

"We get to choose how we're going to live-- what level of energy, what level of vibrancy, what level of excitement."

Brendon Burchard

Next, state how you feel about the belief you just expressed. Think about feelings as single, simple words such as happy, joyful, angry, sad, disappointed, disconnected, frustrated, delighted, or annoyed. Feelings represent our emotional response to either having or not having a universal need met. Our universal needs include respect, trust, connection, and safety, among others.

Person A: *Being at the modern art museum makes me feel inspired and connected. I love how artists express emotions through color, lines, and textures without using images.*

Person B: *Being at a modern art museum makes me feel confused, frustrated, and disconnected because I don't understand what's going on with all those squiggles and blotches of color.*

Acknowledge that you've heard the person by making a simple statement that rephrases what's been said by that person. You are neither agreeing nor disagreeing.

Person A: *I heard you say that the modern art museum is confusing and frustrating to you and that you feel disconnected from the art.*

Person B: *I heard you say you love modern art because this abstract art inspires you and makes you feel connected to artists who express emotions through color, lines, and textures.*

Write your responses to these activities in your journal and share some of your responses with your Voyager Group.

Tell each other about one concrete experience that brought you to your belief. After each person speaks, the listener makes an acknowledgment statement as is done in the example.

End the discussion by thanking each other for expressing their beliefs and feelings about this statement.

Variation Two: Do this with someone you are in a relationship with. Instead of being general about the belief statements, keep them focused on the relationship. If this is a work colleague, the statements should be work related. If this is a personal relationship, the issues should pertain to the relationship.

Go through all the steps above, but ***before*** you end the discussion:

Make a request of each other. This is not an ultimatum or a demand. Ask the other person to do something that would make you feel happier, safer, more respected, better understood, or in some way produce change so that you can feel better or that your life can be easier. For example, you might ask your partner to go to a modern art museum with you.

Respond to the request simply and with a neutral tone. The answers to a request can be numerous: yes, no, maybe, I'll think about it, not likely, I'll have to work on this, etc.

Shake hands or hug each other and express your gratitude for being heard.

Breakthrough/Seven of Worlds
Break through the blockages to success.

Use the Energy of Seven of Worlds to:

Use your talents and resources to set yourself in motion.

Be clear with your vision so you know where you are going.

Work hard with your body fueled by your passions to make your life spectacular.

Dare to succeed!

Caution: Be careful that you don't run over others in your enthusiastic pursuit of your own dreams.

Play with these activities to break through blockages:

✱ **Look for opportunities to interact with people who can help you.** Go to conferences, lectures, classes, meetings. Seek out people you identify with or with whom you want to identify with. Speak up! Be persistent! Tell the people who can help you how they can assist you in achieving a step on your way to your big dream for yourself.

✱ **When an opportunity is offered, go for it!** Follow your interests. See where they lead.

✱ **Put in your hours.** Do the work.

✱ **Revisit your vision statement.** Express this statement so that if your were to run into someone today who could give you an atomic boost on your journey, you could succinctly and clearly say what you wanted.

This is the proverbial "elevator speech." You have one minute, or maybe three, to communicate who you are and what you're doing. If you're writing a book, this would be the pitch you'd make if you had the chance to speak to an agent. If you're looking for a job, this would be the quick summary of what you've done and what position you'd excel at. If you're working on a health issue, this would be the statement that might get you just the help you need to overcome the challenge.

✱ **Listen and appropriately respond when people tell you about who they are and what they want.** Offer help, advice, direction, and names of contacts. Give what you hope to receive.

Two of the biggest blockages to success are the inability to reach out to others and the under utilization of the opportunities around us.

For his book, *The Outliers,* Malcolm Gladwell researched the backgrounds of successful people, and he posits that those who have found themselves in the most rewarding and satisfying positions in their careers are people who have been guided to see and seek opportunity, who have had the inner sense to speak to people who can help them, and who put in the time needed to become experts in their chosen fields (10,000 hours according to his calculations).

Write your "pitch" and practice saying it out loud. Practice at home. Tell the people in your Voyager Group. Make this statement to people you meet throughout the week. Get comfortable with telling people as often as possible who you are, what you want, what you are aspiring to.

Living a spectacular life means that sometimes you make a spectacle of yourself.

Courage/Seven of Wands
Stare down your inner demons.

Use the Energy of Seven of Wands to:

Find the courage you need to bring you to your highest destiny.

Write down your dreams and nightmares to discover your most deeply entrenched demons.

Use art to transform your demons.

Trust that you are protected and that you have everything you need to find your right path, your special destiny.

Caution: Avoiding your fears promotes discouragement. Face them!

Play with these activities to explore how to face your demons:

✱**Take the Buddhist questions as a mantra for yourself whenever you start an internal conversation that isn't productive.** Ask yourself: Is it true? Is it kind? Is it necessary?

✱ **Deal with your inner demons.** Embrace them as part of yourself, and either use them productively or banish them completely.

Facing your demons requires two main steps:

1. Acknowledge the demon exists.
2. Resolve the issue.

Maybe your vision for yourself is to be an artist, but finding time to get to your work or finding the time to explore how to market your paintings proves too challenging for you, so you rarely manage either.

What is the demon here? Is it really lack of time? Or are you telling yourself you're not good enough to be competitive? Most likely, you are being unnecessarily critical. Being your own worst critic is a demon that you can face and a conflict you can resolve.

As your own worst critic, telling yourself you're not capable of producing museum quality work might be true, but the real question is, is it helpful? Does telling yourself that you're not a master painter work in your favor? Of course not!

According to Jose Stevens, author, psychic, psychotherapist, and shamanic healer and guide, the following is a list of irrational fears that keep us from being whole.
We fear that we are
- separate
- unloved
- unlovable
- ignorant
- out of touch with the truth
- without vision

Because of these and other fears, we
- are in pain
- suffer from perceived losses
- create more pain for ourselves
- limit our life experiences
- are unhappy
- are unable to move forward
- feel lost and lonely

From *Transforming Your Dragons*
by Jose Stevens, Ph.D.

✱ Resolve your personal internal conflicts by acknowledging that you may not be an expert, a guru, a renowned artist, yet you are doing your soul work, and that's the way it is.

For example, if you are a visual artist, you could tell yourself that no, you are not a painter at the Georgia O'Keeffe level, but that doesn't matter. You are you with your talents and dreams and only you can produce the work that you envision for yourself.

Being a naysayer to yourself is unproductive, unnecessary, unthoughtful, unkind, and detrimental to your well being. When a thought of condemnation about yourself or one of your creative projects occurs to you, think of someone you love, like your partner or child or best friend, for example, and ask yourself if you would ever say something so destructive and condescending like that to your dear one. Probably not, so don't spew nasties at yourself.

✱ Anytime you hear yourself saying something negative about your capabilities, counter that thought with an opposite and encouraging thought. Tell yourself you are capable of painting. You may have to go slowly, take a class, do more sketching, and play more with color, texture, or perspective. But you can do whatever you need to do to achieve your goal.

✱ Make a list of your demons.

✱ Make a list of how to counter them.

✱ Share both lists with your Voyager Group.

Identify your inner critic, fire the nay-sayer, and continue on!

Satisfy your artistic desires daily. If you're a writer and want to get your work out in the world, keep up a blog and write posts at least five days a week. Announce on social media sites that you've posted to your blog.

No matter what media your artistic endeavors lean toward, invest in this important part of yourself daily. Doing your creative work at the same time everyday is also helpful. Your muse will know when you're ready to be inspired. Your mind, body, heart, and soul will align and be in synch with your artistic expression. Your hour will wind up being especially productive.

Remember the response the musician received when he asked how to get to Carnegie Hall: *"Practice. Practice. Practice."*

Write your responses to these activities in your journal.

Share some of your responses with your Voyager Group.

Chapter Eight
VIII Balance Energies: Align with the Universe

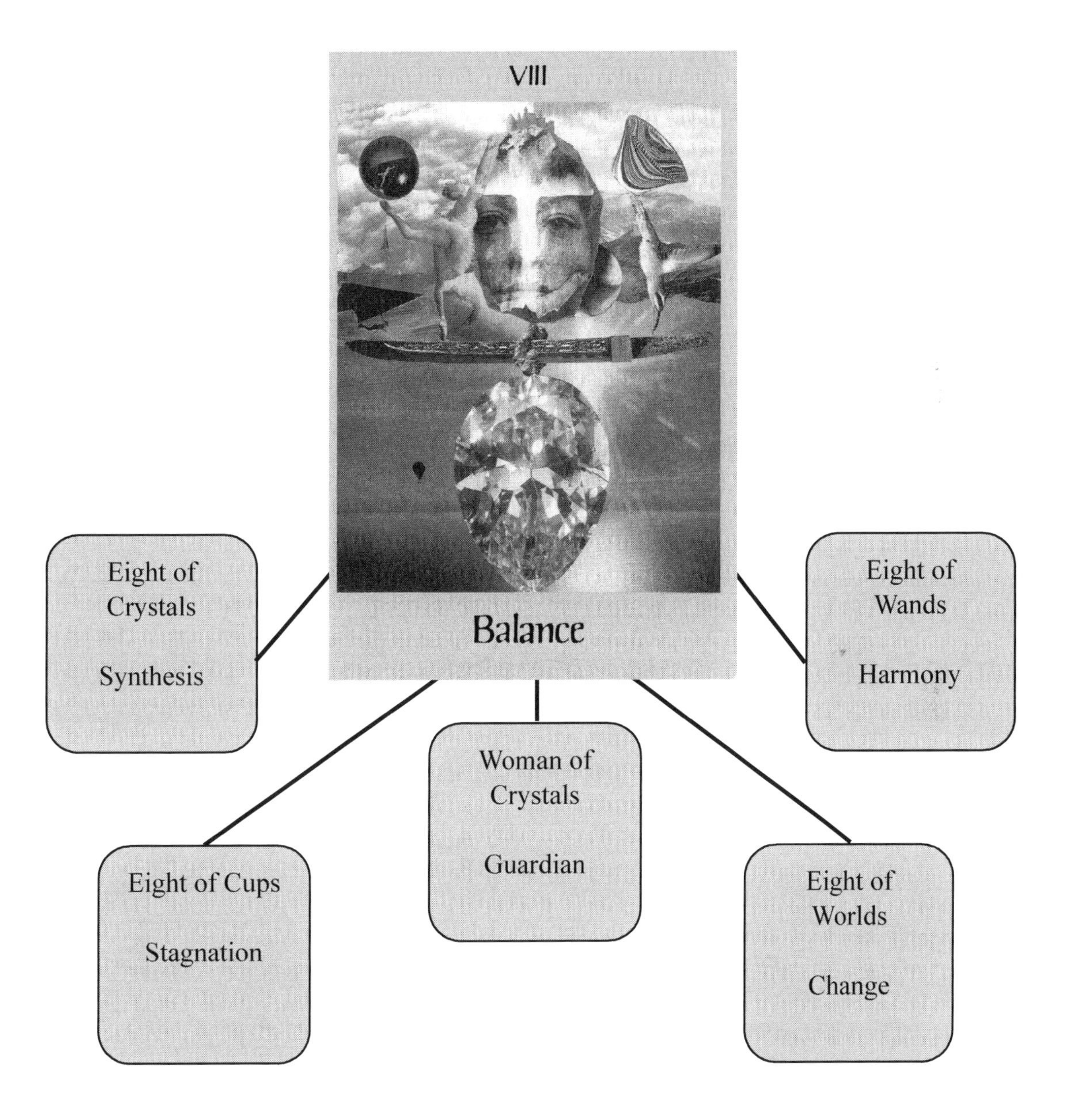

Happiness is not a matter of intensity but of balance, order, rhythm and harmony.
Thomas Merton, 1915-1968
poet, writer, pacifist, Trappist Monk, mystic, and social activist

VIII Balance: Adjust to keep yourself in balance.

Balance is the energy of harmony.

Ballet dancers *en pointe* appear weightless, motionless, but they are anything but still. They have trained their bodies in such a way that movement is subtly occurring from head to toes, especially in the hips and feet.

The glorious sounds from musical instruments occur because of subtle movements from the air or by striking or strumming to cause subtle vibrations.

To be in balance means to be constantly moving, always making subtle adjustments, always checking to see if you're being honest and acting with integrity.

Sometimes you need to make great leaps to achieve your goals.

Sometimes the wisest actions are the more precise movements you make.

Be flexible!

"The good life is the whole life. Structure your life so that your heart, mind, body and spirit are aligned with your life's purpose, work, and relationships."

James Wanless
author, tarot coach, and creator of
The Voyager Tarot Deck

✱ **Everyday, stretch, do yoga, Tai Chi, Chi Gong, martial arts, energy exercises, or dance to slow, rhythmic music.**

✱ **As a meditation, play a slow, constant rhythm on a drum.** If you don't have a drum, you can beat out a rhythm on a desk, a table, or even on your legs. Do this for at least five minutes. Longer if you want.

✱ **Put on some slow music and allow your body to sway and move very, very slowly while listening to the music.** Do this for at least five minutes. Longer if you want.

✱ **Take a slow, meditative walk in nature.** Stop occasionally, close your eyes and listen to the sounds around you.

Comment on your reactions to these activities.

Share with your Voyager Group your responses to either doing or not doing these suggested activities.

Synthesis/Eight of Crystals
Be aware of your balanced mind.

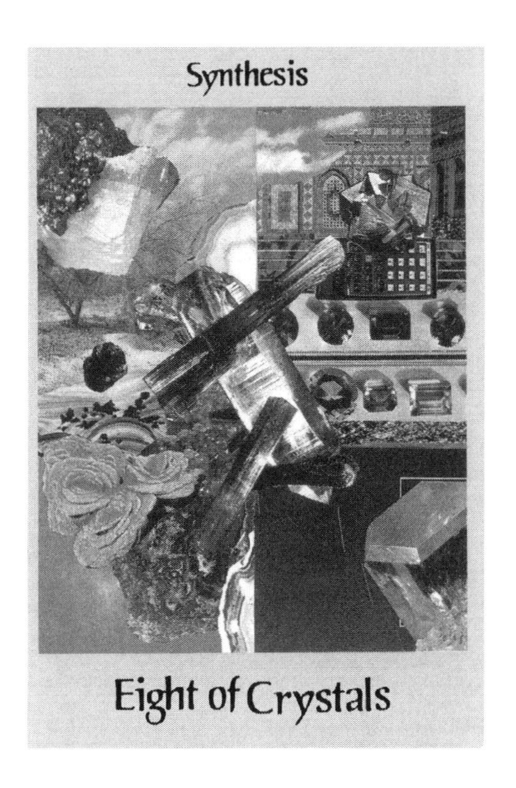

Use the Energy of Eight of Crystals to:

Use both hemispheres equally to make your dreams come true. Combine ideas from the arts and science to come to new conclusions that will help you on your journey.

Be logical and analytical. Be creative and intuitive.

Integrate your logical thinking with your visionary brilliance.

Be a clear thinker who gets new ideas and visions often throughout each day.

Caution: Don't over-identify with either right or left brain thinking.

The right hemisphere of the brain and the left hemisphere have different specialties as well as some shared functioning, which is why developing both sides of the brain is so important.

Right Hemisphere

Specialties:

Copying of designs
Discriminating shapes, such as picking out a camouflaged object
Understanding geometric properties
Reading faces
Comprehending and learning music
Global holistic processing
Understanding metaphoric language
Expressing emotions
Reading emotions

Emotions associated with right hemisphere:

Negative emotions (fearful and mournful feelings)

Neurotransmitters:

Higher levels of norepinephrine

Left Hemisphere

Specialties:

Acquiring and using language skills
Acquiring and using skilled movement
Analytical time sequence processing

Emotions associated with left hemisphere:

Positive emotions

Neurotransmitters:

Higher levels of dopamine

Shared Functions of Right and Left Hemispheres

Feeling sensations on both side of face
Perceiving sound by both ears
Experiencing pain
Experiencing hunger
Being aware of body positioning

✱ **Various exercises are designed to strengthen, and in the cases of brain trauma, to reprogram the nervous system, spinal muscles, and various systems to work optimally together.** The Cross Crawl helps to integrate both hemispheres of the brain, contributing to increased balance, improved coordination, and clear thinking. This easy exercise can be done either standing or seated. Stop at the first sign of fatigue.

March in place by lifting your right arm and left leg as high as possible at the same time.
As you let down your right arm and left leg, raise your left arm and right leg.
Do this very slowly to increase the benefits of control and range of motion.
Ideally, perform between 200 and 500 marches a day—two hundred slow marches or five hundred at a faster clip. Timing yourself might be easier. See how long 200 marches takes and set a timer or use a metronome app to accommodate your pace.

Variations
Touch each hand to the opposite knee cap as you raise your leg.
Move around as you march.
Reach behind your body and touch the opposite foot.
Cross Crawl with your eyes closed.
Use swimming motions with your arms as you march in place.
Cross Crawl on your hands and knees around the floor.

Write your responses to either doing or avoiding this exercise. If you didn't do any of the physical exercises, write down a few thoughts on why you chose not to do them. Share some of your responses with your Voyager Group.

"[Imagination] reveals itself in the balance or reconciliation of opposite or discordant qualities: of sameness, with difference; of the general, with the concrete; the idea, with the image; the individual, with the representative; the sense of novelty and freshness, with old and familiar objects; a more than usual state of emotion, with more than usual order; judgment ever awake and steady self-possession, with enthusiasm and feeling profound and vehement; and while it blends and harmonizes the natural and the artificial, still subordinates art to nature; the manner to the matter; and our admiration of the poet to our sympathy with the poetry."

Samuel Taylor Coleridge, 1732 - 1834
poet, literary critic, philosopher, and co-founder of the Romantic Movement in England

Guardian/Woman of Crystals
Connect with your most authentic, truest, self.

Use the Energy of Woman of Crystals to:

Be at peace with yourself.

Accept with equanimity whatever happens without losing your composure.

Be self-reflective and introspective.

Keep your clarity and focus amidst doubt and distraction.

Be mindful of what you are shown by your inner vision.

Caution: Don't be so self-contained that you zone out and miss your intuitive hits.

Find mental clarity and keep your deep inner knowing sharp through lack of clutter, noise, and distraction. Staying stuck in old problems will distract you from being present.

Play with these activities to help you gain clarity through introspection:

✱ **Name your core issues.** Even if you think you've gotten over something, acknowledge what once controlled you. Food? Alcohol? Drugs? Shopping? Abandonment issues? Perfectionism? Self-righteousness? Paranoia? Security issues? Sex? Feelings of being unworthy or not good enough? Feelings of superiority? Make a list of your core issues.

✱**Over the next month, take some time everyday to write a memoir focused around your core issues.** State the issue and then give specific examples of when you experienced your trauma and how you acted out this addiction throughout your life. Write with vivid details. Use all five senses to capture the scenes you write about so that they come alive on the paper. As you write, be compassionate with yourself and treat yourself as if you were writing about someone you really care about—which I hope is true! Hold yourself and your stories gently and don't judge yourself or the people who created the trauma in your life.

✱**When you feel ready, tell or read your story to others.** Share your story in a safe place with people who have learned to trust each other.

Psychic, author, and radio host, Dougall Fraser, writes about how core issues remain with us throughout our lives. Some psychologists believe that traumas experienced early in life are never far from the surface when we make decisions as adults.

Fraser gives the example of how twenty-year clean addicts still identify as addicts. For a recovering addict, everyday is a day of making the same decision made daily for the past twenty years: today I will not drink/smoke/take pills/shoot up/do drugs/overeat.

If the addict pretended the addiction was now "fixed" or "gotten over," the likelihood of falling back into the abyss of an alcohol or drug shrouded life would be great. Addicts are also encouraged to belong to support groups where they can feel safe to tell their stories, to claim their challenges, and to proclaim their strengths.

People who maintain this lifestyle of claiming their core issue and sharing their weaknesses as well as their strengths in a safe, supportive environment, are the ones who most successfully experience life in loving, productive, creative, caring, and playful ways.

The goal is to accept your core issues so that you can be at peace with yourself, and so that when these issues arise in the future, and they likely will, you can see them clearly for what they are and let them settle back down without the need to act out or berate yourself for being drawn to your old issue.

Being heard, being acknowledged, and being noticed are important steps in the process of gaining clarity and finding inner peace.

Many studies have shown that writing a personal narrative filled with feelings, personal insights, and perceptions can create long-term health benefits.

"Take control of your life by taking control of your attitudes. Pain and disappointment are inevitable, but suffering is optional and tough times are always temporary.

"Live within your means, and when you mess up, fess up. When you're in a hole, stop digging.

"Listen to both your heart and your head. Pursue your passions, but don't confuse feelings with facts, fun with happiness or pleasure with fulfillment.

"Don't sacrifice a thousand tomorrows for a few todays, and don't settle for a little life. Live with purpose and for significance. Respect yourself and others, avoid self-righteousness and be kind rather than right."

Michael Josephson's "One Minute Graduation Speech" from whatwillmatter.com

Mental clarity and deep inner knowing is easiest found in an uncluttered environment. By clearing away items that represent the past and that no longer support you, you can release yourself from these anchors and move into your new life.

✱ Clear your clutter.

Where to begin? Start with your desk or with one room in your house. Look at each object in the room, big and small, and ask yourself these three questions:

- Do I pause and enjoy this item?
- Does this item support who I am now or who I want to become?
- Does this item represent a tie to a past I no longer relate to?

Ask these questions for everything: clocks, books, chairs, lamps, baskets, paintings, salt and pepper shakers, pictures, couches, desks, dressers, tables, clothes, shoes, coats, and on and on.

Remove every item that you don't take time to pause and enjoy, that doesn't support who you are now or who you want to become or that ties you to that past. Sell them, give them to family or friends who say they want them, donate them to charity, recycle them, Freecycle them, throw them out.

Learn to be selective about what comes into your space.

Keep your space as open and as free flowing as possible.

When you clear your clutter, you are taking care of yourself energetically in the same way you would be caring for yourself physically if, for example, you learned you were gluten intolerant, and you cleared out your kitchen of wheat and other grain-based products.

Create an environment that promotes peace and serenity by constantly monitoring the things you bring into your life.

Remember, everything that comes into your life has to be disposed of in some way at some time.

Notice the positive changes that occur as a result of clearing your clutter.

Enjoy having the space you need to create the life you desire.

Stagnation/Eight of Cups
Be still and stop fighting with yourself.

Use the Energy of Eight of Cups to:

Bring new life out of your emotional swamp.

Regenerate, but only after you have allowed yourself to stop the emotional push-pull that indecision inflicts.

Know that new seeds of awareness are preparing to sprout.

Restore your energy in places where you can be still and quiet.

Caution: Don't give in to self-destructiveness or hopelessness no matter how overwhelmed you feel. Just stop and allow the seeds of hope to show themselves.

Play with these activities to explore your emotional state of stagnation:

Everyone gets stuck from time to time. Allow for this down time, but don't wallow in hopelessness.

✱ Rediscover the meaning in your life and your project. Do this by proposing an intention for yourself that has something big as a goal. Check your vision statement now and see if you have challenged yourself enough. Rewrite if necessary. Then, set this aside, and play with something that has nothing obvious to do with your main project.

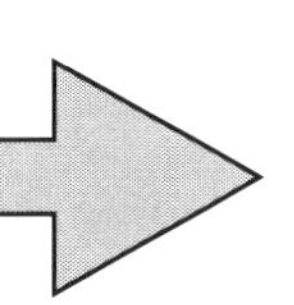

By immersing yourself in something fun and creative, you'll be pulled through the slough of stagnation and be ready to rededicate yourself to your vision statement.

Possibilities of fun projects (a very short list):

✱ Offer something that you make, write, or do to a charity. Sock monkeys for ailing children work just fine as do baked goods for shelters. But spending time thinking about what you could do that's different and more "you" might be even more stimulating. I recently read about a woman who wrote short little inspirational stories, poems, and thoughts for people who are facing cancer and for the people in their lives—their caregivers, children, friends, and family. She printed them up and sent them to as many cancer support centers as she could find, offering her written work as a gift. Soon, she was asked for more, and ultimately, her gifts were gratefully received by people affected by cancer in all fifty states.

✱ Find someone who is going through a difficult time, possibly because of illness or financial or emotional challenges, and learn about a dream they have. Put together an album or computer slide show you can send them of what their dream might look like. Maybe someone always wanted to go on safari. Put together an album or make a CD. Add stories, music, facts that would be interesting.

✱ Create an artistic piece or do an activity to honor someone's memory. Give this memorial to someone who would appreciate your thoughtfulness.

✱ Organize or participate in a collaborative artistic adventure.

Another way to think of that in between time: Actors will show the power of an emotion through "the pause," the silence between the words, phrases, and sentences. The power of a musical composition is in the spaces between the notes. What is unsaid can, in the right situations, be more potent than what is said.

Write about and share some of your responses with your Voyager Group.

Change/Eight of Worlds
Be flexible, adaptable, and versatile.

Use the Energy of Eight of Worlds to:

Stay healthy and whole by adapting to change.

Keep from fighting the constancy of change.

Live a vital and satisfying life by accepting change as part of a loving environment where you can focus on process, having fun, and experiencing joy rather than holding to an illusory goal that may not even be there when you "get everything together."

Embrace uncertainty.

Caution: Don't allow yourself to become irresponsible, unaccountable, or unreliable.

Gregory Berns, MD, associate professor of psychiatry and behavioral sciences at Emory University in Atlanta and author of the book *Satisfaction*, has been studying the pleasure centers of the brain and has concluded that novelty is an important component to happiness and life satisfaction. He asserts that the need to plunge into unknown territory is vital to experiencing happiness. Without the anxiety produced when facing an abyss, whether or not the endeavor is a success, feelings of mediocrity and unhappiness will settle in, and overall levels of satisfaction will plummet.

Embracing uncertainty, he points out, also builds emotional resilience by readying us for the unexpected challenges and hardships we're all bound to face.

Making someone else's life better, creating with a larger goal in mind, getting out of your own limited and limiting space, and working with others are excellent ways to make positive changes in your own and other's lives.

Creativity stimulates creativity! As a result, when you get inspired to help someone else, your own projects and your own life will also be revitalized.

Play with these activities to guide you to be adaptable:

✱ **Seek out new challenges for yourself physically, emotionally, mentally, and spiritually.** Set a time, say about a month, to accomplish something from each category.

Physically challenge yourself by doing something you've always wanted to do, are afraid to do, or wonder if you could do. The activity should produce some amount of anxiety for you. For example, to physically challenge myself, I went to an indoor flying venue where I could have the experience of jumping out of a plane without actually throwing my body into the void. Skydivers frequent this indoor chamber to practice techniques and perfect choreographed routines, so I trust the experience is very similar to the feeling had from dropping to the earth in forty-five seconds. I did this twice and each time, I wondered how long a minute, the time allotted for the experience, could feel. And would I really survive? These thoughts came even as I was in no danger of losing my life. Or so I had been reassured. My body didn't believe danger didn't exist!

Mentally challenge yourself to tackle something daunting by reading, attending a lecture, or having a discussion with someone notable in a field you know little about.

For the mental stretch, I am reading a book on economics, the course I saw as the curse of the devil when I took Econ 1A in college. The title of the book is *Why Success Always Starts with Failure: Adapt* by Tim Harford. His premise is that without experiencing failure and understanding why the failure occurred, systems, governments, structures, and people won't flourish. I'd tell you more, but I have to confess, I'm struggling to finish what feels like an economic textbook. But you have my promise that I will get to the end.

Emotionally challenge yourself by making a connection with someone in a deeply personal way. This could include being open with someone you're close to or by including someone in your life in some new way. I have a friend who often takes a few minutes to speak to homeless people when he comes across them, asking about their day, their concerns, their hopes and dreams.

To emotionally challenge myself, I did a sharing exercise with my daughter. We each told each other a short synopsis of three different stories that changed our lives and that made us see life in a very different way. We simply listened to each other and then wrote a positive statement about what we heard. In other words, I wrote a statement about my daughter based on what she shared, and she did the same for me. This is a very emotionally satisfying exercise and highly recommended.

Spiritually challenge yourself by engaging with something that transcends your normal everyday life and connects you with the greater consciousness of the world. Art, music, and spiritual practices such as yoga and meditation tap into this feeling of connectedness.

To spiritually challenge myself, I've committed to finishing this book that you are reading now and teaching the material both in person and online.

(This activity has been adapted from an article written by Jancee Dunn)

"The greatest danger for most of us is not that our aim is too high and we miss it but that it is too low and we reach it."

Michelangelo, 1475-1564
sculptor, painter, writer, and architect

Write your responses to these activities in your journal.

Share some of your responses with your Voyager Group.

Harmony/Eight of Wands: Unify the mind, body, emotions, and spirit.

Use the Energy of Eight of Wands to:

Allow balance to happen. Listen to what your inner voice tells you and act on these whisperings to align yourself internally and within your world.

Be in harmony with the world by recognizing that you fit in perfectly no matter where you are. Focus on your breath.

Be like the conductor of an orchestra and use your skills to guide and influence your moods and spirit as well as the moods and spirits of others.

Caution: Clean up your messes so that you don't sink into dissonance of spirit.

Play with these activities to feel in harmony with yourself, your family, your friends, your community, and your world:

✱ Act on something that is meaningful to you but that you may not have allowed to come forward yet.

To get at this activity, use this three-step process:
- Ground yourself.
- Tap into your unconscious through guided meditation.
- Step into the activity.

Ground yourself by setting aside twenty minutes just for yourself. This may be inside or outside. Turn off phones, computers, and any electronic stimuli. Wrap yourself in a shawl or blanket that covers your head and leaves only your face exposed. Make yourself comfortable. Sitting on a straight-backed chair is usually best, but you may choose to sit on the floor or on a softer surface.

Take five connected breaths. With each breath, breath in deeply through the nose, exhale completely through the mouth, and feel your belly move with each breath.

Either record the following meditation and play it back or have someone read the meditation to you. Or, make up your own meditation, record it and play it to yourself. Or, simply think through your own meditation.

Be in harmony with your year. Plan things you can do throughout the year to achieve your goal. If you dream of writing a book, for example, and you anticipate the book will be around 90,000 words (which is a good length for a novel), divide that number by the number of weeks you will devote to this writing project. Maybe you want to take a two-week vacation. Christmas may be hectic for you, so plan to take off that week. If you know other things will eat up your time, subtract those weeks, too.

Maybe you're seeing the possibility of working 45 weeks on writing your book to get the first draft down. If you write 400 words a day, five days a week for 45 weeks, you'll have 90,000 words written by the end of the year.

Do this scheduling for whatever you want to accomplish: a product for your business, an art exhibit of your work, a new business plan, or a new job. Decide how much time you will put into accomplishing your goal over the next year or whatever period you choose, and commit that time and your energy to your dream.

You can start your year at any time, even today. One year from now, you can possibly produce something that's important to you—if you get yourself in tune with the rhythm of your year and the rhythm of your dreams.

Meditation: *I offer my gratitude for this opportunity to be in my body in this exact time and place. I thank the universe, and the divine that is me and is all around me and that reaches to all parts of the universe. I thank the angels who guide me always and those who come to my assistance whenever I seek their guidance and advice. I thank the ascended masters, my ancestors, and the energies of father, mother, animals, plants, and gemstones for the guidance they have offered and continue to offer me. I open myself to continued blessings for our earth, my family, my friends, my community, and myself.*

I sit here in the presence of these blessings and feel myself being wrapped in the white light of loving kindness. I sit in this sacred space and allow the golden light of divine love to move into my crown chakra, to fill me with divine love.

I allow the golden light of divine love to move into my throat so I can always speak with words inspired by love and gratitude. I allow the golden light of divine love to move into my shoulders and down my arms into my hands and to the tips of my fingers. I allow the golden light of divine love to move back up my arms and to circle my heart with the warmth of compassion for myself and for all my loved ones, for all who come into my life, for all who have come into my life, for all beings. I allow the golden light of divine love to move into and through my torso, moving down my legs and into my feet to my toes. I allow the golden light of divine love to move through me and into the earth, grounding me in time, place, and the energetic awareness of now.

As I sit here wrapped in the light of loving kindness, I ask to be made aware of the gifts I now possess that are ready to be used and that are ready to be taken into the world now. Please be clear about what these gifts are and how I can best use them now. I thank you. I love you. I am blessed.

Sit quietly for however long you feel moved to be in the quiet, divine space you have just created for yourself. When you are ready, wiggle your fingers and toes, take a deep breath and open your eyes.

Jot down or take careful notes about what came to you during the meditation. Or just write and see what comes forward. Don't judge or censor. Let the words flow.

Assess and act on what comes to you. Follow your instincts, your intuition. If a song comes into your head, play with the ideas in the song or with the connections the song has for you. If the image or the name of a person appears in your mind, you might consider calling or emailing that person just to say hi or even to explain what prompted the call.

Follow through on inspirations.

Share your thoughts with your Voyager Group.

Chapter Nine
IX Hermit Energies: Tap into your Inner Wisdom

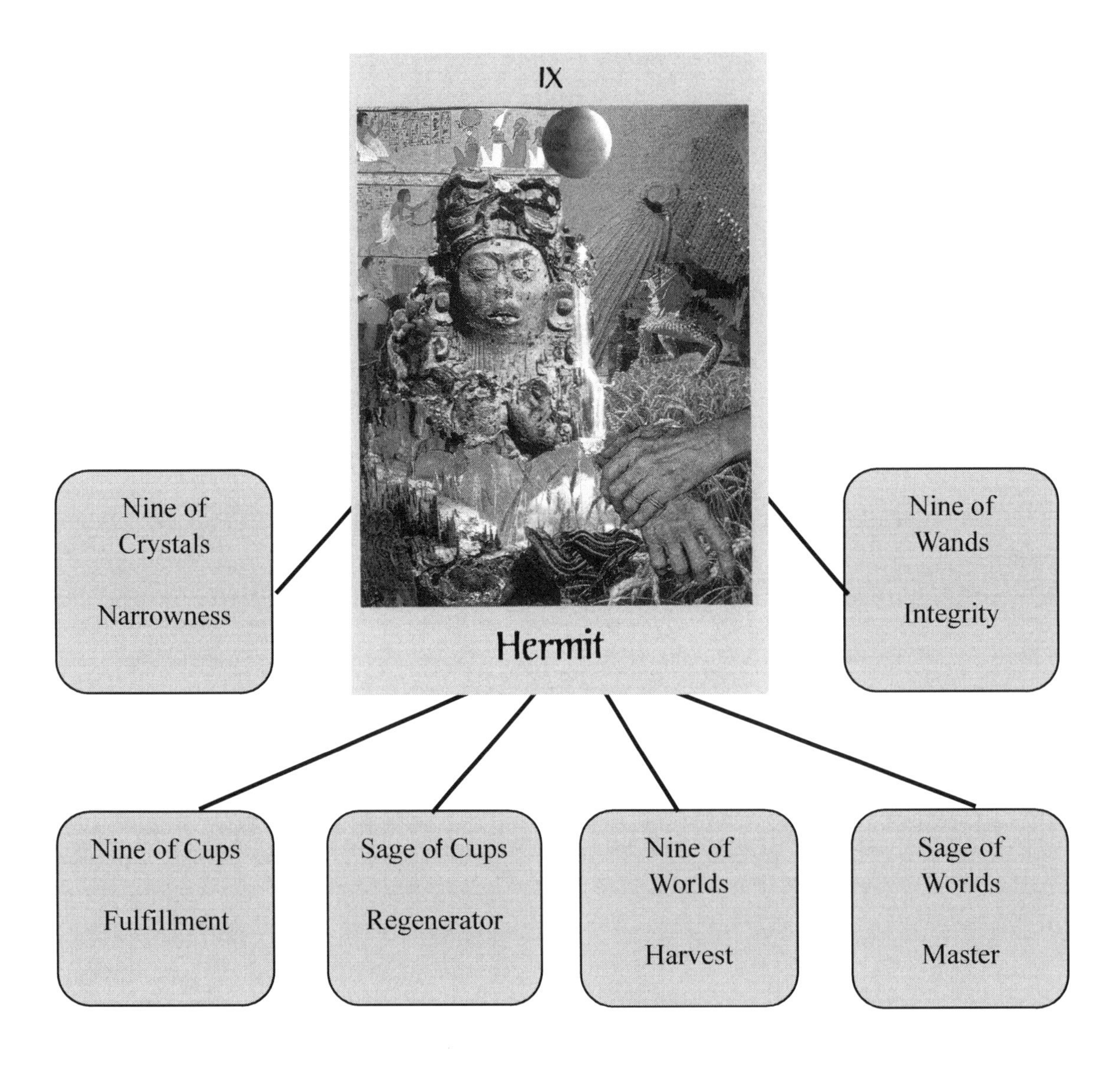

"Everyone has his own specific vocation or mission in life... Therein he cannot be replaced, nor can his life be repeated. Thus, everyone's task is as unique as is his specific opportunity to implement it."

Viktor Frankl 1905-1997
neurologist, psychiatrist, writer, and Holocaust survivor

IX Hermit: Connect your soul with your roles in the world.

Keep your focus, concentrate on learning, and enjoy solitude where answers await you.

Celebrate the harvest of work accomplished.

Seek knowledge through study and meditation.

Inspire and motivate others.

Follow the paths most meaningful to you.

Know that you create your own meaning.

Complete projects or declare them finished just as they are now.

Contemplate new ways to create meaning in your life.

Take time to be introspective.

Initiate new projects that bring meaning into your life.

Be cautious, discerning, and prudent.

Yoda said it all: "Use the force." And as Luke learned, anything is possible when you shut out distractions, when you study in depth something you want to learn, and when you open yourself to knowledge that comes to you in any, in many, forms. Expressing gratitude for all that you have is also key.

✱ **Do something fun, relaxing, and playful!** I'm sure you can think of all kinds of things to do! Do them!

✱ **Host a special awards night.** Invite friends and family to your home. Honor everyone who attends in some way. Be creative in how you shower each person with something that acknowledges how special he or she is. You could have "Eggies Awards." Inside those little plastic eggs that are meant to be filled with candy, enclose a statement that reflects an accomplishment, an attribute, or a talent you admire. Make the presentations a big deal. Have fun!

Share your response with your Voyager Group.

Write in your journal what you did to relax and how it felt to consciously take the time to enjoy some time for yourself.

Cheers!

Narrowness/Nine of Crystals
Focus on what's meaningful to you now.

Use the Energy of Nine of Crystals to:

Focus on your priorities and let distractions slip away.

Be still so you can hear your inner voice guide you to know how to fulfill your dreams.

Concentrate. Be disciplined. Keep your resolve to follow your dreams.

Give yourself a timeline for completion and help you push through until you are successful. Stay true to your dreams.

Caution: Don't be overly critical or judgmental of yourself or others. Don't let fear make you narrow-minded.

✱ Play with this activity to help you focus on something important. These steps will guide you as you productively obsess on your dream.

In his book *Brainstorm,* Eric Maisel writes about the power of the productive obsession, a psychological state which provides opportunity for focus, discipline, resolve, high energy, and constant renewed dedication to our projects.

- Work with a partner for this activity.
- For four weeks, focus on your vision statement. If you haven't yet begun a project, think about what you want to create for yourself. Make this something big, something you really care about, something you feel passionate about accomplishing, and something that matters to you and that will in some way make others' lives better.
- At the end of each week, write to your partner and report on the progress or on the challenges and obstacles you faced.
- Your partner then writes back with a statement of acknowledgement. This is not an evaluation, a judgement, or a critique. The statement acknowledges that the person has been heard by restating, in his or her own words, what was shared.
- If the partner has some resource or contacts to offer, those should be included.
- For the last progress report, write your partner an evaluation of what being focused has meant to you. Again, the response is an evaluation only of what you did as you obsessed on your project. Don't include the correspondence with your partner as part of this evaluation. Do include anything offered by your partner that you followed up on, however.

Remember: this is written correspondence. The partner of the one obsessing on her project only acknowledges or offers resources, but does not include feedback and does not critique the other's progress.

A weekly exchange might look something like this:
Person A: *I am attempting to put a website together. I spoke with a guy who told me I needed to be clear about what I want my website to say. He gave me a list of things to do. I got frustrated and put the list in my drawer. I don't know what I want!*

Person B: *You contacted someone to help you. You felt overwhelmed and confused and are waiting before you move on. My friend Joel just built a website. Here's his phone number and his website. He might be able to help.*

"It's not what you do once in a while; it's what you do day in and day out that makes the difference."

Jenny Craig
co-founder of Jenny Craig Weight Loss

Fulfillment/Nine of Cups
Be aware of what you have accomplished.

Use the Energy of Nine of Cups to:

Feel content with where you are now.

Acknowledge the joy you feel because of the wisdom you've acquired through your hard work.

Remind yourself you are on a journey of consciousness that continues ever onward.

Celebrate all that you've already accomplished as you strive to reach your goal!

Caution: Don't overindulge when you feel good. Toast to good health, but don't drain the bottle!

Play with this activity to relax into the contentment of where you are on your journey now:

✱ **Stopping to allow yourself the joy of being in the present brings deep contentment and relaxation.** A simple, yet powerful relaxation technique is diaphragmatic or abdominal breathing.

- Set a timer for five or more minutes, whatever works for your schedule.
- Sit in a chair or lie comfortably on the floor or on a bed.
- Place one hand on your chest and the other on your abdomen above your belly button.
- Take a deep breath in through your nose. Your lower hand should move more than the hand on your chest.
- Exhale through your mouth in such a way that you hear your breath as it leaves your body.

Practicing abdominal breathing for just five to ten minutes will result in deep relaxation.

✱ **Soak in a warm bath, stretch out on a bed or comfortable mat, or recline on a lounge chair.** Fill the room with scented candles and turn the lights off or down low to give you the feeling of cocooning. Give your body permission to relax. Allow each muscle to soften and your mind to experience only thoughts of joy and peace. If other thoughts present themselves, dismiss them promptly, and return to a thought that makes you happy. Reminding yourself of what you're grateful for can quickly bring you a sense of peace.

✱ **Take a moon shower.** Go naked under the moonlight and notice how your skin feels wrapped in the night air under the gentle touch of the moon's radiance. Offer up words of gratitude for the body you have, just as it is now.

✱ **Have or give yourself a Reiki session.** Let yourself feel the energy flow through your body.

✱ **Get a full body massage.** Besides feeling good, massages help stimulate the lymphatic system, which is responsible for releasing toxins from the body.

Fulfillment is not something to seek or expect because w'eve worked hard. Fulfillment is a state of grace we experience when we're touched by the rightness of the present moment.

Everyday, write a statement in your journal that simply says that you either did or did not do the abdominal breathing exercise.

Regenerator/Sage of Cups
Generate new life vitality through joyfulness.

Use the Energy of Sage of Cups to:

Smile and bring a smile to the faces of others.

Grow through happiness.

Find joy, pleasure, fulfillment, and happiness in being alive.

Create love, joy, and beauty through emotional vitality and happiness.

Be emotionally aligned and congruently expressive of your most authentic self.

Caution: Don't wait around for happiness to come to you. Create happiness for yourself.

Play with these activities to rest, heal, reflect, and renew your spirit of joy:

✱ **Take a walk in solitude and pay attention to the sounds of the leaves rustling, the birds chirping, or water swishing through a creek.** Your heightened awareness of the sounds you hear will help you restore your connection to the world and yourself. Breath in the loamy scents of rich forest soil, the aroma of a flower garden in full bloom or the pungent smells from ripening fruit on trees and allow yourself to be transported to a place of comfort. Feel the wind sweep across your cheek, the sun warm your skin, or the weight of your body as you move along a packed earth path and delight in what the world offers you today and everyday.

Take time out to renew your connection with your deepest, truest, most compassionate self. The best way to do this is to remove yourself from your normal activities and allow yourself time for a retreat.

A retreat away from home, whether for a few hours or a few days, offers the opportunity to be still and to be aware of the world in a more simple yet more profound way.

You can also take a short retreat in your own home.

✱ **With a partner, take turns giving each other neck and shoulder massages, hand massages, foot massages, or head massages.** For hand and foot massages, use a lotion or massage oil, scented or not, and bring a towel to wipe the feet so you don't slip and slide after the lotion has been applied.

✱ **If you're with a group, take turns offering your healing touch to one another.** Have one person lie on the floor or a massage table or sit in a chair and close his or her eyes. The others in the group gently lay their hands on the person's body: on the person's head, shoulders, hands, abdomen, knees, feet, depending on how many people are there. Be instinctive with where you place your hands. Hold these positions for two to five minutes in silence. Let each person have the opportunity to receive as well as give.

The more you sink into the pleasures of your body and enjoy the beauty of the world, the more deeply and joyfully you will come to know yourself. The more joy you present to the world, the higher the vibration of the planet for all.

"Don't ask yourself what the world needs. . . .ask yourself what makes you alive because what the world needs are people who have come alive."
Rainier Maria Rilke, 1875-1926 poet

Harvest/Nine of Worlds: Materialize, manifest, and realize your dreams.

Use the Energy of Nine of Worlds to:

Harvest the fruits of your labors.

Complete all projects that are ready to be finished.

Plant new seeds, and start work on new ideas, now.

Follow your heart to create abundance in all areas of your life.

Be organized, orderly, and systematic about getting things completed.

Caution: Don't work beyond what's needed to be done. Be a realist, not a perfectionist.

Play with these activities to get you to the harvest where your dreams come true:

✱ **Take inventory of your stashed away projects.** Toss out or pass along to someone else anything that no longer holds your interest, that you feel guilty about because the baby you were knitting the booties for is now grown and in college, that reminds you of a time in your life when you were unhappy, or that carries a "should do" rather than a feeling of joy or satisfaction from doing.

✱ **Finish or get someone to complete necessary projects.** Have the ladder, brushes, sealed paint cans, and drop cloths been decorating your living room for months now because you ran out of time or energy to paint the walls? Get help by hiring someone or asking friends to lend a hand.

✱ **Do you have an idea for a new project?** Get a commitment schedule on your calendar so that you have time to devote to your project everyday for the whole month ahead. Then, repeat your commitment when the month ends and a new month begins.

✱ **Within your Voyager Group, discuss how you can help each other.** Offer your time and your expertise to each other. Consider, as a group, dedicating an hour or more at each other's house or office to help get something finished or started. This would be like an old fashioned barn raising meeting.

"It's not that I'm so smart. It's just that I stay with problems longer." Albert Einstein, 1879 - 1955 theoretical physicist

✱ **Within your Voyager Group, your family, or with friends, set aside a time to celebrate what each person has accomplished in a month's or a week's time.** This can be getting together for a cup of tea or coffee or for a glass of wine or just for a sit in the park on a sunny day.

Or you might set aside some time at dinner or at your regular Voyager Group meetings to acknowledge each person's weekly or monthly accomplishments. Be sure to offer up a cheer for each person, no matter how big or how small the harvest is.

Do you have unfinished projects languishing in a drawer, on a shelf, in a closet, or hidden away either out of sight or in plain sight? Take stock of what's waiting for your attention. Anything you've begun and set aside holds energy for you either as a stimulus to express yourself or as an anchor to hold you back from the things that you're now ready to do.

Write your responses to these activities in your journal.

Share some of your responses with your Voyager Group.

Master/Sage of Worlds
Be powerfully productive.

Use the Energy of Sage of Worlds to:

Know that your achievements and productivity are direct reflections of your character.

Acknowledge your power and status.

Share your knowledge, skills, and talents with others.

Guide others to new levels of consciousness and creativity.

Give back to the world in acknowledgement of what has been given to you.

Caution: Avoid being set in your ways and becoming inflexible, fearful, and narrow-minded.

Play with these activities to share your gifts, talents, and power with others:

✱ **Be a mentor to someone.** Who can you guide? If someone comes to mind when you ask yourself this question, think about what you might be able to offer that would be helpful. Contact that person and engage in a general conversation about how he's doing and be alert for ways you can assist him that he might be open to. Offer your guidance or assistance if he appears willing to engage with you as part of his support team.

If no one comes to mind, set the intention that you are open to guide someone and see what happens over the next two weeks.

✱ **Write a story about when you showed the energy of Sage/Master in the world.** Think of a way to focus your story on one incident.

✱ **Start a meditation group where people come together for a regular but short time.** Somewhere around thirty to forty-five minutes works well for this kind of group.

Giving to others is a huge step to being fully conscious and joyful. However, you can also help people simply by living your life with integrity and presenting yourself as someone to model.

The goal of living a conscious life is to learn who you are and to then share your wisdom with others. Now is the time to give back all that you've learned so far. No matter your current age, you carry great wisdom. Acknowledge your gifts, talents, insights, and resources.

A meditation group might use their time by beginning with a poem or a short inspirational essay and either quietly sitting in mediation together or writing for a half hour. The writing is put away and not commented on, but people may want to speak about how they were inspired by either the poem or essay or by the process of writing.

Keep the response time short. Two to three minutes per person would be a good rule of thumb.

Don't go over the allotted time for the meeting. By staying true to the time commitment, you maintain the integrity and peacefulness of the meditation space.

Share your life experiences with others in appropriate settings. Let people hear your story of struggle, defeat, and eventual triumph. The following story was told to me by a woman who carried Master energy with dignity, wisdom, and grace.

Not long ago, I was waiting for the results of a mammogram in a small waiting area at Stanford University Hospital, feeling anxious because I'd been called back for additional screening and because I'd already had breast cancer. Another woman was seated nearby, and I struck up a conversation with her which quickly led to her sharing pieces of her life.

This woman, a Vietnamese immigrant, was probably in her early seventies. In 1975, she and her three young sons, all under the age of nine, were on one of the last evacuation planes out of Saigon as the North Vietnamese stormed the city. She had worked for the US army. Her husband had been a high ranking soldier in the South Vietnamese army, but he had been declared missing in action several months before. As the city fell, she had to leave her country, her family, her home, her connection with her husband, and most of her worldly goods (she could only take 12 pounds of baggage with her for all four of them), and flee for her life and to save the lives of her boys.

Eventually, she ended up in Monterey, California with no job and a stipend of less than $100 a month. Determined to make a life for her sons, she took English classes and became a translator for a social services agency. When her oldest son was ready for college, she moved her family to San Jose so that he, and his brothers when they were ready, could attend San Jose State University and live at home, making it affordable. She was able to find another agency and continue working as a translator.

Several years ago, she had breast cancer treated by surgery, chemo, and radiation therapy. Her annual checkups produce great anxiety for her, yet she smiled to say that her oldest son, now an engineer, always takes the day off from work to drive her, wait for her, and spend the rest of the day with her. He was in the outer waiting room as we spoke.

This woman was someone who appeared content, happy, well cared for, and part of a loving family circle. Yet her life could have given her another outlook. She could have chosen to tell a story of bitterness, resentment, or anger. Instead, she spoke of triumph.

She told me her husband's body has never been found and that she still loves him and has thought about him every day of her life. She spoke with gentleness as she spoke of her struggles and how she managed to survive. She proudly proclaimed her sons are now thriving. All three have graduated from college and work in Silicon Valley in the tech industry. She smiled often. She presented me with a gift of hope and joy that day by sharing this story about her life. This is the energy of Master/Sage.

Another way to share your stories and ideas and to hear the stories others have to tell is to start a discussion group either in person or online. You could continue with this Voyager Group, or you might want to connect with people with other interests.

- Decide on the vision you have for the group. This could be mothers of young children, parents of teenagers, parents of children writing college applications, cancer patients, cancer survivors, people looking for a way to give back to the world, artists or other creatives, political activists, people who want to take time to meditate, or any other type of group that interests you.

- Decide on the number of people you'd like to have in your group. Small makes everyone feel more important and more likely to participate. Six to twelve might be a good number to start with for an in person group. An online group could be larger.

- Choose a time period for the meetings. Four meetings or six meetings might be a good start. If, at the end, people want to continue, start another series of discussions for another specified time period.

- Invite people to join you and give them the details of time and place, as well as the inspiration and expectations for the discussion group. You can, of course, also do this online.

- Begin with introductions. Have everyone introduce themselves by stating their names, of course, and then by saying why they are interested in this particular group.

- Plan each session with a carefully thought out series of topics that you offer for group consideration one week at a time. Begin each discussion group by stating the topic and by responding to the topic with your thoughts on the subject.

- Set up guidelines for your discussion group: no swearing, no name calling, no made up "facts," no sulking or shouting. The idea is to share your thoughts with each other and to respectfully listen to or read what others have to say about an agreed upon topic.

For a writing group, you don't have to focus on bringing writing to the group for feedback and analysis, although this is a valid and worthwhile form. Another focus that is inspirational might include a short discussion of what is important for your writing to proceed and to then spend anywhere from a half hour to an hour to write. When the time is up, the writing is put away. People may then speak about the process of writing or about what writing plans they have between then and the next meeting. The statements should be simple and short.

Integrity/Nine of Wands
Be true to yourself.

Use the Energy of Nine of Wands to:

Have the vision, aspiration, and moral fortitude to take the route of highest integrity as you move toward your dreams.

Remember that you possess everything you need within yourself to fulfill your highest destiny, to reach your loftiest goals.

Have the backbone to walk your own path toward your own dreams.

Act on your own inspirations. Trust your intuition.

Caution: Don't rely on outdated beliefs that keep you so rigid you can't find your way.

Play with these activities to grow through integrity:

✱ **To get at the core of what button is being pushed, try the Big Buddha Question technique of persistently asking "why."** This is best done with another person who is NOT the person who upset you. If you don't have someone to do this with, you can write out the questions and responses.

To do this with another person, sit facing each other. You make a statement about what hurt you. The person sitting in the Buddha seat replies in as neutral a tone as possible: Why does this upset you?

This exercise might look something like this:
You: Jenny said I was selfish.
Buddha Sit In (BSI): Why does this upset you?
You: I left a few things in the sink because I was in a hurry. I was going to clean up later.
BSI: Why does this upset you?
You: She thinks I'm a pig.
BSI: Why does this upset you?
You: I'm not a pig. She doesn't understand how hard I try to keep things clean.
BSI: Why does this upset you?
You: Mother never understood how hard I tried to keep things neat and tidy.
BSI: Why does this upset you?
And so on. . .

Continue with this form of questioning long after the answer seems to have been reached.

In the Zen tradition, this form of questioning often goes on for days or even weeks between teacher and student, but you don't have to let it go on that long to get at the core of the issue. Just try not to stop too soon. You might set a timer for fifteen minutes (or even longer) to give yourself time to get fully immersed in probing through the use of this simple question.

If you choose to do this alone, get out several sheets of paper and do the question and responses yourself, taking on both roles, your own and that of the BSI. Remember, BSI only asks: Why does this upset you? Physically writing allows the body to engage more fully than typing does, and clarity only comes when the resolution is embodied.

If you're doing this alone, say the statements and questions out loud into a recording device. Saying these statements aloud is very powerful!

After you've done this exercise a few times, try to catch yourself in the moment when you are feeling hurt by another's words or actions. In time, you can quickly get past the hurt.

Living, growing, and playing in the field of consciousness affords opportunities to discover more about yourself everyday, in ways big and small. Those FGM's (friggin' growth moments) that torment and irritate can be a growth experience if you allow yourself to transcend the moment.

For example, you may find yourself hurt by someone's thoughtless comment to or about you. Anytime you allow others to control you in this way, you're not standing in your own integrity. Instead, you've chosen to give your power away to someone else. In truth, the comment that upset you is likely something that gets to you because of a deep wound you carry that has nothing to do with the person saying what you're hearing as hurtful words.

At the core of integrity is keeping commitments and showing up for others and yourself. We've all heard about how important showing up is to being successful. But have you thought about what showing up for yourself means?
On the physical level, this means taking care of your body by getting the right amount and kind of exercise. The current suggestion is to take a forty-minute, brisk walk daily. That's all. Anything else you do is "extra."
On the emotional level, be clear about how you feel and express your feelings appropriately.
On the mental level, clear your "to do" clutter. A quick fix for mental clutter is to put on your "to do" list no more than five items at a time. When you've completed those items, you can add more, but no more than you can finish during your workday.
On the spiritual level, act on your inspirations. When you are inspired, you are aligned with your highest self.

Whatever we find irritating in others likely comes from seeing ourselves reflected in the mirror of annoyance or captured by the lens of our own limitations.

Chapter Ten
X Fortune Energies: Be Open to Abundance

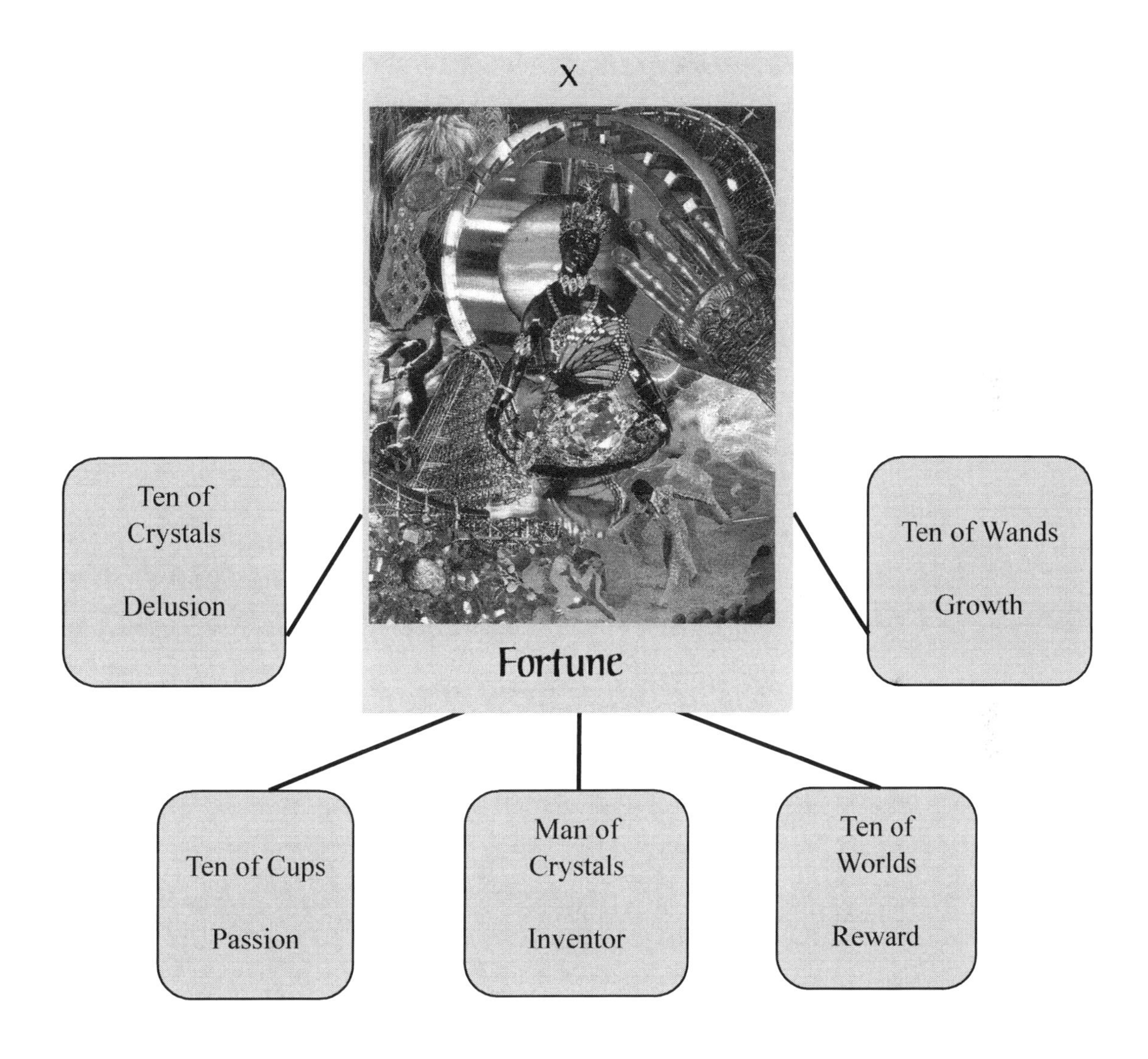

"Appreciation is a wonderful thing: It makes what is excellent in others belong to us as well."

Voltaire, 1694-1778
philosopher and writer

X Fortune: Expect changes! Be receptive to everything that's offered.

Fortune offers abundance.

Expect effortless success.

Know that change is on the way.

Open yourself to receiving the good fortune that awaits you.

This is a good time to take risks if you can get yourself balanced.

Anticipate and adapt to whatever trends arise in your field.

Caution: Accept periods of dullness, boredom, and routine while awaiting the wheel of fortune to turn in your favor.

✱ **Reach out for what's right in front of you.** Read your statement of intention to your Voyager Group. Brainstorm within the group what is possibly readily available to you that will help you get even a little closer to achieving your dreams.

Respond to these activities in your journal. Share some of your responses with your Voyager Group.

✱ **Know what you want.**

Make a list of your top ten desires. Prioritize and place the most wanted item at the top.

Every day for ten days, spend the day pretending you have one item on the list. Really get into the experience of claiming this desire. If you want a new home, find a picture of the dream home and put it in a prominent place. Look at the picture often throughout the day. Check out stores and catalogues for furniture you'd buy for this new home.

Be creative in how you imagine your life will be when you live in this dream home.

On the eleventh day, take your list and, in a safe place, burn the paper. Thank the universe for giving you everything and more that your heart desires.

Bury the paper in your garden or in a potted plant or someplace that you see often.

Let go of the desire to have these things.

In this way you are practicing detachment while remaining open to what is available to you.

Delusion/Ten of Crystals
Be open to new possibilities for your vision.

Use the Energy of Ten of Crystals to:

Expand your thinking.

Be inventive, creative, farsighted, and imaginative.

Be entrepreneurial.

See what no one else can see and act on your vision.

Look for the new, the edgy, and the unprecedented possibilities.

Caution: Avoid seeing only what you want to see, only what you're looking for.

Play with these activities to get inspired to take action on your visions:

✱ **In your journal, speed write whatever comes to you in answer to these four questions:** What do you really, truly, deeply want for yourself? For your family? For your community? For our world?

✱ **Make a list of the top twenty values and beliefs you cherish most.** Reflect on each value you hold and you'll know the secrets of your soul, of who you are.

✱ **Do a meditation on the dream you have for yourself, your community, and your world.** You might use a scripted meditation that you have written or one that is commercially available. You might take a walk or a run in nature and meditate as you move. You might meditate on your dream by sitting and putting your attention on your breath or by listening to meditative music. Take at least fifteen minutes for this meditation. Set your intention and then let your thoughts come and go as they please.

✱**When you finish your meditation, revisit your vision statement.** Or, if you haven't written one yet, go back to the Fool Child and write one for yourself now.

✱ **Evaluate the dream you have for yourself. Is this your dream or is this someone else's dream for you?**

✱ **Rewrite your statement if the vision no longer suits you, if it sounds more like what you think someone else wants for you, or if this is something you think you should do.**

To speed write, write out the question and then quickly write whatever comes to you. Don't think about what to write. Just write. When you stop or slow down, rewrite the question and begin answering again. Keep at the process until you have nothing left to write—for now.

Delusion reminds you to expand your thinking beyond what is seemingly right in front of you.

You're the only one who knows what is right for you, so get moving on your inspirations, ideas, and insights, and make your dreams happen.

Delusion is entrepreneurial energy. The true visionary sees beyond the delusions of the nay-sayers—including the critic who resides inside your own head.

Moonlight deceives the mind by turning red roses gray, gray landscapes blue, and, for most people, the light of the brightest moon erases words from the page in front of them. What is real? What is a delusion?

Inventor/Man of Crystals
See connections in a new and dynamic way.

Use the Energy of Man of Crystals to:

Open up to new ideas. Create and produce.

Brainstorm new thoughts without censorship or judgment.

Be entrepreneurial, constantly coming up with new ideas, inventions, and discoveries.

Seek out the support you need to get your projects to completion.

Caution: Don't let yourself get caught up in just spinning ideas around in your head. Get them into the world.

Play with these activities to make new and more dynamic connections between you and your dreams:

✱ **Answer the following questions to be discussed within your group.** The answer to these questions can be written before you come to the meeting if you choose, but responding spontaneously works well, too.

- What do you look at and think, "Something needs to be done about this?"
- What can you do to transform your community's physical, social, emotional, intellectual, or spiritual environment?
- Who can you enlist to help you?
- What can you do that would transform your life? Your bank account? Your career? Your relationships? Your spiritual connections?
- Who can you enlist to help you do something you are now ready to start?
- When will you take the first step to making a change in your life, in your finances, in your relationships, in your connections with others and with your higher self? Set a date and begin!

Write your responses to these activities in your journal.

Share some of your responses with your Voyager Group.

My friend, John, organized his morning coffee group into guerrilla gardeners. John had noticed big, empty planters around the area where the group congregated, and he suggested they do something with the pots to beautify the environment. A few days later, they arrived with gardening tools, soil, and plants. They created lovely container gardens, and they maintain them for the whole community to enjoy.

Set a date for transformation to begin.

Harness the energy and the drive that you have and put that power into your project. Where you pull back, where you get drained, are things to outsource. Think about hiring someone to help you in these areas. Or you could trade skill sets with someone and help each other out. Maybe a virtual assistant might be the most helpful for you. Maybe you need to take a course or find a mentor to help you. Or if you are working with others, maybe you need to switch hats with one another. Find a way to divert your energy toward things you like to do.

Passion/Ten of Cups
Fire yourself up to live fully and abundantly.

Use the Energy of Ten of Cups to:

Be successful, find your fortune, follow your passions.

Take risks.

Live sensually and brilliantly. Follow your deepest desires.

Be passionate about your projects. Create with great zest and brilliance.

Caution: Be careful not to burn yourself out or burn others up as you drive yourself to achieve your dreams.

Play with these activities to help you find your fortune in your passions:

✱ Where can you push yourself even harder, deeper, smarter, and faster, or where can you take things more slowly?

- Make a list of five things you could do to get closer to your goal that would be easy.
- Make a list of five things you could do to get closer to your goal that are difficult.
- Everyday over the next week, choose first one item from the easy to-do list and one item from the difficult to-do list and do them.
- Continue this process for five weeks. At the end of each week, if you have not accomplished one or both of your items, set them aside and move on to the next set.
- At the end of five weeks, evaluate what you have accomplished and what you have not from your two sets of lists.
- Give a quick report to your group about both what you did and didn't do.

Don't beat yourself up over how this activity turns out. The idea is to see what happens when you attempt things that you find most challenging. Sometimes you'll find this energizes you. Other times you may notice that your excitement drains and your energy falls to zero. You want to be aware of what gets you excited, and what holds no energy for you.

In an interview published in Oprah's online newsletter on July 15, 2011, Michael Cunningham, author of the award winning *The Hours* among other brilliant novels, speaks about what fires burn inside him:

"A writer should always feel like he's in over his head. That's part of what makes good writing compelling—the sense that as readers we're in the company of a writer of vast ambitions, who is always trying to do more than he or she is technically capable of.

"And there, really, resides the pleasure that comes from writing. It's a quirky, sweet-sour, Yankee-ish pleasure; it's more like a plunge into icy water on a hot day than it is like lolling around in the tropics. It's like what runners feel running the 500-yard dash, making good time and feeling pushed slightly beyond their limits, which is great, and feeling at the same time that although they're able to do something remarkable—they can run faster than almost anyone alive—they should nevertheless have done a little better, gone a little faster. They'll try that much harder tomorrow. There may be, in the end, no happiness quite so potent as the anticipation of a greater happiness still to come."

Reward/Ten of Worlds
Open to receiving the rewards you're ready for.

Use the Energy of Ten of Worlds to:

Trust that you deserve material rewards.

Open yourself to receiving the cornucopia of life's abundance awaiting you.

See yourself as rich and prosperous. Trust that everything you can imagine having is there for you and then notice what shows up.

Enjoy the wealth that comes to you and then spread it around for others to enjoy, too.

Caution: Don't fall victim to material consciousness that seduces you into a false sense of where your security comes from.

Play with these activities to open yourself to the rewards awaiting you:

✱ Keep a gratitude journal.

- Choose one day of the week when you set aside ten to fifteen minutes to write down a list of any length about the things you are currently grateful for.

- Once or twice a week, write down three things that you noticed over the past week that made you feel especially good. These statements should be short. Try to keep yourself to one sentence. For example, you might write: An agent asked to read the first fifty pages of my novel. My son set the table for dinner, and I didn't have to ask him. My daughter called just to say hello.

- After you've written your three items, take a few minutes to reflect on them. Why did they make you happy? What do you appreciate about them? Acknowledge the effort you put into making these things happen.

You might write:
I put myself out into the marketplace to attract the attention of an agent.

I've encouraged my son to feel a sense of pride in being part of the family.

My daughter is developing an adult relationship with me because I've gained her trust and respect.

Gratitude opens the heart to noticing the fullness of life and promotes abundance. The mind of poverty will keep you in a state of being without.

Positive psychologists such as Martin Seligman, Sonja Lyubomirsky, Emmet Worthington, and Fred Luskin suggest refocusing your mind to see the best in yourself, the wondrous around you, and the good things that fill your life.

Gratitude doesn't mean you are happy all the time. When you feel the emotion of the moment, you are experiencing life fully, so this means allowing yourself to be aware of when you're experiencing grief, frustration, anger, outrage, sadness, and all those other emotions that represent the "darker" side of life just as you want to always notice when you're happy, joyful, serene, satisfied, and all of the positive feelings you're capable of having.

Gratitude, does, however, give you a place to return to after you've processed those other, less welcome, emotions. Gratitude, in Martin Seligman's model, is not simply about opening to feeling happy but rather as a gateway to developing a truly meaningful life that fully and actively engages you.

Noticing what has gone right in your life will give you a great sense of satisfaction.

Growth/Ten of Wands
Reach for what you need to achieve your dreams.

Use the Energy of Ten of Wands to:

Be on the conscious path of growth. Aspire ever higher.

Use self-knowledge through growth to acquire self-confidence, purpose, and direction.

Reach for your star and become the star that you are.

Stretch yourself to reach new heights and to plumb greater depths.

Caution: Don't give up during times of challenges. Don't shy away from taking necessary risks or from being uncomfortable for a short period of time.

Play with these activities to help you remain inspired to reach your dreams:

✱ **Make a list of five times in your life when you didn't get what you wanted or when things didn't turn out the way you had hoped they would.** These can be big or small "failures."

For each item on your list, write at least five positive things these "failures" gave you or made you aware of. Can you repurpose those so-called failures into successes?

✱ **Stand and stretch your arms above your head.** Take a deep breath in and exhale slowly. Stretch a little higher. Stretch to the right side, facing front and twisting at the waist. Stretch to the left side.

Drop your arms to your sides.

Take another deep breath in and exhale slowly.

Reach your arms above your head again.

Touch your toes—or go as far as is comfortable.

Pat your body as you rise back to an upright position.

When you're standing, gently thump the middle of your chest with clenched fists.

Pat your arms from shoulder to hand and back up again. Shake out your hands. Gently shrug your shoulders. Take a deep breath and exhale slowly.

If you haven't failed somewhere, then you may not be stretching yourself enough to have the full, rich, exciting life you want.

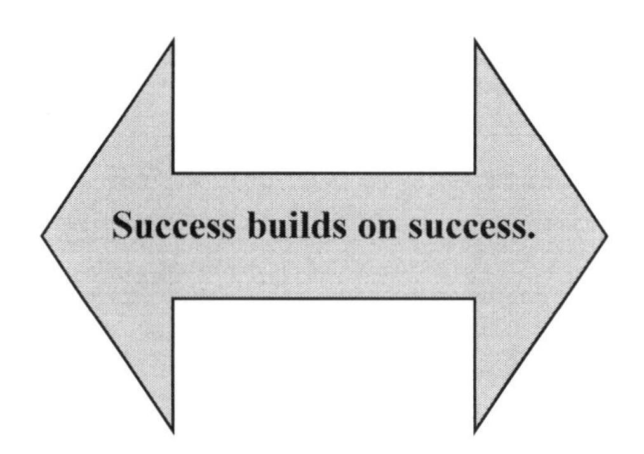

Stretch yourself first to your perceived limits and then beyond those until you've extended yourself far beyond what you at first imagined you could do.

"A display of indifference to all the actions and passions of mankind was not supposed to be such a distinguished quality at that time, I think, as I have observed it to be considered since. I have known it very fashionable indeed. I have seen it displayed with such success, that I have encountered some fine ladies and gentlemen who might as well have been born caterpillars."
from *David Copperfield* by Charles Dickens

Sometimes staying the course can feel downright overwhelming. But the world can be grateful that numerous authors who had their work rejected didn't cave.

Believe in your ability to succeed and remain persistent.

In the 1930s, **Theodor Seuss Geisel** was told his book was "too different from other juveniles on the market to warrant its selling." **Dr. Seuss's** book was turned down by 27 publishers before being accepted for publication. Eventually, he sold over 400 million books around the world.

Herman Melville submitted his manuscript, *Moby Dick* and was told: "We regret to say that our united opinion is entirely against the book as we do not think it would be at all suitable for the Juvenile Market. ... It is very long, rather old-fashioned..."

Vladimir Nabokov heard this about *Lolita* before this now well respected piece of literature found a publisher: "[T]he whole thing is an unsure cross between hideous reality and improbable fantasy. ... I recommend that it be buried under a stone for a thousand years."

J.K. Rowling's *Harry Potter and the Sorcerers Stone* was rejected by 12 publishers. Once accepted, she, who would become the most lucrative writer in the world, was warned to not expect much financial reward from writing children's books.

Carrie, the book that gave **Steven King** his big break was rejected by 30 publishers, one of whom said, "We are not interested in science fiction which deals with negative utopias. They do not sell."

Jean Auel, author of *The Clan of the Cave Bear*, was told, "We are very impressed with the depth and scope of your research and the quality of your prose. Nevertheless...we don't think we could distribute enough copies to satisfy you or ourselves." Her books have sold over 45 million copies worldwide.

Ernest Hemingway, regarding his novel, *The Torrents of Spring,* was rejected with, "It would be extremely rotten taste, to say nothing of being horribly cruel, should we want to publish it."

William Faulkner, author of incredible substance and many classics, was informed by an editor: "If the book had a plot and structure, we might suggest shortening and revisions, but it is so diffuse that I don't think this would be of any use. My chief objection is that you don't have any story to tell." Two years later, he received a rejection that read: "Good God, I can't publish this!"

Alex Haley received 208 rejection letters for *Roots* which eventually sold over six million copies.

Chapter Eleven
XI Strength Energies: Step into Your Power

"Sometimes you reach a point of being so coordinated, so completely balanced, that you feel that you can do anything--anything at all. . . . Simply because [you] feel happy. An extra bit of confidence like that can carry you through, and you can do things that are just about impossible."

Midget Farrelly, born Sept. 13, 1944
winner of the inaugural World Surfing Championship

XI Strength: Fully express yourself by being courageous and powerful, kind and loving.

Feel your power and courage to live fully as who you are in mind, heart, body, and soul.

Be creative.

Use your optimistic personality to create the life you want to have.

Be resolute in all your actions to move forward.

You are charismatic and radiate positivity—you are unstoppable!

Face down your demons.

Be compassionate with yourself and others.

Experience life in wonder and awe.

Be kind and loving, and don't be afraid to be intensely emotional.

You have the power to make your dreams come true. Temper this power with kindness and love.

Think about the story told of the power struggle between ancient British royals in *The Lion in Winter.*

King Henry II and his queen, Eleanor of Aquitaine, have energetic exchanges exerting their personal powers. Even though the queen is the king's captive, she faces down anything he puts in her way, including prison walls. She uses her wit, her cunning, even words of kindness, in her efforts to seek victory. The king softens, showing his vulnerable side. Peace between the couple, within the family, and within the country appears possible.

Unfortunately, this truce doesn't last. Both king and queen resort to exploitative, demanding, oppressive, and intimidating tactics to get what they want: their chosen son as heir to the throne. The family deteriorates into sibling rivalry, jealousy, civil war, treason, and the possibility of murder.

The Lion in Winter shows the dark side of the Strength archetype. But if these royals had used the Strength qualities of reconciliation, they could have healed the rifts within themselves, within their family, and within their country.

Play with these activities to help you see some of your strengths:

✱ **Write your own magical story.**
Do this in your Voyager Group or alone if you don't have a group. A huge benefit of doing this activity is sharing what was written, so if you don't have a group, seek out at least one other person to do this activity with.

Write a fairy tale in the "Once upon a time" tradition. Set a timer for five minutes. During this time, write a story about an animal that sets out from somewhere, goes someplace, does something, and either returns from where it started, stays where it went, or goes off headed toward another destination. This should be very simplistic for this exercise.

To begin, choose an animal, bird, insect, lizard or other non-human creature of the Earth to write about. Don't spend too much time making this decision. This doesn't have to be one of your power animals or most loved creature on the planet.

Trust your instincts. If some animal you never think about pops into your head, go with this creature. If an image of some animal or bird that is common and ordinary presents itself, let it be your creature for now.

Next, write the words: "Once upon a time there was a __________" (fill in the blank with the creature you will write about).

Write until the timer goes off (five minutes).

Whether "completed" or not, encourage each person to read aloud what he or she has written.

Little Mama Mouse: A Fable

Once upon a time there was a little mama mouse whose family was threatened by a huge ogre who sat day in and day out next to their mouse house hole. As time wore on, food was running out.

Mama's baby mice cried themselves to sleep at night as hunger gnawed at their tiny tummies. So, mama mouse decided she had to get out to get food. She knew she could't outrun the ogre, so instead, she talked to him and promised to bring back gold nuggets if he let her go.

He growled, hissed, and threatened her. He didn't believe she could find gold nuggets. Momma mouse persisted, not even sure herself she could accomplish this task, and finally convinced him that gold nuggets could be found. But she'd have to leave her family behind. For insurance. She said she'd agree, but he would have to promise to leave forever if she came back with some enormous amount of gold nuggets. The ogre said okay.

Mama ran past the ogre and had many adventures, faced lots of obstacles, but she managed to find the gold nuggets, return home, appease the ogre, and bring food to her family before it was too late.

After a story is read, those who want to comment can take about two minutes at the most to speak about what the story means personally. Do this by using the phrase, "If I had written this story, the animal would represent/mean/be . . . "

The idea is to give your perspective upon hearing the fable. Whether the author agrees or not is irrelevant. In this activity, you're using the power of story to uncover where you see your power and where you see how you are threatened. What you see in the story is what you can own.

Keep to the "I" point of view.

After feedback is given, have each listener, as well as the story writer, sum up the story that was read aloud with, "And the moral of the story is _________." This statement can be either written and then read or spoken by each person.

An interpretation of "Little Mama Mouse: A Fable" might sound something like this: If I had written this story, the little mouse would mean that I feel very small and insignificant in my world, maybe helpless. But when my little ones are threatened, I'll find a way. My little ones might be my little ambitions, my dreams, which are really important to me, which I know I need to nourish or else they'll die. Because I know they have to be fed, I'm able to figure out a way to save them. I knew I couldn't fight the ogre, but I could be clever enough to start out on my journey. I trusted myself enough to believe I would find what I needed to save my little ones. I had to face obstacles, but I did because my little ones are very important to me.

And the moral of the story is: trust yourself to find what you need to keep your dreams alive even if you don't know every step you have to take when you start out.

Be ***powerful*** without apology.

Exert your power with great ***compassion***.

"All the flowers of all the tomorrows are in the seeds of today." ancient proverb

Chapter Twelve

XII Hanged Man Energies: Be Free of Limitations

"Life just is. You have to flow with it. Give yourself to the moment. Let it happen."

Jerry Brown, Governor of California

XII Hanged Man: Surrender to what is.

Picture yourself in a canoe on a river with a swiftly moving current. What's the most obvious direction in which to paddle?

Imagine yourself a surfer on a board. In which direction would you ride the wave?

Go with the flow and surrender to what is happening now.

Save yourself by letting go of fixed beliefs, negative thoughts, and rigid perspectives.

Be positive. Be compassionate. Forgive yourself and others, and you will transcend any situation.

While it is always important to honor what you're giving up or losing, sometimes a loss can also represent a chance for a new beginning.

Seek out multiple perspectives.

Don't hold onto your perspective just because it's yours.

After a job has ended or a relationship has come to a conclusion, resist the urge to rush into what seems like the next best thing that appears in front of you.

✱ Make a list of possible ways you could fill a newfound "hole" in your life. Possibilities include, but aren't limited to these ideas:

- Create a business of your own.
- Take time to travel.
- Devote a few weeks to learning something new.
- Apprentice yourself to a master.
- Find a teacher who will guide you as you pursue a project you've always wanted to attempt.
- Take a seminar on something you've been interested in but don't know much about.
- Sign up for a class at your community college or through adult ed. or at an extension program with a university.
- Train for a marathon.

✱ Another way to think creatively about finding a new perspective is to explore past life regression. You can do this through a meditation or by having a session with a regression coach. When you allow your mind to seek other planes of information, you can discover lessons your soul strives to understand, talents you have a knack for even if you aren't yet using them, and patterns that you have a tendency to repeat, for better or worse.

Write your responses to these activities in your journal. Share some of your responses with your Voyager Group.

✱ **Write a story from your life that tells about how you learned how to see life from a different perspective.** You may have learned this lesson in the moment, or you may not have realized how influential the incident was until much later. Let your story be as long or as short as is needed to tell the story to your satisfaction.

✱ **Revise a story from your past.** Think back to a time when you had an explosive emotional response to someone. Reconstruct this experience by imagining a way you could have handled it that was more sensitive to the needs of the other person and a teachable moment in the most positive way. If possible, tell the person how you wished you could have managed the situation differently except, of course, you didn't know that then.

Mine was a melt down when my three-year-old son used his freshly wall-papered bedroom wall as a canvass for his creative expression with crayons. I have spoken to my now adult son about how I wished I had taped paper on part of his wall for him to enjoy his own decorating motifs with crayons and markers. I've apologized to him for making him feel bad, even as I still cringe thinking about that day, wishing I could have made the moment a positive learning experience.

Jack Canfield tells a story about a research scientist whose mother set the stage for his successes when he was two years old.

As a two year old, the future scientist attempted to take a bottle of milk from the refrigerator, lost his grip, and spilled almost the entire contents on the kitchen floor. Instead of yelling and shouting about the mess, his wise mother proclaimed that he had created the biggest indoor milk puddle she'd ever seen, and if he'd like to, he could take advantage of having an indoor pool to play around in, an invitation he joyfully accepted. After allowing him some time for splashing around in the milk, his mother explained that all good messes need to be cleaned up, and she asked how he'd like to attack his puddle—with a towel, a mop, a sponge?

They worked together and when they finished she told him that what had happened was he had participated in a failed experiment in milk bottle carrying. She said he had attempted to use two little hands to transport one large and heavy bottle of liquid. She suggested they go into the backyard with the now empty bottle of milk, fill it with water, and see if he could discover how to carry the bottle with his tiny hands. This cheerful learning exercise stayed with this little boy who grew into a lifetime experimenter, doing research that has produced significant medical discoveries.

Sharing your insights with the one you were involved in the trauma with, even if this happened years before, can be healing for you and for the other person involved.

Chapter Thirteen
XIII Death Energies: Let Go and Be Transformed

The dark night of the soul means that something that has been used for survival is no longer working. Face this reality, claim your destiny, and step into what you don't know. Trust the process that comes with telling yourself the truth.

XIII Death: Liberate yourself from bad habits, oppressive attitudes, and outdated ideas.

Rid yourself of mental clutter.

Open yourself to constructive attitudes and beliefs.

Leave behind anything that doesn't serve you well.

Separate from destructive relationships.

Through all the turmoil, remain positive and hopeful.

Embrace change because everything must come to an end.

Make room for your new dreams to come true.

Through loss arises immense opportunity for growth if you have the courage to face the loss and let it go, no matter how painful this loss is.

✱ As you go through change, be aware of pitfalls, the most notorious of which is addiction.

We tend to go to something addictive whenever we attempt to move away from something painful, uncomfortable, or troubling. Anything can be an addiction. Brené Brown, in her inspirational and well researched, *The Gift of Imperfection: Let Go of Who You Think You're Supposed to Be and Embrace Who You Are* lists almost everything we do in our daily lives as holding the possibility of keeping us from being true to ourselves, honest in our relationships with others, and present to what is happening around us.

Addictions numb us from fully experiencing life, both the bad parts and the good parts. To have a life that is rich, full, joyful, challenging, creative, and vital, doesn't mean that we become immune to using addictions to numb ourselves. After all, as Brown points out, we can draw on almost anything to distract us. Food, alcohol, shopping, gambling, sex, video games, television, and work are the obvious and familiar culprits. But we can also separate ourselves from our true natures by plunging into worthy causes that consume our days and keep us from being in present time, from feeling the pains and joys of the moment with the people around us. The point is to be aware of what is motivating us to do what we're doing. Are we investing our time to distract ourselves or to escape from something? If yes, break free from the addiction.

Play with these activities to let go of what needs to die and to make room for what is ready to be born:

✱ **Write a list of your "addictions."** These are the comfortable methods you rely on for numbing yourself or for taking the edge off of feeling vulnerable, uncertain, and fully present to both the good and the unpleasant, painful feelings.

✱ **Throughout the coming week, be aware and mindful whenever you notice that you are caught up by one of your addictions when any of these behaviors kick in.**

✱ **Now that you can label an activity an "addiction," are you willing to let go of the hold this has on you?** If the answer is yes, congratulate yourself. If the answer is no, ask yourself why and when you'll be ready to let go of the unhealthy behavior.

Caution: Don't make a habit of wearing black. Every color has a vibration, and each color brings benefits. You want to take advantage of all possible ways of being in touch with your most creative, vibrant, and energetic self. Color is a great way to make connections that move us into our most powerful and dynamic ways of being in the world.

Share some of your responses to these exercises with your group.

Thinking about Black

In Feng Shui, black is the color associated with the energy of your career, and within this ancient Chinese system of energy, career embodies your sense of self-esteem, your feelings of self-worth, and your very reason for being alive. Black captures your spirit and leads you on your soul's journey of offering your gifts and talents to the world in your own positive way.

Black is the color of mystery, power, and protection (black keeps you from being noticed in the dark of the night). Black also gives definition in open spaces (outlining a drawing makes the form pop off the page).

✱ **To feel grounded and stable, wear black.**

✱ **To seek out your true identity, wear black.**

Wearing black gives you a sense of power and safety, an excellent place to discover who you are.

However, wearing all black reduces light intake, so be sure to either add a spot of color to your attire or after dressing, picture yourself surrounded by the white light of protection.

✱ To create a sense of power and an opportunity to experience in-the-moment personal integration, try the following ritual in your Voyager Group:

- You will need a black or dark colored piece of cloth around six and a half feet long and at least three feet wide and a ceremonial rattle. A massage table is good to use, but this can be done on a sofa, a bed, or on the floor.

- One person lies on the table and is covered with the black cloth. To assist in breathing, this person might want to place one or both hands slightly cupped on his or her cheeks to keep the material from being too close to the mouth.

- Divide into two groups. One group will be under their black cloths first and the other group will act as assistants. Only one rattle is used but each person should have his or her own piece of cloth.

- Each person under a cloth has an assistant who stands or kneels by the person's head.

- To begin, each assistant offers a blessing and invocation out loud. The blessing might sound something like this:

(Name) is here to ask for new insight. (Name) is willing to let go of anything that restricts or restrains him or her from being the new person he or she desires to be. May all the spirits, guides, and angels of the seen and the unseen worlds assist in this new journey.

- One of the assistants rattles for five minutes. Watch the clock.

- After the rattle stops, each assistant, in turn, says: You, (name), will now return refreshed with new energy, wisdom, and resolve.

- The assistant moves to the person's feet and pulls the cloth either slowly or quickly down the person's body until the cloth is completely removed.

- The person stands and faces the assistant and in some way they acknowledge each other. This acknowledgement can be a "Namaste" or a bow or a hug or whatever feels appropriate.

- Switch roles so that everyone has opportunity to be under the cloth.

✱ Form a circle after this activity for a sense of completion. While in the circle, each person can either say how he or she felt or what was experienced before, during, or after the activity or what they hope to take away from the activity. The idea is to make a statement that acknowledges something has occurred that was out of the ordinary and that each person in the circle will attempt to be open to new inspirations that may come in the very near future.

Write a response to the ritual.

Chapter Fourteen
XIV Art Energies: Transform through Art

Everything that happens to us can be transformed into something that supports us if we invest our own personal meaning into these situations, good or bad.

XIV Art: Explore, discover, synthesize, and integrate external and internal resources to create the fullness of your life.

Channel your vision into a creative expression of what you want.

Be outrageous in how you show the world who you are and where you are going.

See the big picture, and then widen your vision. Be a multi-sensory creative.

Consider yourself an artist in all areas of your life. Think creative thoughts. Be fully expressive emotionally. Physically express yourself in big ways. Imagine your divine essence is leading you to make your dreams come true.

Make your mantra: Create! Create! Create!

✱ **Do something creative to get those juices flowing**. Move to the music. Write a poem. Write a children's story. Write a song. Decorate your home with flowers, leaves, vines, twigs—whatever you find in your own garden. Sculpt out of clay. Do an art project you've never done before just to see what you can create. Be spontaneous.

Share what you created with your Voyager Group.

The Art archetype stimulates you to express yourself.

Think about a group of kindergarteners. Set out art supplies and they're painters. Let them loose in front of clay and they're sculptors. Turn on music and they're dancers and singers. Allow musical instruments to be in reach, and they're musicians. Give them access to discarded material, old clothes, wigs, hats, purses, tool belts, and they're actors.

When you were young, you easily and readily expressed yourself through images, through metaphor, through sound and movement.

Don't forget—that need remains. The soul speaks the language of symbols. Emotions demand to be expressed.

Be fully expressive, be outrageous!

✱ **In your Voyager Group, connect with each other through the Sufi heart dance.** Play some soft, meditative music. Stand in an inner circle and an outer circle. In silence, face the person in the circle in front of you. Each person places a hand on the upper middle chest, near the top of the collarbone, of the person they're facing. Remain silent throughout the dance. Make eye contact and maintain eye contact throughout your dance with this person. Slowly rotate around a fixed point so that you are both moving in a small circle. Stop when you have completed a full rotation. When everyone in the group has stopped, move to the next partner. Do this until you have connected with everyone in the circle opposite you. Now form one circle. Continuing in silence, make eye contact with everyone in the group. Put your hands on your own upper chest. Close your eyes and notice if you feel your heart beating. Open your eyes and drop your hands to your sides. The dance has concluded.

✱ **Teach someone something that you enjoy and that you know how to do well.**

✱ **Explore something that interests you.** Discover something new through your exploration, and express your new insight through some creative form such as film, clay, storytelling, paint, music, dance, baking, flower arranging, writing, woodworking or ?? Integrate your creative desires into your life by finding new ways to make your vision your reality.

Write your responses to these activities in your journal. Share some of your responses with your Voyager Group.

✱ **In your Voyager Group, put on some music and dance**! Be lively. Smile and laugh.

✱ **When you're almost exhausted, sit in a circle and share your vision statement and what you plan to do tomorrow that will stir up these juices again to stimulate you to take action on your vision.**

Speak one at a time. Maintain eye contact with each speaker. Passing a "talking stick," which can be a stone, a stick, a bowl, or anything that is pleasant to hold, helps the group focus on the individual. When the person holds the "talking stick," no one is to interrupt. This is a time for sharing your intention. Remember, an intention shared is much more likely to happen than one kept to yourself.

After the person has spoken, everyone in the group offers an acknowledgement such as thank you, yes, amen, or some other word or phrase that recognizes that the speaker has been heard. You can decide ahead of time if you'll say your concluding word or phrases all at the same time, or individually, and whether they'll be the same or whether they'll be spontaneous and individual expressions.

No other comments are made by the members of the group. The "talking stick" then passes to the next person.

In his book, *A Whole New Mind*, business guru Daniel Pink says we are moving away from the information age to the conceptual age and that people who can think creatively as well as logically will be the people enjoying the most opportunities and the greatest rewards the culture has to offer.

Many researchers, thinkers, and futurists claim that the ability to be compassionate, mindful, and co-creative will be the most important qualities for fashioning a livable world. People who will be influencing and shaping the way we live, work, communicate, eat, travel, interact, celebrate, and grieve will be those developing their artistic sensibilities to invent, communicate, care for, and manage the needs of the human and natural environment.

Pink emphasizes that in the imminent future an MFA degree will serve you better than an MBA, because global business and industry now require creative, emotionally intelligent, out-of-the-box, intuitive thinking to meet the divergent and evolving climate of business and life.

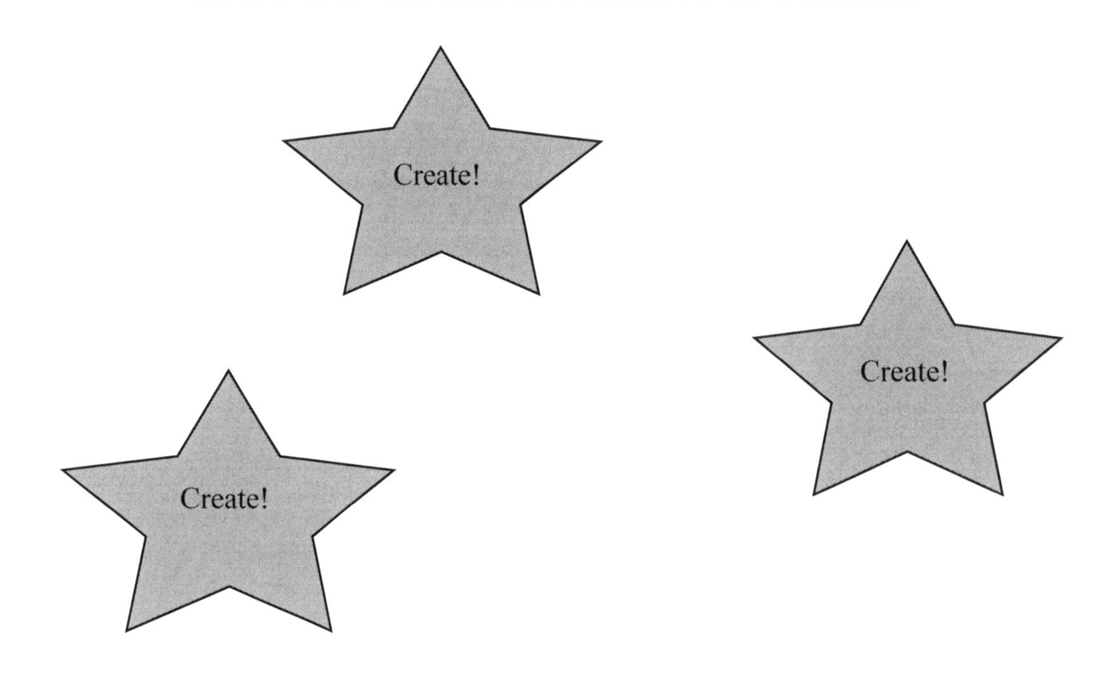

Chapter Fifteen

XV Devil's Play Energies: Live Fully and Creatively

Security is mostly a myth perpetuated to keep people from setting off on their own heroic journeys of enlightenment. To live a conscious life, shed the trappings of restrictive thinking imposed by religious and secular institutions and by cultural superstitions. Choose the daring adventure that is the authentic life. Choose to live!

XV Devil's Play: Live fully, live provocatively, live with uninhibited joy.

Enjoy life.

Let the world know you have big dreams for yourself.

Play the devil's advocate to stimulate creative thinking, acting, and expressing.

See with multiple perspectives.

Laugh! Laugh often! Laugh with ease!

Express yourself sexually and sensually.

Live a creative life.

Set your inhibitions aside and find new ways to enjoy life.

Succeed at what you set out to do just because you can even if you have to find a new way to see how to succeed.

Be playful and get others to play with you. Stretch to reach your dreams.

Embrace this moment right now just because you are here. No matter what else is going on, there are still parts of life that can be hugely enjoyable. Notice them. Enjoy them.

When Devil's Play energies are active, you are likely to see life as one gigantic playground where you're like a ten-year-old on an "explore." Everything appears interesting to the curious ten year old filled with wonder and joy. The child might come across a dead bird in a park, experience sadness, and then just as quickly let go of this debilitating emotion. To do this, he or she might create a story about how happy the bird was when it was alive, chirping sweetly in the leafy branches of the trees in this park where children play. The child might say something kind to the little creature, throw leaves over its lifeless body, and then move on to enjoy the world of the nearby playground.

✱ **Laugh out loud.** Right now. For no other reason than it's good to laugh. Laughing reduces stress by sending endorphins to your brain which ease pain and enhance your feeling of well being. You may notice that just smiling makes you feel pretty good.

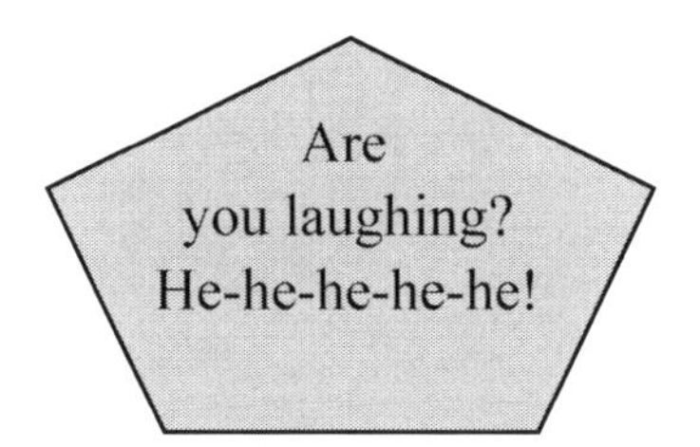

Allow yourself to play! Open yourself to the joy around you! Give in to happiness!

To do this, don't hold onto any emotion. Emotions are fleeting. They rise up. They're experienced. They dissipate. This is a wonderful part of being human. You don't want to deny any emotion that presents itself. And you don't want to hang onto any emotion because when you do this, you're missing out on a new emotional experience. We've all been caught up in the euphoria of new love. Remember how difficult it is to concentrate because all you want to do is think about your beloved. Everyone and everything else fades into the background as you entertain only thoughts of this very special person. The same is true for anger. "Blinded by rage" is something we can all relate to, I'm sure. All we have to do is remember the betrayal, the hurt, the violence, and we're steaming with hostility, ready to punch out the first person who annoys us. Familiar feelings, yes?

✱ **Today, set a timer to ring every hour for several hours throughout the day.** When the timer goes off, notice what you were thinking and feeling. Were you here, in the present moment? Were you worrying about something that has not occurred yet? Were you remembering something from the past? Write down where your mind and emotions were or just notice them.

✱ **On another day, set your timer, and when the buzzer sounds, no matter what you were thinking or feeling, bring yourself to the present and concentrate fully on what you're doing.**

Notice the language I've used. We have to "think" about the loved one. We have to remember, or conjure, the image of the evildoer. What's happening here is that our minds are reminding us of an old emotion. We're not experiencing those emotions in the present moment. We're bringing experiences to consciousness so that we can remember and reactivate old feelings. Doing this, we're missing out on present emotional experiences, and we're superimposing old ones on the present moment. We're ignoring what's in front of us which could be pleasant or unpleasant, but whatever emotion is ready to be experienced is one that can lead us to greater awareness of ourselves, others, and our environment. Imagine all the wonderful solutions to problems, all the amazing creative thinking, all the extraordinary interactions with others and our world that could be experienced if we were fully present. Eckhart Tolle has written many books and spoken widely on, as he calls it, "the power of now."

Find some way to experience joy in this moment, no matter what is going on around you.

✱ What can you change your mind about right now so that instead of seeing a situation as bleak and hopeless you can find a way to enjoy the moment you are currently experiencing in spite of the pain—and the reality—of a grief you are also experiencing?

The movie *Life is Beautiful* showed me what it means to be present no matter what. In the movie, a Jewish father and young son are in a concentration camp during the Holocaust, and the man creates a beautiful world in the mind of his little boy in the midst of violence and depravity. The father couldn't change his hideous surroundings. And, in spite of all the dangers, the Nazis couldn't take from this father his creative, generous, and loving mind, heart, and soul, and he used his talents and resourcefulness to help his son know life as fun, full of love, interesting, imaginative, and hopeful.

Respond to these activities in your journal.

Share some of your responses with your Voyager Group.

Maureen Carroll, a Stanford University researcher, offers programs to help companies get their creative juices flowing to solve all manner of problems.

In one activity, Carroll put people into small groups to brainstorm their best and worst airline experiences. At the end of the brainstorming session, the best experiences were ignored, and the groups were directed to turn their disasters around so that passengers would look forward to flying with the airline. Funny and outrageous solutions emerged!

The airline noted for losing baggage became "Weight Loss Air" where you could lose your excess baggage by dieting during your flight.

"Angry Air," which guaranteed your misery, transformed itself into "Angry Birds Air," where every flight was filled with fun and games.

The crying baby flights offered a nanny for every baby brought on board.

While these are not the most practical solutions, the ideas come from a positive mindset, where creativity abounds. Not everything that pops out of our mouths when we're brainstorming will resolve our problems, but we're much more likely to find nuggets and gateways to solutions in thoughts that delight, make us laugh, and give us the courage to keep trying than we are if we keep the circuitry going in circles of negativity.

Chapter Sixteen

XVI Tower Energies: Expect Fast, Sudden Change

"Everything can be taken from a person but one thing: the last of human freedoms--to choose one's attitudes in any given set of circumstances, to choose one's own way."

Victor Frankl, 1905 - 1997
neurologist, psychiatrist, writer, lecturer, and Holocaust survivor

XVI Tower:
Develop a more profound sensibility and create a new life by disrupting your untenable trajectory.

Expect disruptions in your life.

Be prepared for sudden loss.

Give up old structures and develop new ways to be in the world.

Give up old patterns, beliefs, attitudes, and ideas that no longer serve you.

Remain positive and hopeful in the midst of change and disruption.

Trust that your dreams will come true.

Commit to doing whatever is needed in the most positive and productive way to make your dreams come true for your personal benefit and for the good that you offer the world.

✱ **Make a list of events that have recently occurred in your life that have made you feel unsettled, unnerved, or uncomfortable.** Don't judge them. Simply acknowledge them.

✱ **Make another list of events that have recently occurred that have cheered, encouraged, pleasantly surprised, or in some way made you feel good.** Again, don't judge them. Acknowledge them.

✱ **Share these lists with little or no comment from you or from those to whom you read your lists.**

Can you trust that the beauty of a new way of being in the world will arise no matter how challenging recent events may have been?

Tower energy is a time of growth and development.

As the saying goes, "*Shift happens.*"

The current astrological Age of Aquarius is ushering in rapid change, shaking us to our foundations. Nothing will be the same. Hierarchies, patriarchies, and authoritarian structures of the past two thousand years are breaking down. We will realize that security is an illusion. The mind of consciousness is rapidly expanding as we prepare to explore other and unknown realities.

A Zen story tells of the farmer whose son longed for a horse, but the farmer didn't have the means to buy one. One day, a wild stallion appeared in their fields and over many days, the boy lured the animal closer and closer until he could circle his neck with a rope and lead him back to the barn.

"This is very good, father!" He shouted. "I now have a horse."

His old and wise father simply replied, "Who knows what is good, who knows what is bad?"

Everyday for weeks, the boy arose early to feed and care for his horse and to do his chores so that he could continue to work with his stallion in the afternoons.

One day, the horse threw the boy from his back, the boy broke his leg, and the horse ran off.

"Oh father!" the boy cried. "This is horrible! This is the most miserable day of my life."

The father simply replied, "Who knows what is good, who knows what is bad?"

The son was laid up with his broken leg, unable to help his father with his chores and fruit rotted on the trees because the father couldn't do everything himself. A neighbor saw the father in town and offered her condolences about the farmer's misfortunes.

The farmer simply replied, "Who knows what is good, who knows what is bad?"

The next day, soldiers descended on the town, conscripting all boys of the appropriate ages into the army to fight in the war raging on the far border of their country. When they came to the farmer's house, they said they came for his son, but when they saw him, they said they couldn't use someone with a broken leg. They then looked around for any horses they could take, but the farmer didn't have any.

When the soldiers left, the son smiled and said, "Father! This is a great day."

His father simply replied, "Who knows what is good, who knows what is bad?"

Chapter Seventeen

XVII Star Energies: Know How Connected You Are

Physicists have concluded that 93% of the mass of our individual bodies is stardust. This means that in a time long past, someone may have wished upon a star and that star is now part of you.

XVII Star: Recognize your radiance and illuminate the darkness for others to find their way.

Be compassionate with yourself.

Be compassionate and in service to others.

Do your part to inspire others to shine.

Recognize that you are a star, a source of light for others, a model of optimism, joy, and hope.

Make the world a beautiful place by offering your beauty, your genius, and your many gifts to the world.

Inspire others to find their own starlight. Be innovative and creative.

Trust that amazing things can happen when you let your radiance shine out into the world.

Model optimism and hope.

Be self-sufficient and self-confident.

Trust your visions. Act on what you know the world now needs.

Know that your dreams—or something better—will come true.

We are all connected, each of us golden and worthy of living in the garden that is this earth and this universe. We live in a closed energetic system and everything we do has an impact on our own energetic, chemical, and biological systems, on the systems of untold others on our planet, on life throughout our world, and likely throughout our universe.

✱ **Acknowledge the gifts, talents, and abilities in the people you interact with.** For example, you might comment to the person serving your table in a restaurant how much you appreciate how patient he was with you after you changed your order three times. Or you might tell your struggling college student how much you admire her persistence and self-discipline. Or consider thanking your neighbor with the beautiful roses in her front yard for making the neighborhood so cheerful and colorful.

✱ **Over the next week, notice how often you acknowledge the gifts, talents, and abilities you see in others.** Write in your journal about what you noticed and what you did.

✱ Acknowledge your own gifts, talents, and abilities. Make a list of people you respect, admire, love, or appreciate. For each person, list the qualities that each person has or give examples of what each person has done to elicit positive responses in you.

Acknowledge that each of these characteristics that you admire in others are qualities you have yourself. You likely wouldn't be able to see them in someone else if you didn't first know about them through personal understanding.

You may not be able to achieve the level of expertise of quality, talent, or gift the person you admire has achieved. For example, you may not be able to paint like Picasso, but you can be persistent in your creative expression, you can gather around you other creative people for inspiration, you can show your work with pride no matter how others judge your offerings, and you can be productive in whatever way you choose to focus your creative expression—some of the characteristics this great and innovative master exhibited and which you can develop, too.

✱ Look for "ahas!" in all areas of your life. Star energizes your self-confidence and intuition and brings more clarity to what you pay attention to. Be sure to pay attention because some of the awarenesses may be subtle. Don't let them slip away. There are numerous stars in the sky waiting for you to notice them. Keep track of these "hits of brilliance" in your journal.

✱ Acknowledge your limitations and claim those aspects of yourself that you've been reluctant to embrace in the past. Star energy acknowledges your readiness to unfold in a new, transformative way as you grow more fully and completely into embracing the best of who you are while also accepting the qualities you may not be so proud to claim. These may be either negative traits or positive qualities that you've hidden away for whatever reason seemed reasonable when you tucked them into your deep inner being.

✱ Be careful not to overextend yourself or, like a shooting star, you're likely to plummet and burn yourself out. Pace yourself. Pay attention to your body. A twenty-minute power nap in mid-afternoon is a much more effective revitalization technique for lethargy and fatigue than is pushing through with a caffeine or sugar boost. Also good would be taking a walk outdoors, playing a game, or reading a novel for a short break.

✱ Star energy is meant to be joyful, loving, balanced, calm, and thoughtful. When you find yourself stressed, take time to get yourself balanced. Take a long, pleasant walk, a leisurely bath, get a massage, do yoga, tai chi, chi gong, jog, participate in a sport, meditate, dance. Find an activity that will calm you.

✱ For a quick rejuvenation, take a Ten Zen Second break.

Think of a short saying that will work for you and your situation at hand. Eric Maisel, who developed this system, refers to them as incantations. If you're feeling anxious or overwhelmed, try: "I am completely stopping." If you're feeling distracted or scattered, "I am completely present" might be good. When trying to accomplish a difficult task, "I accept this challenge" might work. Or, when feeling really challenged, "I embrace this moment," or "I am open to joy" might ease your stress or pain. Any short phrase that helps you will work for this exercise.

Break the phrase into two parts.
"I am completely / stopping."
"I am open / to joy."
"I accept / this challenge."
"I embrace / this moment."

Breathe in for five seconds and think the first part of the phrase, such as "I am completely." Time yourself with a clock until you get a sense of what five seconds feels like.

Exhale for five seconds and think the last part of the phrase, "stopping."

Take Ten Zen Seconds throughout your day for clarity, insight, and bringing yourself back to a more balanced state of mind whenever the stress levels begin to rise.

(Adapted from Eric Maisel's *Ten Zen Seconds*)

By staying calm when energized by the Star archetype, you will be able to see projects, relationships, and life, with a deeper, broader, and more inspirational vision. You will be able to act with clarity, wisdom, and certainty. You will be able to transform any situation.

"We all have a genius within us and when one of us doesn't develop or use our special gift, a cosmic void takes place."

From the online newsletter, "Daily Om,"
Friday, June 3, 2011

Write your responses to these activities in your journal.

Share some of your responses with your Voyager Group.

Chapter Eighteen
XVIII Moon Energies: See Through Illusions

"I dreamt a dream! What can it mean?"
William Blake 1757 - 1827
poet, engraver, printer, mystic

XVIII Moon:
Allow for cycles of lightness and darkness, reality and illusion, integrity and deception, knowing and not-knowing.

Expect to receive intuitive inspirations and act on them in positive, helpful ways.

Let emotional tidal waves recede before making decisions.

Enjoy being a romantic. Feel deeply and express your feelings exuberantly.

Be cautious.

Embrace and accept all your feelings, intuitions, dreams, and imaginings.

Write down your dreams and look to these metaphoric landscapes for visionary insights.

See yourself clearly in the world you are creating for yourself.

Be introspective and open yourself to more ideas. Taking time to be discerning gives you more options because you're not acting on the first impulse to do something. Remember, being "loony" comes from the word "lunar" which refers to the moon.

When you can separate yourself from the emotional pull of Moon energy to act impulsively, you give yourself time and thought to make wiser decisions. Being in touch with your emotions is healthy. Acting without regard to what happens next will get you trouble.

✱ **Expect to receive intuitive inspirations.** Act on these insights in positive, helpful ways. However, be cautious of making impulsive decisions. When Moon energy takes hold of you, you may be inclined to react rather than to take deliberate action. When a new idea or plan of action comes forward play with the concepts, write about how you can use the intuitive inclination you're entertaining, test the premise with forward thinking imagery, discuss the idea with teachers and mentors, and be introspective.

✱ **Set an intention to know the answer to a problem you're facing.** Draw a Voyager tarot card or open this book to any page and write about what the card you've chosen is telling you about how to respond to your concern.

Open any book to any page and read a paragraph. Write about what this passage is telling you about how to respond to your concern.

Use a photo album to choose a photo at random and imagine what the picture is telling you about how to respond to your concern.

Moon energy is about love, and loving yourself is your number one project. Love yourself enough to act in your own best interests by balancing your intuitive instincts and your emotional urges with your calm, detached, intellectual evaluations.

✱ **Make a list of changes you would like to make in the next six months or year.** Be as exhaustive as possible about issues big and small you would like to see resolved.

✱ **Prioritize the changes you believe are possible.** Be a realist. Highlight these. Don't worry about how many you highlight, but do be honest with yourself.

✱ **Put the changes you've highlighted on separate index cards and set them on your desk or in some prominent place.** As you accomplish each change, throw away the card and look at the next card.

✱ **Be creative in your approach to addressing these changes.**

✱ **Do the same process for projects you would like to begin or end this year.** Make a lengthy list, prioritize, and write the important ones on separate index cards. Place the cards in a prominent place and throw out each one as a project is completed.

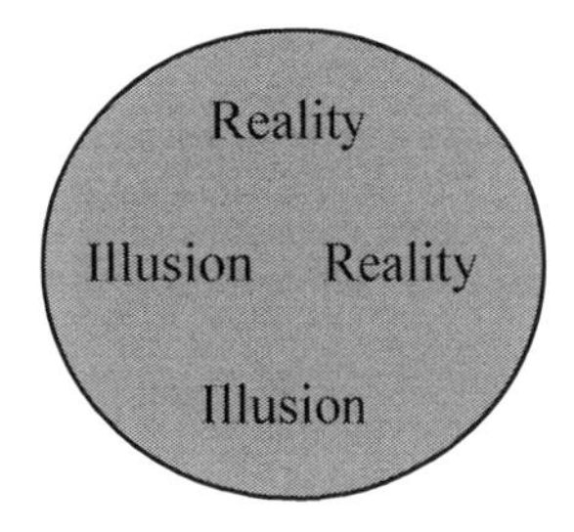

Through conscious choice, you can create new realities, sustain and maintain current realities, and release and let go of realities that no longer serve you.

As you grow more and more uncomfortable with old ideas that no longer feel "right" for you, decide what changes you need to make to get yourself and your life more balanced. Is a minor change in attitude or behavior called for? Do you need to revamp an area of your life that isn't working? Job? Relationship? Living situation? Diet and exercise practices?

✱ **Make a collage that shows many of your qualities.** Focus on shining a light on qualities you don't easily claim. The positive qualities you ignore are referred to as your "Bright Shadow" and the negative aspects that you don't claim are your "Dark Shadow" qualities. Use pictures, photos, colors, words, and objects that capture pieces of yourself.

Moon energy guides you to reflect on your authentic self, the self that is talented, thoughtful, loving, creative, full of potential, weak, dispassionate, prejudiced, angry, imperfect, and all the other qualities that make up the whole of who you are. Embrace them all and love yourself as you are.

✱ **Consider sharing your collage with your Voyage Group or with one person you trust.** Briefly explain what the images, words, and objects mean.

Or maybe you want this collage to be just for your own inner reflection, and that's a fine choice, too.

✱ **When you take time to look at and think about your collage, keep in mind what you want for yourself.** Notice what represents you when you are in your highest integrity. Keep these thoughts in mind when you make decisions.

✱ **After doing these activities, review your vision statement.** Any changes you want to make? Make adjustments, big or small, that better reflect what you hope to achieve.

Share some of the changes you want to focus on with your Voyager Group.

"You yourself, as much as anybody in the entire universe, deserve your love and affection."
Buddha

✱ **Do the following activity with another person to reflect on how you respond when seen in a positive light.**

- To begin, both of you write down three qualities you admire in the other person. When you both have these qualities listed, decide who will be Person A and who will be Person B.
- Person A tells Person B the three qualities and why those qualities were chosen.
- Person B says nothing while Person A speaks. After hearing the explanation for each quality, Person B responds with a simple, "Thank you."
- After the last "Thank you" is said, Person A asks Person B the following questions:

How did that feel to hear these positive statements about yourself?
Did you notice any physical reactions when listening to these compliments?
How do you usually respond to compliments?
Do you believe what you heard?

After Person B responds to the questions, switch roles. Now Person A receives the compliments and gets asked the questions by Person B.

After you have both received your compliments, discuss your experiences of this process.

Chapter Nineteen

XIX Sun Energies: Be Filled with Light and Joy

The sun shines,
the flowers blossom

Choose
Which flowers
you will pick

XIX Sun: Awaken to the abundance of energy, wealth, vitality, and joy that's all around you.

Collaborate with others, with the world of nature, and with the energy of the life force.

Get out in the world where you can shine.

See yourself and the world in the most positive of ways: abundant, creative, fertile, energetic, vital, active, light, colorful, and radiant.

Create a healthy and optimistic mind.

Expect to be prosperous.

Be sunny, joyful, wise, happy, energetic, and creative.

Pace yourself appropriately. Be careful not to get burned out or not to burn up from too much exuberance or from over-indulgence.

Share your abundance.

Be delighted with your life!

Create a life that supports you fully.

Own your true identity.

Research psychologists have scientifically concluded that we are all happiest when we are doing what we do best and when we're using our greatest, our strongest, our most well-developed strengths (those core qualities that make us the unique people we are) in a group setting with the goal of accomplishing something we value, something we consider worthwhile.

Creating the life of your dreams means not only bringing to fruition a relationship or project—your novel, your piece of sculpture, your new business, your blog, your travel plans, your non-profit, your theatre group, or whatever you've chosen as your focus—but also making your life meaningful in a complete way: financially, relationally, spiritually, emotionally, and intellectually.

Your identity, as characterized by the Sun energy, represents the fullness of who you are.

Who are you today?

✱ For each question that follows, identify yourself on a scale of 1 to 10, with 1 representing feeling less satisfied and 10 suggesting you're feeling great.

1. How do you rate your financial health?
2. How do you rate your relationship with your partner or spouse? If you aren't in a relationship, how do you rate your emotional satisfaction with not being in a relationship?
3. How do you rate your ability to focus on something that's really important to you?
4. How do you rate your emotional equilibrium?
5. How do you rate your ability to express yourself in public situations?
6. How do you rate your ability to express yourself through a creative outlet?
7. How do you rate your ability to feel connected to the world in general?
8. How do you rate your understanding of important issues facing our world?
9. How do you rate your ability to give yourself the time, space, and mental awareness for a project that's important only to you?
10. How do you feel about your understanding of what it means to you to be spiritual?
11. Anything else you want to add to your list?

✱ For each answer that was less than "9," go through a variation of the Buddha Sit In exercise: Ask yourself, write out, or have someone else ask you, "How do you know this is true?" Repeat this question until you feel you've gotten at the core for what you can do to boost your rating to a "9" or a "10."

✱ On a scale of 1 to 10, with 1 being "Not so much" and 10 being "Wow! All I could ask for!" how would you say each of the following would rate how lovable you are?

1. Your partner?
2. Your child, children or grandchildren?
3. Your parents, including step parents?
4. Your siblings, including steps and halves?
5. Your closest friends?
6. Your in-laws or your partner's family?
7. Anyone else you think should be on this list?

✱ On a scale of 1 to 10, with 1 being "Not so much" and 10 being "Wow! I know how honored I am to be in this work related or professional relationship!" how would you say each of the following would rate how respectful you are of them?

1. Your business colleagues?
2. Your employees?
3. Your employer?
4. Your professional associates?
5. The people who provide products or services to you at work?
6. Anyone else you think should be on your list?

✱ If you didn't rate yourself a 9 or 10 in every category, determine what needs to be done to boost your rating.

Chapter Twenty
XX Time-Space Energies: Change Old Patterns

"A great many people think they are thinking when they are merely rearranging their prejudices."

William James 1842 - 1910
psychologist, philosopher, and writer

XX Time-Space: Change your psychological and behavioral patterns, change your life.

Time-Space energy directs you toward changing old patterns and getting you to a place beyond outdated and unnecessary habits and restrictive beliefs.

A belief crucial to finding peace within and peace throughout the world, centers on embracing a new way to think about forgiveness.

Discriminate, be judicious, aware, wise, and astute.

Reflect and evaluate where you act out of habit and where you make thoughtful decisions about beliefs, attitudes, and behaviors.

Be analytical. Thoroughly examine old beliefs and discard those that no longer serve you.

Keep your body still while your spirit soars. Touch the universe with your mind and spirit.

Remain in touch with your dreams. Bring long forgotten dreams to your current awareness.

Take steps to make your dreams come true.

Don't get spaced out. Use behaviors that serve you well.

Acknowledge that your thoughts are manifesting.

Know that your visions, your dreams, are becoming your reality.

Everett Worthington, a psychologist who specializes in forgiveness, offers ways to change old patterns after being hurt. Typically, in Western culture, when a person is hurt, the forms of "solace" often include one or more of the following unhelpful responses: revenge; anger turned outward or within; dependency on drugs and/or alcohol; reliance on addictions to work, driving recklessly, sex, food, exercise, therapy or anything else; constantly speaking about being a victim; and refusing to speak about what happened.

To forgive, it is necessary to move beyond outdated and unnecessary habits and restrictive beliefs.

To forgive does not mean to accept, condone, or in any way support abusive, manipulative, or hurtful behavior.

Worthington's new model is the challenging but life altering process, REACH.

Recall the hurt without infusing it with emotion. Be reflective in an evaluative, critical, discriminating, and analytical way. Neither cast the other as evil nor see yourself as stuck in pain and self-pity. Visualize what happened as if from above the scene in an all-knowing position. Make up the story if you don't know what really happened.

Empathize with the one who hurt you. Why might he/she have done this? Again, make up possible scenarios. Was this person feeling threatened? Was this person in some kind of intolerable, hurtful situation?

Altruistically offer the gift of forgiveness. Remember a time when you were the transgressor in a situation and the person you hurt forgave you. Recall how grateful you felt to be relieved of the burdens you carried of guilt, embarrassment, shame, fear, humiliation. When you can fully accept yourself as fallible and human, you can step out of yourself and give freely the gift of forgiveness not to make yourself feel better, but because it's the right thing to do.

Commit yourself to forgive publicly. Worthington suggests something written, such as "a certificate of forgiveness," a letter of forgiveness to the offender, a song, or a poem. Or make a public statement within a family setting or circle of friends who were involved or knowledgeable of the transgression.

Hold onto forgiveness. Following the REACH guidelines doesn't eradicate the memories of the pain, the hurt, or the loss. But when thoughts of the transgression return, remind yourself not to dwell on vengefulness and not to wallow in self-pity.

Worthington personally experienced the benefits of his program when he followed his own principles after his elderly mother was beaten, raped with a wine bottle, and murdered one New Year's Eve by two intruders who had broken into her home after she had gone to bed.

The REACH model is adapted from *Authentic Happiness* by Martin Seligman, PhD

✱ **Do the REACH exercise within your Voyager Group.** Focus on a small transgression that you experienced and help each other with each step of the process so that you can eventually move on to doing the exercise to forgive something even more painful that happened to you.

The length of time that has passed matters little with issues of forgiveness. Sometimes, you will find yourself needing to forgive something that happened thirty, forty, fifty, or more years ago.

Releasing old patterns, especially in the area of forgiveness, is challenging and can be a very difficult process. Be mindful that Worthington's forgiveness process has been scientifically shown to bring people to a place where they were less angry and more optimistic. Their health also improved as stress in their bodies was lessened.

Fred Luskin, author, psychologist, and head of the Forgiveness Project at Stanford, has developed programs on helping people through the process of forgiveness. When we've been emotionally hurt, betrayed, humiliated, abused, or harmed, we often cling to the rage we feel toward the people or circumstances that caused us pain, extending the insult for years and even decades. This turmoil affects our minds, bodies, emotions, relationships, and spirits. Luskin offers relief through his process for forgiving, described in his book, *Forgive for Good.*

Luskin's process, in summary:

- Be clear about how you feel about the problem, and why you feel harmed. Be as specific as possible. Then share this information with one or two trusted confidants.
- Commit to the healing process.
- Make your goal that of finding a place of peace, of stillness within yourself, not of condoning the actions that caused the pain.
- Be aware of your feelings in the present rather than focusing on the feelings felt at the time of abuse.
- Stop expecting to get what can't be given to you by another person.
- Give up on ruminating on what might have been. Create your own life now by doing things for yourself.
- Stand in your own personal power.

"Out beyond ideas of wrongdoing and rightdoing there is a field. I'll meet you there.
When the soul lies down in that grass, the world is too full to talk about.
Ideas, language, even the phrase 'each other' doesn't make any sense."

Mevlana Jelaluddin Rumi 13th century Persian poet

Chapter Twenty-one
XXI Universe Energies:
Feel the Power of Completion

You are a blessed and well loved child of the Universe. Use the power of this divine connection to engage with the abundance of the Universe. Create the life you want to live. Contribute to the world you want to see flourish.

XXI Universe: Everything is available to you.

Feel complete.

See your successes as opportunities to continue on to more successes.

Have a clear vision for yourself and take daily actions to make your dreams your reality.

Be adaptable.

Be flexible.

Keep your dream alive until you reach fulfillment.

See how you and your dreams fit into the big picture of life.

Continue to dream and create new dreams to achieve even greater success.

You have a universe of possibilities available to you.

Be grateful for all that you have and for all that you have yet to receive.

Remember that everything and everyone is whole, complete, and perfect in all our imperfect ways.

Have a fully realized vision in your head so that you can see your dream come true before you even take the first step toward actualizing this dream.

Take the first step, no matter how big or how small this move feels.

You are the artist of your life. Like the sculptor, see fully what is hidden in the block of stone. Like the painter, allow the vision for the blank canvas to appear in its own time. Like the writer, listen to what the characters have to say as they come alive on the paper or the computer screen. Evolve with your never-ending project of integration and enlightenment.

Keep your dream alive until you take the last step: fulfillment.

Everything that has manifested began as a thought, a vision, a dream.

Fill your day with love, passion, and gratifying experiences, and you'll soon find yourself living with more of the same in your life.

Ritual is a powerful way to express your connection to yourself, your loved ones, your community, your sense of the divine, and your creative ideas and projects. We use rituals throughout our lives in big and small ways. I recommend using some ritual, even something as simple as lighting a candle and declaring your positive intention at the beginning and end of every endeavor. Sometimes, something bigger is needed to acknowledge your transition. We know how important marriage, birth, birthday, graduation, anniversary, and burial rituals are for helping us connect more deeply to the new person we become during these times of passage; however, we often neglect to acknowledge other meaningful transitions like new careers, new homes, launched or at least finalized artistic projects, relationship completions (a term I learned recently to substitute for the harsher sounds of "divorce" or "break up").

Over the past several years, I have been privileged to participate in and lead a special ritual that is meant to acknowledge our connection to each other, the earth, and the universe. A Peruvian couple, both shamans, taught a small group of us the ritual I will now share with you. They asked that we share this ritual with as many people as possible because the gift was given to them so that the earth and all life on our sacred planet can be healed through this ceremony of love and sharing.

The Flower Ritual

Prepare for the ritual by collecting red, yellow and white flower petals.

Red represents our connection to each other and the earth through our open hearts.

Yellow represents our connection to each other and the earth through our open minds.

White represents our connection to each other and the universe by opening us up to the divine in all.

The basic ritual is simple: one person takes handfuls of these flower petals and sprinkles them over another person.

The variations on the ritual are as many as are our imaginations. You may choose to include music and meditation. In two of the ceremonies conducted by the Peruvian shamans, they played trance-inducing music on their flutes and spoke a single word or short phrase to each of the participants as they gently dropped the flower petals over us. Magic filled the air!

You can also play recorded music.

Blessings can also be added.

For "blessings," I've used what I also refer to as "statements of wonder." I've written these myself, and I encourage you to write your own. Each statement is written on a card and chosen randomly by the person receiving the blessing. One person reads for the person being blessed with the flower petals. Here are some samples:

Quiet your mind and listen for the soft sounds around you. Open your heart to the love that settles into your every cell. Feel the flow of creation. At the right time, express what wants to and what is ready to be brought forward.

Be still and listen for your inner guidance. Ask to make choices that are wise and that will lead you in the direction of where you can be most of service. Know that you will be aware of what you need to know. Know that you will be taught all the lessons you need to learn. Know that you are blessed, and the world is blessed because of what you offer.

Walk in stillness. Bask in love. Relish forgiveness for others and for yourself.

Feel the protection of the universe. Embrace the love that is showered on you. Breathe. Enjoy.

Take your journey. Walk into the vastness of all possibility. Allow your vision to be clarified with each step you take. When the mist falls, keep walking—or stop to dance. Notice the crispness of the air. The scent of violets wafting from the garden nearby. The gurgle of the brook. When your senses are full, resume your journey.

Feel at peace and live in stillness. Feel the love of your family, friends, and relatives. Feel the love of the universe. As you walk through the world, open yourself to appreciation for every aspect of nature, for every breath breathed by you and by all living things.

Listen to your inner voice calling to you to explore your interior world. Listen for the wisdom that will arise from deep within you. Now picture something or someone familiar. Look deeply and take in the magnificence of what you see. Notice something you haven't seen before. Offer compassion. Feel the joy. Sense the connection. Know that you are totally and wholly loved.

Offer no resistance to what is. Allow the present moment to be and accept the impermanent nature of all things and conditions. Allow the people in your life to be who they are. Allow yourself to be who you are. Now. This is the way to peace. This is the way to enlightenment. You are all things at all times. Be.

Each day, begin with thoughts of gratitude. Each night, end your day with thoughts of gratitude. Feel blessed.

Know that you are a loved and blessed child of the universe. Feel the inspiration that arises, offering you a life bigger and better in all the right ways. Accept that you are the creator of your life. Feel your radiance. Smile. You are filled with de-light!

I've used this ritual to celebrate birthdays by asking individuals who have known the birthday celebrant during the different decades of the person's life to say something about the person during that age of her life and then sprinkling the person with the flowers.

This is a wonderful ritual to play with.

Keep in mind what the flower petal colors symbolize:

Red holds the energy of connection through the heart.

Yellow holds the energy of connection through the mind.

White holds the energy of connection through the soul.

Use this ritual now, even if your group only consists of two. Gather the flowers. Find, make, or write something that symbolizes the project or transition you have just completed or that symbolizes that you have completed a full Voyager journey.

Use the symbolic object, the flower petals, music if you prefer, and blessings in your ritual.

Feel the love the universe offers in all the forms possible for you to experience, then pass this love along.

The new definition of success will have to include living a life of meaning, purpose, and abundance. When we are fully aligned within ourselves physically, mentally, emotionally, and spiritually, we can infuse our lives with meaning and we can live a purposeful life. When we share this authentic expression of ourselves with the world, benefits abound for each of us individually, for the world in present time, and for the future ad infinitum.

Appendage A

Soul of Success Curriculum for a Three Month Program that Meets Weekly

This is a 14 meeting curriculum meant to take place over three months. However, it can also be extended to serve as a six month curriculum meeting every other week. The facilitator should look ahead to the requirements for each meeting. Although the preparations are never huge, some planning will be necessary to make each meeting run smoothly.

The time will depend on the size of the group. For groups of two to four, two hours should work well. For groups of four to eight, three hours will likely be needed.

To maintain the integrity of the group, meetings should start on time and end as close to the designated time as possible. Ending a little early is almost always appreciated more than is going over the prescribed time.

If the group is meeting for three hours, a short, no more than ten minute break should also be included.

Group Guidelines should be agreed upon by everyone. Suggestions:

- Confidentiality is a priority. Don't share personal information outside of the group.
- Gossip is an unhealthy addiction. Don't speak about other group members or what the members have shared except to explore something that might be helpful and supportive.
- When people speak, honor their time. Don't carry on side conversations while someone is speaking.
- Decide on a way for the group to show acknowledgement and support. This might be something like offering breath blown over open hands in front of the mouth, the sound of "Ahhhhhhh," or by saying a quiet, "thank you." Or you might think of something else.
- When someone is obviously feeling vulnerable, allow the person space to experience his or her emotions by being quiet and by keeping your attention focused on the person. Open your heart to the person.
- If you have shared something that made you feel vulnerable, when you're ready, ask the group for an acknowledgement of support.
- Honor the needs of others.
- Ask for what you need from the group.
- I encourage you to enter into the process of dream creation in the spirit of joy, fun, playfulness, and openness. The more open and vulnerable you can be, the more inspiration and creativity you will experience.
- Enjoy the process!

Meeting 1

The facilitator lights a candle if this is possible, welcomes people to the group and suggests a name be chosen for the group at the end of this meeting. Group members should think about this name and at the end of the meeting, try to choose one.

The facilitator introduces him or herself by name and provides a single sentence stating the intention he or she holds for the meeting. This is meant to be a personal intention.

Each person in the group states his or her name and the intention held for the meeting.

The facilitator chooses something from Chapter Zero—Fool Child Energies: The Journey Begins to read out loud. This might be one of the quotes, one of the descriptions of the cards, or one of the stories offered in this section.

The facilitator leads the group to do the following:
- Write a vision statement.
- Share the statement with the group. After each person reads his or her vision statement, go around the group so that each person can either offer something specific that is supportive or simply say something supportive, such as, "I hope your dream comes true."
- In your journal, write a list of positive, healthy beliefs that you hold as part of your core belief system.
- In your journal, write a list of beliefs you would like to claim.
- Share these two lists, or some of the statements on the list, with the group.
- Share a dream, big or small, that you have for yourself that has no connection to your vision statement.
- In your journal, take ten to fifteen minutes to write about something that's meaningful to you. This can take the form of a story, an essay, a poem, or just a note to yourself. This isn't meant to be shared tonight, but if you feel like expanding on what you begin, do this over the time between meetings.
- Decide on a name for your group.
- Decide who will be the facilitator for the next meeting.
- Go around the group and read your vision statements again. After each person reads, no one comments other than to say, "thank you." Allow a short moment of silence between readings.
- After the last person has read their vision statement, take three connected breaths together and sit for a moment in silence.
- The facilitator ends the meeting by reading another quote, description of a card, or story from Chapter Zero—Fool Child Energies: The Journey Begins.
- Hug everyone in your group. Extinguish the candle.

Between Meetings
- Do the activities not done for Learner/Child of Crystals and for Feeler/Child of Cups.
- Find a game to bring to the next meeting or find a scene from a movie or play to bring.

Meeting 2

The facilitator lights a candle if this is possible, and welcomes people to the group, stating the name chosen for the group.

The facilitator introduces him or herself by name and suggests each person state his or her vision statement. After each person speaks, allow a short moment of silence before the next person speaks. This is not a time for commentary about the vision statement.

The facilitator chooses something from Chapter One—Magician Energies: Express Your Personal Power to read aloud. This might be one of the quotes, one of the descriptions of the cards, or one of the stories offered in this section.

The facilitator leads the group to do the following:

- Share the activities done between meetings.
- Do something active for about ten or fifteen minutes. Charades is always easy to put together, but any game that's active and fun is good. Or put on music and dance. Or if you brought a scene from a play or movie, act this out, reader's theatre style.
- Have everyone take several deep breaths in unison. Set a timer for ten minutes and have participants either close their eyes or stare into the candle flame (if one has been lit) and allow their minds to travel to wherever their thoughts take them. When the timer goes off, take another ten minutes to write in your journal. Write whatever comes to you. Don't share what you write. Let the ideas just "be" for a while.
- Go around the circle and share your vision statement and then talk about ideas, actions, or people who could possibly help you take even one small step toward making this dream come true. If anyone else in the group has other thoughts, allow for them to be shared.
- Look at the story on the page for I Magician: Make It Happen.
- Go around the circle and have each person read out loud the story by filling in the blanks. This is meant to be spontaneous for this read through.
- After the last person has read, take three connected breaths together and sit for a moment in silence.
- The facilitator reads another quote, description of a card, or story from Chapter One—Magician Energies: Express Your Personal Power.
- Decide who will be the facilitator for the next meeting.
- Hug everyone in your group.
- Extinguish the candle.

Between Meetings

- Do activities from Seeker/Child of Wands, Magician, and Brilliance/Ace of Crystals.

Meeting Three

- The facilitator lights a candle if possible, welcomes people, and states the name of the group.
- The facilitator introduces him or herself and invites each person to share their vision statement. After each person speaks, everyone says a quiet, "thank you." Allow a short moment of silence before the next person speaks. This is not a time for commentary about the vision statement.
- The facilitator chooses something from Chapter One—Magician Energies: Express Your Personal Power to read aloud. This might be one of the quotes, one of the descriptions of the cards, or one of the stories offered in this section.

The facilitator leads the group to do the following:

- Share some of the activities you did in between meetings.
- With a partner, play the Silly Faces Game under Ecstasy/Ace of Cups.
- Go around the group and let each person tell what award or awards they would like to win or be presented with that acknowledges their vision statements. If no such award exists for the vision statement chosen, make up something.
- Set a timer for ten minutes. If possible, play some soothing instrumental music. As a group, take several deep breaths in unison and then spend the ten minutes visualizing living the life you'll be living when your vision statement is your reality.
- Take another ten minutes to write in your journal about whatever comes to you. This is not to be shared. This is just for you.
- Look at the "State Your Objective" activity under Actor/Man of Wands. Either pair up or do this activity in the group by talking it through rather than writing it down. As you do this activity, notice how you feel in your body as you talk about what you will do. Tell your partner, or the group, where you feel something. This might sound like: "When I said I'd call and make an appointment, my throat felt tight." Or, "When I heard myself say I had a client, I felt like I wanted to breathe a great sigh of relief."
- Take a healing break: Have each person sit in a chair with one person sitting on either side of the person in the "healing chair." These people will each hold one of the person's hands between their hands. Another person stands behind the person and gently sets both hands on the person's shoulders. Hold this position in silence for two to three minutes. Switch off so that everyone has opportunity to be in the "healing chair."
- Return to your circle, take three connected breaths together and sit for a moment in silence.
- The facilitator reads another quote, description of a card, or story from Chapter One—Magician Energies: Express Your Personal Power.
- Decide who will be the facilitator for the next meeting.
- Hug everyone in your group.
- Extinguish the candle.

Between Meetings

Do activities from Ecstasy/Ace of Cups, Success/Ace of Worlds and Illumination/Ace of Wands. Come to the next meeting dressed as you will dress when your vision is your reality.

Meeting Four

- The facilitator lights a candle if possible, welcomes people, and states the name of the group.
- The facilitator introduces him or herself by name and invites each person to share his or her vision statement. After each person speaks, everyone says a quiet, "thank you." Allow a short moment of silence before the next person speaks. This is not a time for commentary.
- The facilitator chooses something from Chapter Two—Priestess Energies: Use Your Inherent Wisdom to Live a Purpose Driven Life to read out loud. This might be one of the quotes, one of the descriptions of the cards, or one of the stories offered in this section.

The facilitator leads the group to do the following:

- Share the activities you did between meetings.
- Explain why you chose to dress the way you did.
- If you have a visualization recording to play, do this as a group. If you don't have a recording for guidance, set a timer for ten minutes and either stare into the candle if one is lit or close your eyes and allow your mind to travel to wherever it chooses.
- At the end of the ten minutes or the visualization, take another ten minutes to write in your journal. Write whatever comes to you. This is not meant to be shared.
- Take an energy break: Do the energy exercises under Equilibrium/Two of Cups.
- Do the activity "Eliminate Outdated Thoughts and Beliefs" under Purity/Two of Wands.
- Do the activity that follows on the next page: "As a group, share belief statements."
- After the last person has spoken, take three connected breaths together and sit for a moment in silence.
- The facilitator reads another quote, description of a card, or story from Chapter Two—Priestess Energies: Use Your Inherent Wisdom to Live a Purpose Driven Life.
- Decide who will be the facilitator for the next meeting.
- Hug everyone in your group.
- Extinguish the candle.

Between Meetings

- Do some activities from Priestess, Two of Crystals, Two of Worlds, and Woman of Wands.

Meeting Five

- The facilitator lights a candle if possible, welcomes people, and states the name of the group.
- The facilitator introduces him or herself and invites each person to share his or her vision statement. After each person speaks, allow a short moment of silence before the next person speaks. Everyone says a quiet, "thank you." This is not a time for commentary.
- The facilitator chooses something from Chapter Three—III Empress Energies: Use the Power of Love to Heal and Transform to read aloud. This might be one of the quotes, one of the descriptions of the cards, or one of the stories offered in this section.

The facilitator leads the group to do the following:

- Share the activities you did between meetings.
- Look at the statements about making a commitment to your vision under Empress. Fill in the blanks for these statements and share them with your group. If you want to change your vision statement, that's fine, too.
- Play the "I Can Do One More" game under Creativity/Three of Crystals either in groups of two or three or in the whole group. Share your lists.
- Get with a partner. Set a timer for 90 seconds and during that time, tell your partner how great you are. Talk about your accomplishments, talents, personality traits that are endearing, and your special abilities. Really elaborate on how great you are. At the end of the time, switch and listen to your partner tell you about how great he/she is for 90 seconds. Notice how you feel as both speaker and listener.
- Write a six word autobiography and three or four six word biographies. This activity is found under Creativity/Three of Crystals. Share these with the group.
- After the last person has spoken, take three connected breaths and sit for a moment in silence.
- The facilitator reads another quote, description of a card, or story from Chapter Two—Priestess Energies: Use Your Inherent Wisdom to Live a Purpose Driven Life.
- Decide who will be the facilitator for the next meeting.
- Hug everyone in your group.
- Extinguish the candle.

Between Meetings

Choose from activities under Love/Three of Cups, Nurturing/Three of Worlds, Preserver/Woman of Worlds, and Compassion/Three of Wands.

Meeting Six

- The facilitator lights a candle if possible, welcomes people, and states the name of the group.
- The facilitator introduces him or herself and invites each person to share their vision statement. After each person speaks, everyone says a quiet, "thank you." Allow a short moment of silence before the next person speaks. This is not a time for commentary.
- The facilitator chooses something from Chapter Three—III Empress Energies: Use the Power of Love to Heal and Transform to read aloud. This might be one of the quotes, one of the descriptions of the cards, or one of the stories offered in this section.

The facilitator leads the group to do the following:

- Share the activities you did between meetings.
- Working in pairs or small groups, create a virtual support group as explained under Achiever/Man of Worlds.
- Do the activities under "Play with these activities to explore how to let go of expectations" in the

Disappointment/Five of Cups section. Be sure to do the activity where you give yourself a big hug and warm caresses, too.
- Do the word collage activities under Setback/Five of Worlds. Share these with the group.
- After the last person has spoken, take three connected breaths together and sit for a moment in silence.
- The facilitator reads a quote, description of a card, or story from Chapter Four—IV Emperor Energies: Ignite Your Thrust towards Success.
- Decide who will be the facilitator for the next meeting.
- Hug everyone in your group.
- Extinguish the candle.

Between Meetings

- Choose from activities under Emperor, Logic/Four of Crystals, Anger/Four of Cups, Aspiration/Four of Wands, and Seer/Sage of Wands.
- Write either the mini-bio as explained under Commencement/Four of Worlds or your legacy as explained under Seer/Sage of Wands.

Meeting Seven

- The facilitator lights a candle if possible, welcomes people, and states the name of the group.
- The facilitator introduces him or herself and invites each person to share his or her vision statement. After each person speaks, everyone says a quiet, "thank you." Allow a short moment of silence before the next person speaks. This is not a time for commentary.
- The facilitator chooses something from Chapter Five—V Hierophant Energies: Commit to Personal Growth to read out loud. This might be one of the quotes, one of the descriptions of the cards, or one of the stories offered in this section.

The facilitator leads the group to do the following:

- Share the activities you did between meetings.
- Share the mini bio or your legacy.
- Do a visualization if you have one or make one up. This visualization should focus on walking somewhere outside where animals, insects, birds, lizards appear. Allow creatures to come into view to be observed. When the visualization or meditation is completed, take ten minutes to write in your journal about these sightings. See the activities under Confusion/Six of Crystals for more details.
- Do a group tarot reading. Either use a Voyager Tarot deck or use this book. See the activity under Confusion/Six of Crystals for more details.
- Go around the circle so each person can briefly sum up anything they care to share about either the visualization or the tarot reading.
- After the last person has spoken, take three connected breaths together and sit for a moment in silence.

- The facilitator reads a quote, description of a card, or story from Chapter Six—VI Lovers Energies: Integrate Oppositions, Polarities, and Paradoxes within the Self, Between Another, and Within Communities.
- Decide who will be the facilitator for the next meeting.
- Hug everyone in your group.
- Extinguish the candle.

Between Meetings

- Choose from activities under Hierophant, Five of Crystals, Sage of Crystals, Five of Cups, Lovers, and Rejoicer/Woman of Cups
- Practice the Ho'oponopono Prayer as explained under Oppression/Five of Wands.
- Do the "pity letter" activity as explained under Sorrow/Six of Cups.

Meeting Eight

- The facilitator lights a candle if possible, welcomes people, and states the name of the group.
- The facilitator introduces him or herself and invites each person share his or her vision statement. After each person speaks, everyone says a quiet, "thank you." Allow a short moment of silence before the next person speaks. This is not a time for commentary.
- The facilitator chooses something from Chapter Seven—VII Chariot Energies: Be Committed, Determined, and Emotionally Invested in Your Dreams to Keep Yourself Moving Forward to read aloud. This might be one of the quotes, one of the descriptions of the cards, or one of the stories offered in this section.

The facilitator leads the group to do the following:

- Share the activities you did between meetings.
- Do all the activities under Trust/Six of Wands.
- Reread your vision statement to the group. Change anything that needs to be changed.
- Do Dr. Judith Orloff's Three Minute Meditation as described under Dullness/Seven of Crystals.
- Take three connected breaths together and sit for a moment in silence.
- The facilitator reads a quote, description of a card, or story from Chapter Seven—VII Chariot Energies: Be Committed, Determined, and Emotionally Invested in Your Dreams to Keep Yourself Moving Forward.
- Decide who will be the facilitator for the next meeting.
- Hug everyone in your group.
- Extinguish the candle.

Between Meetings

Choose activities from Synergy/Six of Worlds, Dullness/Seven of Crystals, Fear/Seven of Cups, Surfer/Man of Cups, Breakthrough/Seven of Worlds.

Meeting Nine

- The facilitator lights a candle if possible, welcomes people, and states the name of the group.
- The facilitator introduces him or herself and invites each person to share his or her vision statement. After each person speaks, everyone says a quiet, "thank you." Allow a short moment of silence before the next person speaks. This is not a time for commentary.
- The facilitator chooses something from Chapter Eight—VIII Balance Energies: Align Yourself with the Harmony of the Universe to read aloud. This might be one of the quotes, one of the descriptions of the cards, or one of the stories offered in this section.

The facilitator leads the group to do the following:

- Share the activities you did between meetings.
- With a partner, do the activity under Surfer/Man of Cups.
- Choose some physical activity to use as a meditation. See Balance and Synthesis/Eight of Crystals for details.
- Look at Change/Eight of Worlds together as a group. Discuss possible ways you could challenge yourself.
- Take three connected breaths together and sit for a moment in silence.
- The facilitator reads a quote, description of a card, or story from Chapter Eight—VIII Balance Energies: Align Yourself with the Harmony of the Universe.
- Decide who will be the facilitator for the next meeting.
- Hug everyone in your group.
- Extinguish the candle.

Between Meetings

Choose activities from Seven of Wands, Woman of Crystals, and Eight of Cups.

Meeting Ten

- The facilitator lights a candle if possible, welcomes people, and states the name of the group.
- The facilitator introduces him or herself and invites each person to share their his or her vision statement. After each person speaks, everyone says a quiet, "thank you." Allow a short moment of silence before the next person speaks. This is not a time for commentary.
- The facilitator chooses something from Chapter Nine—IX Hermit Energies: Connect Your Soul with Your Roles in the World to read out loud. This might be one of the quotes, one of the descriptions of the cards, or one of the stories offered in this section.

The facilitator leads the group to do the following:

- Share the activities you did between meetings.
- Do the meditation as explained under Harmony/Eight of Wands.

- Set up the partner activity under Narrowness/Nine of Crystals to carry you through the next four weeks.
- Do the Big Buddha Question activity under Integrity/Nine of Wands either with a partner or on paper.
- Take three connected breaths together and sit for a moment in silence.
- The facilitator reads a quote, description of a card, or story from Chapter Nine—IX Hermit Energies: Connect Your Soul with Your Roles in the World.
- Decide who will be the facilitator for the next meeting.
- Hug everyone in your group.
- Extinguish the candle.

Between Meetings

Choose to do activities from Hermit, Fulfillment/Nine of Cups, Regeneration/Sage of Cups, Harvest/Nine of Worlds, and Master/Sage of Worlds.

Meeting Eleven

- The facilitator lights a candle if possible, welcomes people, and states the name of the group.
- The facilitator introduces him or herself and invites each person to state his or her vision statement. After each person speaks, everyone says a quiet, "thank you." Allow a short moment of silence before the next person speaks. This is not a time for commentary.
- The facilitator chooses something from Chapter Ten—X Fortune Energies: Open Yourself Up to Your True Destiny of Abundance, Prosperity, and Expansion to read aloud. This might be one of the quotes, one of the descriptions of the cards, or one of the stories offered in this section.

The facilitator leads the group to do the following:

- Share the activities you did between meetings.
- Do the "speed writing" activity under Delusion/Ten of Crystals.
- Again, under Delusion/Ten of Crystals, make a list of the top twenty values and beliefs you cherish most.
- Take a stretch break. Move. If you have dance music, put it on. Dance! Dance together. Dance alone. Do a circle dance. Let each person dance in the middle of the circle. Keep the music on for at least ten minutes.
- Sit in your circle when the music stops and take three connected breaths together and sit for a moment in silence.
- The facilitator reads a quote, description of a card, or story from Chapter Eleven—XI Strength Energies: Step into Your Power without Apology, but with Great Compassion.
- Decide who will be the facilitator for the next meeting.
- Come prepared to do the ritual as described in the XIII Death section at the next meeting.
- Hug everyone in your group.
- Extinguish the candle.

Between Meetings

Choose to do activities from Inventor/Man of Crystals, Passion/Ten of Cups, Reward/Ten of Worlds, and Growth/Ten of Wands.

Bring materials for the ritual as explained under XIII Death.

Meeting Twelve

- The facilitator lights a candle if possible, welcomes people, and states the name of the group.
- The facilitator introduces him or herself and invites each person to share his or her vision statement. After each person speaks, everyone says a quiet, "thank you." Allow a short moment of silence before the next person speaks. This is not a time for commentary about the vision statement.
- The facilitator chooses something from Chapter Twelve—XII Hanged Man Energies: Make the Decision to Let Go and Move On to read aloud. This might be one of the quotes, one of the descriptions of the cards, or one of the stories offered in this section.

The facilitator leads the group to do the following:

- Share the activities you did between meetings.
- Write, read, and play with a magical story as explained in the XI Strength section.
- Do the ritual as described in the XIII Death section.
- After writing your responses to the ritual, take three connected breaths together and sit for a moment in silence.
- The facilitator reads a quote, description of a card, or story from Chapter Thirteen—XIII Death Energies: Let Go and Be Transformed Into a New Phase of Hope.
- Decide who will be the facilitator for the next meeting.
- Hug everyone in your group.
- Extinguish the candle.

Between Meetings

Choose from activities under XIV Art, XVII Star, and XVIII Moon to do.

Meeting Thirteen

- The facilitator lights a candle if possible, welcomes people, and states the name of the group.
- The facilitator introduces him or herself and invites each person share his or her vision statement. After each person speaks, everyone says a quiet, "thank you." Allow a short moment of silence before the next person speaks. This is not a time for commentary.

- The facilitator chooses something from Chapter Fourteen—XIV Art Energies: Revolutionize Your Transformation Through Your Creative Impulse to read aloud. This might be one of the quotes, one of the descriptions of the cards, or one of the stories offered in this section.

The facilitator leads the group to do the following:

- Share the activities you did between meetings.
- Read the instructions for the activity under XV Devil's Play: What can you change your mind about right now? Set a timer for ten minutes and write a response to this question.
- Do the Sufi Heart Dance as described XIV Art.
- Do the list making activities described under XV Tower.
- Share these lists with little or no comment from you or from those to whom you read your lists.
- After sharing your list, take three connected breaths together and sit for a moment in silence.
- The facilitator reads a quote, description of a card, or story from Chapter Fifteen—Devil's Play Energies: Live Fully and Celebrate Your Creative Spirit.
- Decide who will be the facilitator for the next meeting.
- Decide who will bring what for the flower ritual to be experienced at the next meeting. This is described under XXI Universe.
- Hug everyone in your group.
- Extinguish the candle.

Between Meetings

Choose from activities under XVII Star, XVIII Moon to do.
Bring what is needed for the flower ritual as described under XXI Universe.

Meeting Fourteen

- The facilitator lights a candle if possible, welcomes people, and states the name of the group.
- The facilitator introduces him or herself and invites each person to share his or her vision statement. After each person speaks, everyone says a quiet, "thank you." Allow a short moment of silence before the next person speaks. This is not a time for commentary.
- The facilitator reads aloud the Zen story from Chapter Sixteen—XVI Tower Energies: Expect Fast, Sudden, and Absolute Change, Ready or Not.

The facilitator leads the group to do the following:

- Share the activities you did between meetings.
- Do the activity, "Who are you today?" under XIX Sun.
- Be sure to do the Buddha Sit In exercise that accompanies this activity.
- Do the REACH activity under XX Time-Space.
- Do the Flower Ritual as described under XXI Universe.

- After the Flower Ritual, return to your circle and take three connected breaths together and sit for a moment in silence.
- The facilitator asks each person to choose a quote, description of a card, or story to read aloud from Chapters Seventeen, Eighteen, Nineteen, or Twenty.
- The facilitator invites each person to offer a statement of gratitude for the other members of the group.
- Hug everyone in your group.
- Extinguish the candle.

Appendage B

Bibliography and Resources

Alarcon, Francisco X. *Snake Poems: An Aztec Invocation.* San Francisco: Chronicle Books, 1992.

Arrien, Angeles. *The Tarot Handbook: Practical Applications of Ancient Visual Symbols*. New York: Jeremy Tarcher, 1997.

Atwood, Janet and Chris. *The Passion Test: The Effortless Path to Discovering Your Life Purpose.* New York: Plume, 2006.

Ball, William. *A Sense of Direction: Some Observations on the Art of Directing*. New York: Drama Books Publishers, 1984.

Brown, Brené. *The Gifts of Imperfection: Let Go of Who You Think You're Supposed to Be and Embrace Who You Are.* Center City: Hazeldon, 2010.

Canfield, Jack. *100 Ways to Enhance Self-esteem in the Classroom: A Handbook for Teachers and Parents.*

——————— with Janet Switzer. *The Success Principles: How to Get From Where You Are to Where You Want to Be.* Fort Collins: Collins, 2005

Choquette, Sonia. *Trust Your Vibes: Secret Tools for Six-Sensory Living*. Carlsbad: Hay House, 2004.

Craig, Gary. EFT Tutorial as free download on www.emofree.com.

Daily Om. www.Dailyom.com.

Dworkin, Hale. *The Sedona Method: Your Key to Lasting Happiness, Success, Peace, and Emotional Well-Being.* Sedona: Sedona Press, 2007.

Eden, Donna. *The Energy Medicine Kit: Simple, Effective Techniques to Help You Boost Your Vitality and Feel Better.* Boulder: Sounds True, 2004.

EFT (see info under Craig, Gary)

Fraser, Dougall. Website: www.DougallFraser.com

Fulghum, Robert. *All I Really Need to Know I Learned in Kindergarten*. New York: Random House, 1986.

Gladwell, Malcolm. *The Outliers: The Story of Success.* New York: Little Brown and Co., 2008.

Greer, Mary K. *Tarot for Yourself: A Workbook for Personal Transformation*. North Hollywood: Newcastle Publishing Co., 1984.

Gordon, Jon. Newsletter on line. 6/6/2011. www.jongordon.com.

———— *The 10-Minute Energy Solution: A Proven Plan to Increase Your Energy, Reduce Your Stress, and Transform Your Life.* New York: G. P. Putman's Sons, 2006.

Houston, Jean. Newsletter on line. 4/16/2011. www.jeanhouston.org.

Katie, Byron with Stephen Mitchell. *Loving What Is: Four Questions That Can Change Your Life.* New York: Three Rivers Press, 2002.

Larsen, Michael. San Francisco Writers Conference Newsletter. Dec. 2011. www.Sfwriters.org.

Luskin, Dr. Fred. *Forgive for Good: A Proven Prescription for Health and Happiness*. San Francisco: HarperCollins, 2003.

Lyubomirsky, Sonja. *The Myths of Happiness.* New York: Penguin Books, *2013.*

Maisel, Eric. *Ten Zen Seconds: Twelve Incantations for Purpose, Power and Calm*. Naperville: Sourcebooks, 2007.

————*The Creativity Book: A Year's Worth of Inspiration and Guidance.* New York: Jeremy Tarcher/Putman: 2000.

———— *Coaching the Artist Within.* Novato: New World Library, 2005.

———— *Rethinking Depression: How to Shed Mental Health Labels and Create Personal Meaning.* Novato: New World Library, 2012.

McGonigal, Jane. *Reality is Broken: Why Games Make Us Better and How They Can Change the World.* New York: Penguin Press, 2011.

Nichols, Sallie. *Jung and Tarot: An Archetypal Journey*. York Beach: Samuel Weiser, Inc., 1980.

Orloff, Judith. *Dr. Judith Orloff's Guide to Intuitive Healing: 5 Steps to Physical, Emotional, and Sexual Wellness.* New York: Time's Books, 2000.

Psych K, a psychological-kinesthetic approach to emotional blockage release. See official website: psych-k.com.

Riso, Don Richard and Russ Hudson. *Understanding the Enneagram: The Complete Guide to Psychological and Spiritual Growth for the Nine Personality Types.* New York: Bantam Books, 1999.

Ruiz, Don Miguel. *The Four Agreements.* San Rafael: Amber-Allen: 1997.

Schoeninger, Kevin. "How to Break Free of Old Habits." www.EnergyMeditationSecret.com.

Seligman, Martin. *Authentic Happiness: Using the New Positive Psychology to Realize Your Potential for Lasting Fulfillment.* New York: Free Press, 2002.

Stevens, Jose, Ph.D. *Transforming Your Dragons: Turning Personality Fear Patterns into Personal Power*. Santa Fe: Bear & Company Publishing, 1994.

Taylor, Jeremy. *Basic Hints for Dream Work.* Sausalito: Dream Tree Press, 1988.

————— *Dream Work: Techniques for Discovering the Creative Power in Dreams*. New York: Paulist Press, 1983.

TED Talks: Ideas Worth Sharing. www.ted.com/talks.

Tolle, Eckhart. *The Power of Now: A Guide to Spiritual Enlightenment.* Novato: New World Library, 1999.

Wanless, James. *Voyager Tarot: Way of the Great Oracle*. Carmel: Merrill-West Publishing, 1989.

————— *Voyager Tarot Deck*. Carmel: Merrill-West Publishing, 1985.

————— *Star Tree: Voyager Tarot Self-Development Course*. Carmel: Merrill-West, 1997.

————— www.voyagertarot.com.

Winokur, Jon. *Zen to Go: Bit-Sized Bits of Wisdom.* Seattle: Sasquatch Books, 2005.

Worthington, Everett. *Dimensions of Forgiveness: Psychological Research and Theological Perspectives.* Philadelphia: Templeton Foundation Press: 1998.

About the Author

Betty Dietz is a creativity, life, and empowerment coach, writer, speaker, and teacher. The purpose of her programs and individual coaching is to guide people to empowerment, purposeful decision making, and creative and enlightened action by helping them gain clarity and by being more aware of the power of their intuition.

Betty has been teaching, coaching, and guiding individuals and groups to create their lives of purpose and joy using a variety of educational channels and methods for over forty years. She has been involved with personal transformation and consciousness raising as a college instructor in English literature and writing, a high school English teacher, a speech and debate coach, a writer, a blogger, and a writer, producer, and director of children's theatre. For the past twenty years, she has been developing expertise in the esoteric and energetic arts which include tarot reading, reiki healing and teaching, space blessing, counseling, guidance, hypnotherapy, past life regression, and forgiveness and compassion training.

Betty also has a strong writing background and loves to help other writers with their projects. She has an MA in English with an emphasis in Creative Writing. Along with *The Soul of Success: A Guide to Living a Life of Meaning, Purpose, and Abundance*, she has written two compilations of short stories and two novels and is in the process of completing a book on the art of creativity for writers. She has edited many books, articles, and short stories and has helped guide numerous books, stories, and articles from idea to publication.

Visit her website at BettyDietz.com

Acknowledgements

To be inspired means to understand a truth or to recognize how an idea can be transformed into an action. In the writing of this book, numerous people, including friends, family, authors, poets, speakers, leaders, teachers, holistic healers, activists, mystics, and children have offered me truths and ideas. The initial inspiration came from James Wanless, tarot guru, teacher extraordinaire, and all round big-hearted wise one. He listened to my kernel of an idea and talked me into thinking more expansively. He offered me the use of his beautiful Voyager Tarot images and has periodically, almost magically, popped up in my inbox to supply more encouragement throughout the writing of the book.

Once the initial material was set down on paper, my brilliant, creative, supportive, and tech savvy daughter Lauri offered on-going inspiration and hands on labor, including how to revamp the material into a more interesting format and getting the ebook online. She has never been far from the more expanded version that this project became. In truth, if Lauri had not been as close to the book as she has been, the project would never have come to fruition. She is a source of inspiration and support beyond measure—as well as joy.

Many others need to be acknowledged for their thoughtful suggestions, inspirational encouragement, and positive actions. Jim O'Hara and I walked each other through the self-publishing process, holding each other up with words, wisdom, and wine. My husband Bill Dietz and my son Patrick Dietz helped to keep me on top of the project by reading the material and poking, prodding, and playfully teasing me toward completion on a constant basis.

Brian Allen, June Chan, Ron Blandford, and Tori van Zanten invested many hours into first convincing me that the project was worthwhile and then into encouraging me to continue when I experienced bumps and trenches along the way. Tori also stepped in with her design and technical skills, for which I am both grateful and humbled by her generosity.

Jeff Aalfs and Sally Araki-Aalfs must be acknowledged for inspirational support and practical guidance.

Scot Federman jumped in to offer his amazing technical know how. His wizardry with a Mac and his generous heart brought an early ebook version to life.

Superhero Bill Geary took the initiative to get the electronic file for my book made into a real book. This prototype appeared at a time when I was almost convinced the book was a dead project, impossible to be resuscitated after devoting over a year in fruitless attempts to get the material in a publishable format.

My careful, keen-eyed, and talented copyeditor, Jen Finstrom, fine tuned the manuscript and offered encouragement and good cheer.

Numerous others supported and inspired me in their own special ways throughout the writing, formatting, and publishing of the book. I acknowledge many by name here, and apologize for any oversights to others left off the list. These angels in my life include Mary Lou Ceh, Rachel Fitzgerald, Mark Shumway, Mark Behr, Margaret Heffermen, Susan Shear, Steve Shear, Andy Pabst, Eiko Amano, Emily Levy, Janet Kornblum, Karla Huebner, Denise Minor, Kathleen White, Joyce Weaver, Marsha Jacobson, June Hebb, Danny Johnson, Matthew Pearson, Pamela Dunford, Cathy Russo, Dougall Fraser, Eric Maisel, and Katie Brown.

Made in the USA
San Bernardino, CA
30 April 2015